The Past
That Would Not Die

Books by Walter Lord

THE PAST THAT WOULD NOT DIE

PEARY TO THE POLE

A TIME TO STAND

THE GOOD YEARS

DAY OF INFAMY

A NIGHT TO REMEMBER

THE FREMANTLE DIARY

TENNESSEE

ARKANSAS

Memphis

Holly Springs

Sardis Reservoir

Mississippi River

Clarksdale

Oxford

Tupelo

Tallahatchie R.

Indianola

Greenwood

ALABAMA

Greenville

MISSISSIPPI

Kosciusko

Yazoo R.

Yazoo City

Philadelphia

Pearl R.

Forest

Meridian

Okatibbee Creek

LOUISIANA

Vicksburg

★ Jackson

Natchez

Laurel

Pearl R.

Hattiesburg

ALABAMA

McComb

LOUISIANA

Biloxi

0   25   50
Miles

WALTER LORD

The Past
That Would Not Die

HARPER & ROW, PUBLISHERS

NEW YORK, EVANSTON, AND LONDON

To

Charles Dewees Dilworth

Contents

The Past
That Would Not Die

1

"The Worst Thing I've Seen in 45 Years"

"THE EYES OF THE NATION AND ALL THE WORLD ARE UPON YOU and upon all of us," said the President of the United States, speaking from the White House on Sunday evening, September 30, 1962. It was a national TV hook-up, but these particular words were addressed to the students of the University of Mississippi. John F. Kennedy was appealing to them to accept on their campus at Oxford a young Negro Air Force veteran—the first of his race ever to win admission to the University.

James H. Meredith had arrived there that afternoon, armed with 60 hours of academic credits, an order from the Supreme Court and several hundred federal marshals. That should have been enough, but for days Mississippi had been in turmoil at the prospect. The Governor had called for defiance, the Confederate flag seemed to fly from every car aerial, and one youth in Jackson was urging that it would be perfectly practical to mobilize private planes and bomb the U.S. Army with napalm.

So President Kennedy had gone on the air at 10:00 (8:00 Mississippi time) and was using every argument he knew. There was the sanctity of the law: if the courts could be defied, "no citizen is safe from his neighbors." There was his duty to enforce the laws even if he had to use troops, but he carefully stressed that local means were best. There were the other Southern states that had set such a fine example. There was the rest of the nation that must share the blame for "the accumulated wrongs of the last 100 years." And most important, there was the honor of Mississippi —her bravery on the battlefield, courage on the gridiron, the patriotism of Senator (later Justice) L. Q. C. Lamar, the great Mississippian who put the nation first.

"Let us," concluded the President, "preserve both the law and the peace, and then, healing those wounds that are within, we can turn to the greater crises that are without and stand united as one people in our pledge to man's freedom."

Few of the students even heard. By now a full-scale riot was on, swirling about the federal marshals who were deployed around the Lyceum, the University's administration building. Meredith had been whisked to a dorm, but few knew that. Bricks, bottles, pipes showered down on the marshals, and even before Kennedy began speaking, the federals were fighting back with tear gas. By the time the President finished, a roaring battle was on.

Kennedy went to the Cabinet Room and sank into his black leather chair. Behind him hovered a handful of aides. Beside him sat his brother Robert, the Attorney General, relaying bulletins that came over the phone from the riot. The news grew steadily worse— 10:58, marshals running out of gas . . . 11:02, the Mississippi Highway Patrol, the chief hope for law and order on the spot, reported pulling out . . . 11:22, former General Edwin A. Walker, militant right-winger, rumored on the campus . . . 11:23, a marshal shot through the leg . . . 11:42, "state trooper hurt bad."

About 11:45 Kennedy was on the phone with Mississippi's Governor Ross Barnett, urging him to get the Highway Patrol back. Barnett said he'd do everything he could. But the bad news flowed on—11:55, FBI radio monitor reported Highway Patrol still without orders to return to campus . . . 11:58, still no orders to the Patrol . . . 12 midnight, gunfire spreading.

Now Deputy Attorney General Nicholas deB. Katzenbach, in

charge of the federal forces on the scene, came on the phone. Reluctantly he said the time had come for troops. It was the last thing the President wanted to do, but he didn't hesitate a second. Walking to his oval office, he phoned the Pentagon and put through the orders.

The minutes dragged on, punctuated by more depressing bulletins —12:10, only 67 local National Guardsmen immediately available . . . 12:13, U.S. Army regulars, flying down from Memphis, not airborne yet . . . 12:21, troops still not airborne . . . 12:52, 13 wounded now . . . 12:57, state patrolmen still sitting out on the highway. Once, spirits briefly rose with a flash that the troops were at last on the way, but at 1:02 word came that this report was wrong —they hadn't left Memphis yet. Then another message that the men were airborne . . . and at 1:47 another heart-breaker, that they were really still in Memphis.

In the end, it was after 2:00 when the little group in the Cabinet Room knew for sure that the troops had not only left but were actually arriving at Oxford's miniature airport. Now at last the White House could breathe easily. It was only a half-mile to campus —General Billingslea and his men should be there in three or four minutes. Such calculations made it all the more frustrating when word arrived at 2:55 that there was no sign of the Army yet . . . only new, high-powered rifle fire. Worse, at 3:33 word came that the troops were still at the airport. The General—struggling to assemble his men and equipment—thought they could reach the battlefield by four.

John F. Kennedy was not a man to throw his weight around, but the long delay, the mounting bloodshed and, above all, the dashed hopes had done their work. At 3:35 the White House line to the communications base at Oxford crackled with a stern command: tell General Billingslea to move *now*. The General got and obeyed the order, but he didn't learn the actual text until two hours later, when his men were clearing the campus and the crisis was over. "People are dying in Oxford," ran the anguished message. "This is the worst thing I've seen in 45 years. I want the military police battalion to enter the action. I want General Billingslea to see that this is done."

Where did the blame lie for the "worst thing" in the President's 45 years? Certainly not with the troops—they were moving as fast as they could. Nor with the decision a few days earlier to rely on federal marshals—that was in the best tradition of civilian government. Nor was it the fault of a month ago, when the Administration first plunged into the Meredith case—it was the President's duty to enforce court decisions. No, the real blame lay still further in the past—beyond the Supreme Court's ban on school segregation, beyond dark decades of apathy and misunderstanding . . . all the way back, in fact, to the blunders and bitterness of a people fighting a desperate civil war.

2

"Lest We Forget, Lest We Forget . . ."

SPLINTERS FLEW IN EVERY DIRECTION AS THE UNION TROOPS hacked away at the chairs and tables of Edward McGehee, a wealthy cotton planter in Wilkinson County, Mississippi. It was October 5, 1864, and Colonel E. D. Osband's men were simply acting on the philosophy expressed by General Sherman when he told a group of protesting Mississippians, "It is our duty to destroy, not build up; therefore do not look to us to help you."

Soon the work was done, the house in flames, and Edward McGehee left contemplating his only remaining possession—a gracefully carved grand piano. It was no comfort to Mr. McGehee, once the owner of hundreds of Negro slaves, that these deeds were done by a company of stern, efficient Negro soldiers.

Ruin upon ruin, the destruction continued for six more grueling months of war. By the end, Mississippi seemed but a forest of chimneys. The whole town of Okolona could be bought for $5,000. There was not a fence left within miles of Corinth, not a clock running in Natchez. The capital, Jackson, was in ashes—the Confederate Hotel as complete a wreck as the cause it honored.

The first visitors from the North were stunned. Approaching old Charles Langworthy's home near Aberdeen, a man from Chicago recalled spending two pleasant weeks there back in 1855. Greeting the owner, the visitor quickly asked after Mr. Langworthy's five boys and two girls.

"Where is John, your oldest son?"

"Killed at Shiloh."

"Where is William?"

"Died of smallpox in the Army."

"And the other boys?"

"All were killed. . . ."

The Langworthy daughters came forward, dripping with mourning. Not only were their brothers gone; both also had lost their husbands in the service.

The incident was all too typical. Mississippi had sent 78,000 into the fight; only 28,000 came back. Whole companies were wiped out—the Vicksburg Cadets marched off 123 strong; only six returned. The legacy of this sacrifice was 10,000 orphans.

Nor were those who returned always able to play their full part. Surgery was not one of the happier aspects of the Civil War. Empty sleeves flapped everywhere. At a town meeting in Aberdeen a visitor noticed that 100 of the 300 men present had lost either an arm or a leg. It's not surprising that in the first year after the war Mississippi spent one-fifth of its entire revenue for artificial limbs.

Painfully, the people of the state struggled to live again. Nearly everyone was wiped out. The greatest source of wealth—436,000 slaves worth over $218 million—had vanished with Emancipation. The farm animals that meant so much to a rural people had been carried off—one out of every three mules gone. Most of the cotton was confiscated as Confederate property; any that escaped was mercilessly taxed by Washington. Land values crashed—on December 13, 1865 alone the Vicksburg *Herald* advertised 48 plantations for sale or lease. After five years of war Mississippi tumbled from the nation's fifth wealthiest state, per capita, to the very bottom of the list.

"My children, I am a ruined man," Thomas Dabney told his daughters one evening in November 1866. In happier days Mr.

Dabney had endorsed some notes. At the time there seemed little danger—the risk was good and Dabney was the wealthy owner of Burleigh, a fabulous plantation near the town of Raymond. But now times had changed, and the sheriff was downstairs.

Ultimately, Burleigh was auctioned off, and Dabney managed to buy it back only by consigning his cotton crop for years to come. Meanwhile, the family had nothing—even the "loyal" Negro servants had vanished. As the once pampered Dabney girls faced the novel prospect of housework, it looked like a major victory for General Sherman's boast that he would force every Southern woman to the washtub.

But this time the General had met his match. "He shall never bring my daughters to the washtub," Dabney thundered. "I'll do the washing myself!" And he did. Dabney was now 70 years old, but for the next two years he scrubbed away, grimly satisfied that here at least he was foiling the hated Yankee.

There were other consolations too, as the people of Mississippi struggled to recover. There was relief that the war was over—whatever their original feelings, most Mississippians were heartily sick of destruction. There was also hope that the state could get back into the Union rather painlessly; President Andrew Johnson had decided to carry on Lincoln's lenient plans for restoration. Best of all, there was the land. Mississippi's towns might lie in ruins, but her matchless asset was the soil itself. If only cotton could get going again. . . .

But that was the problem. If the key to prosperity was cotton, the key to cotton had always been slaves—and there weren't any slaves any more. Over 380,000 freedmen aimlessly roamed the state, living where they chose, eating off the federal troops, nearly all of them at loose ends.

The former owners had no influence. Most Negroes felt this was what freedom meant—no work. And there were plenty of people around the Union Army camps who advised them not to go back to their old masters. There were even rumors that Washington soon would be dividing up the plantations—forty acres and a mule for everyone.

Actually Washington was never more at cross-purposes. President Johnson suffered from being a states' rights Democrat from Tennessee, and as his prestige waned so did the chances for his lenient program. The Radical Republicans in Congress were winning control over national policy, but beyond a thirst for revenge, they had no clear-cut plans at all. As late as October 1865 the Radical leader Thaddeus Stevens was asking his friend Charles Sumner if he knew of any good books on how the Russians freed their serfs.

The Negroes themselves could be of very little help in solving their problems. Over 95% were illiterate. In the old days it had been illegal to teach the slaves to read or write, and now they were hopelessly ignorant. Few had any idea of citizenship, law, suffrage or responsibility. Hauled before a court for stealing a bag of corn, one ex-slave happily camping on Jefferson Davis' plantation was asked if he wanted a jury trial.

"What's that?" was all he could say.

From the white Mississippian's point of view, the Negroes seemed dreadfully immoral too. Informal alliances had been the custom among plantation slaves, and the freedmen couldn't understand why all this was changed. Of 240,000 in a cross-section of Mississippi counties, only 564 applied for marriage licenses in 1865. Petty stealing was another plantation tradition; and there seemed nothing wrong with it now. Chickens and corn meal were never safe, and horse thieves at Olive Branch stole 16 mules in the space of two weeks.

The whites felt cornered and helpless. For years they had done as they wanted with these people, and now the tables were turned. They were generally outnumbered, and in the rich cotton areas the margin seemed appalling—Bolivar County was 87% Negro; Issaquena County had 7,000 Negroes, only 600 whites.

But most frightening were the Negro troops. When the U.S. Army's XVI Corps went home in August 1865, 9,122 of the

10,193 Union soldiers still in the state were Negroes. Their mere presence seemed to invite the most hideous trouble. In Jackson Major Barnes, commanding the 5th U.S. Colored Infantry, urged the local Negroes to defend their rights even to the "click of the pistol and at the point of the bayonet."

And incidents did happen. William Wilkinson was murdered at Lauderdale Springs by five of his former slaves for selling his plantation—they claimed it was rightfully theirs by Christmas. This sort of bloodshed was rare, but it was enough to set off the whites.

Terror bred fantastic rumors. The Natchez *Courier* warned that the county's Negroes were supposed to rise on New Year's Day. In Yazoo City the date was Christmas. The Brandon *Republican* set no date but reported, "They are evidently preparing something and it behooves us to be on the alert and prepare for the worst." There was nothing, of course, to any of these reports, but each rumor hardened the feelings of the whites.

They soon developed a fierce callousness toward the Negro, no matter how harmless he might be. On a quiet Sunday afternoon in Natchez an elderly freedman protested to a small white boy raiding his turnip patch. The boy shot him dead, and that was that. In Vicksburg the *Herald* complained that the town's children were hitting innocent bystanders when using their "nigger shooters."

Nor was it just the specter of Negro supremacy that aroused white Mississippians—Negro equality was just as bad. "God damn your soul, get off this boat!" raged the captain of the Memphis-Vicksburg packet, Christmas morning, 1865. The greeting was directed at a Negro couple who had dared ask for first-class passage. As their luggage was pitched ashore, the captain turned back to his work muttering, "They can't force their damned nigger equality on me."

Even when the principle of equality was acknowledged, the practice must have mystified the beneficiaries. "Take off your hat, you black scoundrel, or I'll cut your throat," a Mississippi state legislator yelled at his former slave; later he explained, "Sam, you've got just the same rights as a white man now, but not a bit better, and if you come into my room again without taking off your hat, I'll shoot you."

The case of Negro suffrage showed that even token equality was too much. In 1865 President Johnson—already fearing for his generous Reconstruction program—urged Provisional Governor Sharkey to make some gesture toward Negro enfranchisement. It might allay Congressional doubts, for instance, if Mississippi gave the vote to those who could read the Constitution, write their names and who owned at least $250 in property—perhaps 5% of the Negro population. Governor Sharkey couldn't have been less interested.

But the greatest anathema was Negro education. It was not so much a question of integrated schools; it was a question of any schools at all. At Oxford an angry band drove off the missionary assigned to the local freedmen's school, even though he was a Southern man. At Okolona someone fired four shots at Dr. Lacy, the old Episcopal minister who was trying to teach the town's young Negroes.

"If any man from the North comes down here expecting to hold and maintain radical or abolitionist sentiments," warned the *Nation's* correspondent, "let him expect to be shot down from *behind* the first time he leaves his home." Visitors were shocked by the sheer violence of the state's reaction. Lulled by a carefully cultivated tradition of moonlight and magnolias, they forgot that life in Mississippi had always been closer to the frontier than the Tidewater.

Harder to explain was the stream of contradictory assurances that soon became so familiar. Negroes? "The Southern people are really their best friends," a planter told author John T. Trowbridge in 1865. "We're the only ones that understand them," someone explained to Whitelaw Reid, another visitor. Just give the Southerners time, begged the sympathetic editor of *DeBow's Review*: "If let alone to manage affairs in their own way, and with their intimate knowledge of Negro character, everything possible will be done in good time for the social, physical, and political advancement of the race."

There was also an odd element of fantasy in it all—almost as if the war hadn't been lost . . . in fact, as if Mississippi were dealing with Washington as an equal. When Whitelaw Reid doubted that Congress would seat the ex-Confederates who swept Mississippi's first postwar election of 1865, his listeners scoffed at the very thought. Of course they would be seated—"because of the tremendous pressure we can bring to bear." The Natchez *Courier* agreed: "The State of Mississippi still stands in all its grand individuality. Massachusetts has no more right to dictate to us now about our internal laws than she had five years ago—nor has she half the power. . . ."

Occasionally a voice of doubt popped up, but the moderates seemed, in the *Nation*'s words, "somewhat bewildered . . . bullied . . . humbugged." Usually they could be quickly silenced. When one Mississippi planter suggested in August 1865 that the Negroes might be trained to use their rights, his companion shot back the clincher that was also getting familiar: "They'll be wanting to marry your daughters next."

And this was the heart of the matter. To the ordinary Mississippian political equality automatically led to social equality, which in turn automatically led to race-mixing. It was inevitable—and unthinkable. To a people brought up to believe that Negroes were genetically inferior—after all, that was why they were slaves—the mere hint of "mongrelization" was appalling. And all the more so in view of the homage paid white Southern womanhood. It was she who had sacrificed so much, whose purity, in fact, carried on the whole system. She was everything.

Of course there were other factors too. Cotton planters didn't want their field hands getting out of line; the red-neck farmers worried about Negroes taking their bread. Yet these were areas where something might be worked out; but there could be no compromise—not an inch—on anything that might open the door to race-mixing. Emancipation made absolutely no difference. "A monkey with his tail off," explained the Natchez *Courier*, "is a monkey still."

It didn't matter that the position was illogical. Northerners might snigger that if the Negro was so backward, why might he advance so far? Other visitors might wonder about the high percentage of Negroes with white blood—surely race-mixing must have once been all right with somebody. None of this made any difference. So in November 1865 it was easy for the Jackson *Daily News* to lecture the state's first postwar government: "We must keep the ex-slave in a position of inferiority. We must pass such laws as will make him *feel* his inferiority."

Mississippi's new government understood. Under President Johnson's generous terms the state had freed the slaves but done little else. A new constitution had been drafted—but it seemed pretty much along prewar lines. A new state legislature had been chosen—but it featured many old leaders. A new governor had been elected —but he was Benjamin G. Humphreys, an outstanding Confederate general who hadn't even been pardoned yet. On November 20, 1865 Governor Humphreys set the tone of things in a message to the legislature: "Under the pressure of federal bayonets, urged on by the misdirected sympathies of the world, the people of Mississippi have abolished the institution of slavery. The Negro is free, whether we like it or not; we must realize that fact now and forever. To be free, however, does not make him a citizen, or entitle him to social or political equality with the white man."

A series of laws, later known as the Black Code, swiftly put the Negro in his place. He was allowed to marry, own property, sue and be sued, even testify if he was a party—but that was all. No Negro could vote, keep firearms, rent a home outside town, ride in a first-class railroad car with whites or "make insulting gestures." Any unemployed Negro over 18 was declared a vagrant, fined $50 and turned over to whoever paid up. Any unsupported Negro under 18 could be apprenticed out. If he tried to run away, "the master or mistress" (the law easily slipped back into ante bellum language) had the right to pursue and recapture.

Reaction was not long in coming. "We tell the white men of Mississippi," exploded the Chicago *Tribune* on December 1, "that the men of the North will convert the state of Mississippi into a frog pond before they will allow any such laws to disgrace one foot of soil in which the bones of our soldiers sleep and over which the flag of freedom waves."

Northern fury grew as one Southern state after another followed Mississippi's lead with Black Codes of their own. Finally, in 1867 Congress threw out President Johnson's Reconstruction program, launched a far harsher one of its own. The Confederate-dominated state governments were scrapped and the South divided into five military districts, each under martial law. Negroes were given the vote, new constitutional conventions held. No state could get back in the Union until Congress approved its new government . . . until it granted Negro suffrage . . . until it passed the Fourteenth Amendment, guaranteeing (among other things) "equal protection of the laws" to all persons in a State.

Mississippi eventually knuckled under, but only after three more years of rear-guard defiance. By 1870, however, the state was "reconstructed," and by 1873 the local Radical Republicans were riding high. The electorate was 57% Negro—mostly illiterate and easily controlled. The legislature boasted 64 Negroes and 24 carpetbaggers. The Speaker of the House, the Lieutenant Governor, the Superintendent of Education were all Negroes. The new Reconstruction Governor himself was an ex-Union officer—General Adelbert Ames, a remote, tactless New Englander who seemed to stay away from Mississippi as much as he could.

It would later be argued that this state government turned in an impressive performance, and indeed there were many bright spots. The Negro legislators included at least 15 well-educated, conscientious clergymen. The carpetbaggers were often solid Middle Westerners who had come not to loot but to farm. The Negro troops had all been withdrawn, and only a token force of Federals remained —for instance, 59 at Natchez, 129 at Vicksburg, about 700 men altogether. The state debt never got out of hand. There was little stealing—the only major case involved the carpetbag treasurer of the state hospital in Natchez who took $7,251.81. And all the while important things were being accomplished—war-damaged bridges repaired, Northern innovations like free hospitals established, courts expanded to take care of the freedmen, and a whole public school system launched.

All this was done, but it would take the perspective of a century to appreciate it. At the time the white people of Mississippi felt only bitterness. They didn't care if most of the troops were gone; one blue uniform was too many. They didn't know about worthy projects; they only knew taxes were soaring—up 1300% in five years. They didn't notice that most key officials were honest; in their frayed poverty, they only saw any sign of waste: why, the state contingency fund even paid for Governor Ames' bedpan. And perhaps most important, they knew little about the conscientious work of many Negroes in top-level positions; they only knew their own county, where they were in daily contact, and that was often appalling.

Negro sheriffs, clerks and magistrates thrashed about in confusion and ignorance. In Warren County the sheriff couldn't write a simple return. In Issaquena County not one member of the Board of Supervisors—responsible for handling the county's business—could read a contract. There wasn't a justice of the peace in Madison County who could write a summons.

Petty corruption spread everywhere, often induced by light-fingered whites. Hinds County ran up a bigger printing bill in nine months than the whole state paid in 1866-67. The Wilkinson County Board of Supervisors shelled out $1,500 for three bridges —containing 4, 8 and 20 planks apiece. Vicksburg's Republican candidate for mayor staggered under 23 indictments. Nor were the dethroned Democrats entirely innocent. An officer in Vicksburg's clean government group was caught charging the city $500 to move a safe from the river to the courthouse.

Little matter—it was all the same to most of white Mississippi. Reconstruction was to blame, and that meant the Negroes. Free voting and the shadow of federal bayonets might make them invulnerable to ordinary political tactics, but there were other ways. . . .

The shifting seasons merged into one long blur of desperate violence. There was the sunny October morning when Thomas Dabney's daughters heard a hail of shots and watched a Negro's riderless horse race across the Burleigh lawn . . . the starlit winter night in Monroe County when carpetbagger A. P. Huggins knelt on a lonely road as the KKK delivered 75 lashes with a stirrup strap . . . the bright March day when the Meridian courthouse erupted in rifle fire and the Radical judge fell dead on his bench . . . the lazy summer afternoons near Yazoo City when small boys drilled with real guns, wearing the sacred Confederate gray. An intercepted letter had told of 1,600 rifles buried at Satartia by Negroes "all prepared for Bussness."

Violence and more violence. Partly it was a case of bitterness and frustration, but it also went deeper than that. To Northern visitors it seemed that Mississippians were just made that way. Perhaps it was the lingering spirit of the frontier, or perhaps the lush, richly scented countryside itself: it so invited languor—and sudden storms.

"Life is not sacred as it is in the North," wrote correspondent Charles Nordhoff:

Everybody goes armed, and every trifling dispute is ended with the pistol. The respectable people of the State do not discourage the practice of carrying arms as they should, they are astonishingly tolerant of acts which would arouse a Northern community to the utmost, and I believe that to this may be ascribed all that is bad in Mississippi—to an almost total lack of a right opinion; a willingness to see men take the law into their own hands; and, what is still worse, to let them openly defy the laws, without losing, apparently, the respect of the community.

In this atmosphere there was no hope for a man with the "wrong" attitude, whatever his credentials. At Aberdeen the town teacher, Dr. Ebart, had an impeccable Southern background, but he favored Negro schools, and that was the end of his job. On the other hand, if a man thought "right," anything could be forgiven. General C. E. Furlong was an ex-Union officer on the hated Sherman's staff, but he helped rout the Negroes at the Vicksburg riots—and became an instant hero.

The pressure was too much. The white Republicans soon melted away. Many crossed over to the Democratic fold; others fled North; only a few stood by the helpless mass of Negroes. The moderates, who might have been a third force, seemed mesmerized by the fury of the blast. "The quiet, sensible and orderly people," mused a puzzled Charles Nordhoff, "seem to have almost entirely resigned the power and supremacy which belong to them."

This was the picture by 1875, when the Democrats decided that the time had come formally to recapture the state. A skillfully conceived strategy—to be known as the Mississippi Plan and later copied throughout the South—took care of the two chief obstacles: the Negro majority and federal bayonets.

"We are determined to have an honest election if we have to stuff the ballot box to get it," shouted one Democratic leader, and this was only a small part of the plan. Newspaper notices warned Negroes that they would be thrown off their land if they voted the Republican ticket. Democratic "rifle clubs," usually sporting conspicuous red shirts, drilled endlessly near Negro sections. In Hinds, Lowndes and other counties, cannon appeared and fired "salutes" near Republican rallies.

The Negro voters got the message, but the Democrats still faced the danger of federal intervention. The trick here was not to let things go too far, and the Democratic campaign chairman, General

J. Z. George, proved a past master at the art of intimidation by indirection. Still, it was a delicate tightrope. The embattled Governor Ames was calling Washington for help, and the slightest slip might bring in the federals. . . .

A crash of rifle fire scattered the 1,200 Negroes swarming around the Republican barbecue at the little town of Clinton on September 4. Here and there men fell—not all of them black. Two young white hecklers were cut down by return fire as they scurried from the scene. It seemed that Negroes too could feel strongly about elections.

Wholesale shooting began, and for days undeclared war raged around Clinton. On September 8 Governor Ames appealed to General Grant for troops to restore peace and supervise the coming elections. The whole future of Mississippi hung in the balance. A nod from the President, and all of General George's intricate strategy would fall apart.

Grant looked the other way. "The whole public are tired out with these annual autumnal outbreaks in the South," the President sighed, "and the great majority are ready now to condemn any interference on the part of the government." Word was passed to Governor Ames through Attorney General Pierrepont to try harder, exhaust his own resources before calling on Washington for aid.

It was really not Grant's fault. The country was indeed tired of Reconstruction, and the President was but echoing the national mood. Most people had never been for Negro civil rights in the first place. Freedom, yes; but that didn't necessarily mean all the privileges of citizenship. At the end of the war only six Northern states let Negroes vote, and in 1867 the District of Columbia rejected Negro suffrage 7,337 to 36. Nor did anyone feel the Fourteenth Amendment had much to do with education. In fact, stalwart Union states like New York, Pennsylvania and Ohio all had segregated schools. Congress itself set up a segregated school system in Washington only weeks after approving the Fourteenth Amendment.

These feelings were rising to the surface, now that the initial exhilaration of winning the war was over. Other forces were at work too: the implacable Thaddeus Stevens had died . . . anti-Grant Liberals were happy to attack everything about the Administration, including Reconstruction . . . Northern investors were anxious to resume "normal" relations with the South . . . the nation's eyes were turning to fresh, exciting visions in the Far West.

The new mood showed itself in various ways. Congress had indeed passed the Civil Rights Act of 1875 (protecting the Negro in public places like trains and restaurants), but it was the dying gasp of a lameduck session. Besides, it was a shaky victory. A school integration provision had been defeated; also a force bill giving the measure teeth. Even more significant, the Supreme Court was now nibbling away at the earlier Reconstruction Acts. And in the background came a steady chorus from the press, "Let the South solve its own problems." The President understood and gave the nation its way.

The Silver Cornet Band led the Jackson victory parade to General George's house on Election Night, November 2. The returns were rolling in, and huge Democratic majorities were piling up: Morton, 233 to 17 . . . Deasonville, 181 to 0 . . . Yazoo City, 4,052 to 7. In the end the Democrats carried 62 of the state's 74 counties. In the time-honored fashion of all political leaders everywhere, General George gave full credit to the rank and file "for the redemption of our common mother, Mississippi."

Governor Ames was a practical man. Exactly 146 days later, in exchange for the Democrats' withdrawing a set of impeachment charges, he resigned his office, packed his bags and left the state forever. In the word of the times, Mississippi had been "redeemed."

To Mississippi's Negroes redemption meant a loss of power but not the trappings. The men now running the state came from the old cotton-planting gentry, who got along well with their former slaves. Some of these leaders, like L. Q. C. Lamar, were far more interested in corporation law than 8-cent cotton, but they still had a tradition of *noblesse oblige* and gave the Negroes considerable leeway—as long as they were "good."

This arrangement was further cemented by a sort of gentlemen's agreement with Washington after the election of 1876. The South accepted Hayes' dubious claims to the Presidency, and in return the grateful Republicans adopted Grant's hands-off attitude as the new Administration line. The last troops were withdrawn and the old Confederacy left free to work out its own problems. But at the same time it was always understood that the Negroes would retain at least their surface gains. The redemption leaders happily agreed. In fact, the Jackson *Clarion* accepted the obligation on the very morning after the great 1875 victory. Observing that Negroes helped make the triumph possible, the paper declared that the state must now "carry out in good faith the pledges of equal and even justice to them and theirs in which they placed their confidence."

So the Negroes continued to vote and often held minor offices. Nor were they barred from most public places. The two races drank at the same bars and ate at the same restaurants, though at separate tables. In Jackson, Angelo's Hall echoed with Negro laughter one week, white the next. And when life was done, both races could rest together in Greenwood Cemetery.

With the Negro's role settled, Mississippi's redemption government launched a massive economy wave. The conservative land-owning leaders had been hit hardest by the staggering taxes of Reconstruction, and now they were determined to end all that. State expenditures were slashed from $1,430,000 in 1875 to $518,000 in 1876. Teachers' salaries alone fell from $55.47 a month in 1875 to $29.19 the following year.

In a way it was all justifiable. Mississippi remained wretchedly poor. In 1877 the state's per capita wealth was only $286, compared to $1,086 in the Northern states. Even as late as 1890 there were only 46 banks in the state with combined cash assets of but $635,-000. The war had wiped out Mississippi, and there just seemed no way to get going again. In these days the idea of federal recovery aid was unknown—between 1865 and 1875 Washington spent $21 million on public works in Massachusetts and New York, but only $185,000 in Mississippi and Arkansas.

Still, whatever the justification, Mississippi paid a high price for her sweeping economies. Letting roads disintegrate meant even more stagnant communities. Appropriating merely $5,392 a year for health meant the end of nearly all services. Spending only $2 a head on schoolchildren (against $20 in Massachusetts) meant mounting illiteracy and a new generation utterly untrained to advance in life.

Nor was cost-cutting the answer. Despite all the economies, conditions continued to slide. From the mid-'70s to the early '90s cotton sagged from 11 cents to 5.8 cents a pound. Field hand pay fell from $15 to $12 a month . . . when there was any cash at all. More often there was the sharecropping system, which saw little money ever change hands. Yet the plantation owners themselves were certainly not getting rich. Under a vicious system of liens, they mortgaged their future crops for months or even years ahead to get the tools and supplies needed for tomorrow.

Everything seemed to conspire against Mississippi. While crop prices fell, the farmer's costs soared. Freight rates rigged in the East increased his shipping charges. Combinations like the jute-bagging trust raised the cost of his supplies. Ever higher tariffs added more to his burden. Creditors insisted that he plant only cotton; and shackled to a one-crop system, his land quickly eroded. Even nature joined the conspiracy—a flood, freeze or drought usually came along to spoil the all-too-few good years. Whether holding out in some paint-peeled mansion or hanging on in the squalor of a dog-trot cabin, most Mississippians knew only the bitterest poverty.

The state's landed leaders proved utterly unable to cope with the situation. They came from the lowlands—the cotton belt that ran everything in prewar days. They owed their authority to an odd combination of ante bellum nostalgia and redemption heroics—certainly not new ideas. They easily took to the laissez-faire views of Eastern business—tax concessions, hard money, railroad grabs like the Texas-Pacific. They shied away from new panaceas like government regulation and flexible currency. Their most lustrous figure, L. Q. C. Lamar, shuddered at the Greenback movement's "boundless, bottomless, and brainless schemes."

Such men neither understood nor even liked the upcountry farmers who scratched away at the red clay hills to the east. Desperately these red-necks—along with a growing number of poor white tenants all over the state—turned to new and more radical sources of hope, like the Farmers' Alliance and later the Populists.

And all the while they smoldered with growing hate—hatred for the Yankee banks and railroads that squeezed them so tightly . . . hatred for the Black Belt leaders who seemed to care so little . . . and, above all, hatred for the Negroes to whose level they were sinking so fast.

Jim Crow laws began to sprout . . . the first in twenty years. In 1888 Mississippi became the first state to have segregated waiting rooms. In 1890 Jackson extended the racial barrier beyond death by establishing a separate cemetery for Negroes. The rules grew ever more strict as the margin narrowed between white and colored living standards. If race was all the whites might have left, then all the more reason to guard this sacred heritage. Woe to the Negro who flirted with crossing the line.

Lynchings multiplied at a fearful rate—nobody knows how many, for the press handled the incidents as casually as the weather. "Four Negroes were lynched at Grenada last week," remarked the Raymond *Times* on July 18, 1885, "also one at Oxford." That was the whole item.

With Mississippi in this mood, it certainly didn't help matters when the big landowners met the red-neck challenge with thousands of Negro votes from the black counties they controlled. A weird political duel developed as the '80s wore on, utterly lacking in logic or principle. The old conservative leaders represented traditional white supremacy, yet relied on Negro votes to hold their power. The mass of poor whites had much in common with the Negro, yet fought him as a mortal enemy. The remaining Republicans in the state stood for the Negro's freedom, yet deserted him as a hopeless handicap. No wonder the Negro himself soon lost interest. Untrained in politics anyhow, he found Mississippi's brand far too confusing. Usually he just sold his vote to the highest bidder or was thrust aside while someone else cast it for him.

The situation proved too sordid to last. In 1890 a special convention assembled in Jackson to draw up a new state constitution. "Let us have the questionable and shameful methods of controlling the ballot box stopped," urged Delegate Miller of Leake County. "These methods are demoralizing to our young men and there is general outcry that they must cease."

The solution, most people felt, was to take away the Negro's vote. Even the Black Belt leaders now agreed—the advantage it gave them was outweighed by the cost (usually a dollar a vote) and the ever-haunting possibility that the Negroes might some day decide to go back into politics for themselves. It was, of course, a little odd to keep Negroes from casting votes in order to stop white people from stealing them, but nobody worried too much about that. A far greater problem was how to do it. The Fifteenth Amendment specifically guaranteed the Negroes the right to vote.

Clearly, the trick was to frame a set of qualifications that would technically apply to everybody but actually eliminate the Negro without touching the white. A poll tax alone was not enough—it might discourage more whites than Negroes. Nor would a literacy test do—there were thousands of good white voters who couldn't even write their names. In the end the convention came up with a series of devices which were, in the words of one delegate, "a monument to the resourcefulness of the human mind."

Most important were the new qualifications: all voters had to be able to read any section of the state constitution, or understand it when read to him, or give it a reasonable interpretation. This, of course, dumped the final decision into the lap of the examining registrar . . . who would know exactly what to do.

Reregistration began immediately. In 1885 over 1,600 Negroes had qualified in Panola County; by 1896 the figure stood at 114. The same thing happened everywhere: in Coahoma County only 4% of its once-eligible Negroes now could vote; in De Soto only 5%; in Tunica only 2%. Loyal Mississippians held their breath—how would the nation react to this giant wink at the Fifteenth Amendment?

They need not have worried. The White House was in friendly hands—first under the conservative Grover Cleveland, later under the benign William McKinley. Congress was no threat either—in 1894 it repealed most of the remaining civil rights laws. The Western Populists were bitter at the Negroes for sticking by their old masters. The Southern progressives felt that white solidarity would weld all classes more closely together. Eastern liberals recalled the reactionary leaders who engineered Reconstruction—and found it easy to sympathize with Mississippi. And above all, there was the American mood—a moment of bursting national pride and pious imperialism. As the liberal *Atlantic Monthly* noted with a touch of gentle irony: "If the stronger and cleverer race is free to impose its will upon the 'new-caught sullen peoples' on the other side of the globe, why not in South Carolina and Mississippi?"

The Supreme Court added its blessing in 1898. In *Williams* v. *Mississippi* the justices solemnly declared there was no reason to suppose that the state's new voting qualifications were aimed especially at Negroes. It was a predictable decision, for the Court had already shown its hand. In 1883 it had greatly diluted the civil rights laws by ruling that the Fourteenth Amendment only protected a Negro against discrimination by a state, not by private parties like stores and restaurants. In 1896 the Court went a step further: it said that a Louisiana Negro named Homer Plessy had no right to ride in a railroad car reserved by state law for whites as long as there were also "separate but equal" accommodations for Negroes. This time a state was clearly involved, but the Court maintained there was no discrimination. The Fourteenth Amendment required equality, Justice Brown conceded, but "in the nature of things it could not have been intended to abolish distinctions based on color. . . ."

"Our Constitution is color-blind," countered Justice John Marshall Harlan in a lone dissent, "and neither knows nor tolerates classes among citizens." He went on for two pages but caused little stir. The majority opinion in *Plessy* v. *Ferguson* prevailed. "Separate but equal" was good enough for most Americans.

As the new century dawned, it was clear that the Negro—stripped of his gains, abandoned by the courts and rejected by the country —was in a highly vulnerable position. And for the Negro in Mississippi—the state which had invented the Black Codes in 1865, pioneered the "Mississippi Plan" in 1875 and led the way to disenfranchisement in 1890—the future looked bleak indeed. If it needed any underlining, that came from Massachusetts where Adelbert Ames, Mississippi's ex-Reconstruction governor, pondered in retirement. For championing Negro rights, he had been forced out and nearly impeached; but by 1900 even he had finally come around. "I did not know then," he reflected, "that a superior race will not submit to the government of an inferior one."

The "superior race" was taking no chances. When Mississippi fell under the progressive spell and adopted direct primaries in 1902, the Democratic leaders made sure they were open to whites only. It seemed the progressive movement had nothing to do with the Negro. In fact, it actually worked against him, for the red-necks and poor whites who supported the trend most strongly were still the very people who feared and hated the Negro most bitterly.

This was fully appreciated by the eloquent man with the flowing locks who ran for governor in 1903. James K. Vardaman lived in Greenwood in the cotton-planting Delta, but his appeal lay with the people of the hills. He campaigned in a great lumber wagon drawn by eight white oxen, adding drama and excitement where before there was none. He pulled coarse, vulgar jokes to the delight of an electorate weary of proper aristocrats. And above all, he struck the right chord. "The Negro, like the mule," he cracked, "has neither pride of ancestry nor hope of posterity."

Vardaman's appeal proved irresistible. He was swept into office in an election that saw the triumph of the hills over the lowland conservatives who had so long ruled the state. And out with the aristocrats went their sometimes apparent sense of *noblesse oblige* toward the Negroes.

"The way to control the nigger is to whip him when he does not obey without it," thundered Vardaman, "and another is never to pay him more wages than is actually necessary to buy food and clothing." It soon turned out there were other ways too. The Holly Springs Normal School—the state's only institution for training Negro teachers—had an annual budget of only $2,500 and hadn't been painted for 17 years. But even that was too much. Vardaman swiftly vetoed the 1904 appropriation: "I killed the bill and I killed the school!"

Tighter Jim Crow laws cemented the Negro in his place. One new measure segregated streetcars for the first time; another drew the color line in hospitals; another required Negro nurses for Negro patients.

Nor could the Negro look to his old white friends for any real help. The conservative leaders, seeing how the wind was blowing, vied for red-neck support with ever more incendiary speeches. Campaigning against Vardaman for the Senate in 1907, John Sharp Williams—a patrician to his fingertips—reassured crowds that he matched his opponent on racial matters. All men running for office, declared Williams, "are paying no more attention to Negroes in Mississippi than they are to the mules tied up by those Negroes."

For the next thirty years Mississippi's white leadership never relaxed its pressure. In 1922 a new Jim Crow law kept up with the times by segregating taxis. In 1930 another new law prohibited "publishing, printing or circulating any literature in favor of or urging inter-racial marriage or social equality." And if anybody stepped out of line, there were always stronger measures. Lynching happily declined all through the '20s (thanks mainly to the efforts of the very Southern women it was supposed to protect), but the figure was still high—and Mississippi led the union.

These were the days of the revived KKK, fundamentalism and the Scopes trial, and it followed that there was less patience than ever with Negro education. In 1930 there were about 3,700 colored schools in the state, but 3,243 of them were one- and two-teacher affairs, often housed in old churches, sheds and cabins. Half had no desks, and the blackboard was usually a strip of oilcloth tacked to a wall. Perhaps it made little difference, for 2,719 of the teachers had never finished high school—half of those in Sunflower County tested around the fourth-grade level.

On those rare occasions when public money filtered down, it was quickly siphoned off for white use. For 1928-29 Bolivar County received $99,368.24 from the state school fund, earmarked for the county's Negro children. A hungry Board of Education quickly diverted $50,562.60 of this amount to white schools instead, then added all the available local tax money. In the end Bolivar spent $45.55 per white child, $1.08 per Negro. At that, neither got much of an education—during the same period California's rate was $115 per child.

The depression only made matters worse. New Deal pump-priming rarely touched the Mississippi Negro. Through 1935, for instance, there was only one PWA Negro school project in the state. Mississippi itself was already reeling from floods and the crop-killing boll weevil of the '20s. Now with cotton sinking to 5 cents a pound, nobody could spare any money for "niggers." Negro wages fell to 10 cents an hour.

World War II saw better jobs and pay, but no change in status. And with peace, Mississippians were no different from many others—they only wanted to get back to the way things used to be. An official committee examining Alcorn, the state Negro college in Claiborne County, was horrified to detect strong traces of a liberal arts program. "There has been too much of a nonrealistic feeling that the purpose of a college education has been to prepare youth for white collar jobs," scolded the committee. It urged that Alcorn return to the program established in 1878 and concentrate again on things like sanitation and domestic arts—"skills which actually prepare people to make a living."

Negro voting also called for attention. The Supreme Court had outlawed the white primary in 1944, and now the returning Negro veterans were showing signs of interest. Running in the Democratic primary for the Senate in 1946, Theodore Bilbo—the spiritual heir of James K. Vardaman—called on "every red-blooded American to get out and see that no nigger votes."

When Negro clergyman T. C. Carter tried to cast his ballot at Louisville that July, four white men twice blocked his way. When Mr. and Mrs. V. R. Collier attempted to vote at Pass Christian, a crowd of men threw Collier down and threatened to kill him if he tried to vote that day. It happened all over the state.

"A certain patience," suggested the gentle Mississippi poet, William Alexander Percy, "might well be extended to the South; if not in justice, in courtesy." Nor was Percy the only moderate to ask for more time as the turbulent '40s unfolded.

The trouble was, "more time" all too often meant that the Negro simply drifted farther back. When Mississippi tightened its voting qualifications in 1890, it was argued that the Negroes were not yet ready, since 60% were illiterate. By 1950 the figure had fallen to less than 9%, but fewer Negroes than ever were allowed to register.

In Panola County, where the number of Negro voters had dropped from 1,600 to 385 in the 1890s, the number was now down to 2. During the same period the figure in Holmes County fell from 434 to 8; in Tallahatchie County from 245 to 1.

Nor did "more time" mean more money for Negro education. In 1886 Negro teachers averaged $27.40 a month; in 1939 the figure was $28—a gain of 60 cents. During the '40s take-home pay increased, but so did the gap between Negro and white teachers. The ratio stood at three to two in 1890, but 2.5 to one in 1950.

In 1900 the state spent three times as much on a white student as it did on a Negro; in 1950 the margin was the same.

Moreover, the quality of Negro education fell steadily behind. In 1945 half the teachers still hadn't been through high school. There were only seven regionally accredited Negro schools in the whole state. A Negro boy had less than one chance in 20 of going to a school where he could learn a foreign language.

"More time" was equally meaningless on jobs. In 1902 a Negro church in Jackson listed members in a wide range of interesting occupations—a bakery owner, a fashionable dress designer, a representative of tailoring firms, numerous painters and craftsmen. Negro William H. Smallwood was Jackson's leading expert on leases and deeds in the '80s. In 1905 Greenville listed numerous Negro doctors, lawyers, bookstore owners, cotton samplers. By 1950 all this was over. White workers had crowded out Negroes and monopolized the field. After World War II Greenville experimented with an imaginative plan for training Negro auto mechanics, but the results were disappointing. It proved impossible to place them.

In social life "more time" also found the Negro drifting back. In the 1890s prominent Negroes like J. R. Lynch had lived on Capitol Street, not far from General George himself. By 1950 this was unheard of. All the time, an elaborate system of social taboos continued to multiply, putting the Negro ever more firmly in his place—don't shake hands with one . . . don't let one in the front door . . . and never, never call one "Mr." or "Mrs."

Oddly enough, many Mississippians remained very fond of the Negro. "It is an historic fact," declared Senator James Eastland, "that the Southern white people are the best friends he has ever had." An overstatement, but still it was true that countless white people took care of Negroes when they were sick, fed them when they were hungry and lent them money when they were broke. To a sensitive person like Will Percy, life seemed an endless stream of good deeds: one day he would offer legal help to Nick, a field hand arrested for a shooting scrape . . . the next, he would have to forgive Lege, the gardener, for wrecking the Percy car . . . then he would be intervening for Jim, a houseboy in trouble with the sheriff.

The picture wasn't all that rosy. Even those whites who felt most deeply the spirit of *noblesse oblige* had to trim their sails during hard times. And more and more whites didn't have the spirit at all, as lumbering and other industries crowded out the plantation tradition. In any case, the Negro had to be "good" and "know his place." Still, it was often a happy relationship, and to most visitors the mystery was how so many white people could be so devoted to the Negro and at the same time so firmly hold him down.

A Clarksdale housewife inadvertently supplied an "answer," while trying to set a newcomer straight. "People up North," she explained, "just don't realize all the things we do for Negroes. We don't hate them at all. We're always untangling their problems —which is anything but easy, for after all they're animals, simply animals." A farmer from Calhoun County put it a little more bluntly: "The best way to understand how people here feel is to put it the way my daddy put it: the nigger has no soul. He is like a duck, a chicken or a mule. He just hasn't got a soul." Certainly not all people in Mississippi felt this way, but a surprisingly large number—probably a majority—unconsciously agreed with the redneck logger who summed it all up: "Let's face it; the nigger is a high-class beast."

Once this curious premise was accepted—that the Negro was something less than a real person—everything fell into place. It explained why the people of Marks were so proud of the paved streets in the Negro section—something that might elsewhere be taken for granted. It explained why a Delta housewife felt she was making a major concession when she said she was willing to let her cook use her bomb shelter in the event of nuclear war. It explained why a different standard of justice was meted out to

Negroes—lenience when the matter was between Negroes, harsh treatment when a white was involved. And, of course, it explained the whole strange mixture of kindness and meanness. A man might feel kindly toward a "duck, a chicken or a mule," but he certainly wouldn't want to vote with one, or especially send his child to school with one.

Above all, it explained white Mississippi's deepest fear and obsession: "the mongrelization of the race." If a man really believed a Negro was "like a duck, a chicken or a mule," he understandably didn't want his daughter to marry one. And, paradoxically enough, he seemed sure she might. The inevitable progression was still at work: incidental contact at school must lead to social contact outside, which in turn must lead to mixed marriages and inferior offspring.

It did no good to point out that, even assuming any basis for such weird racial theories, all the experience of integrated schools elsewhere indicated that there would be no significant trend to intermarriage. The standard answer: why take any chances? "We just don't want any of those black babies with blue eyes," declared a plantation manager near Perthshire.

Nor did it do any good to suggest that Negroes might want to go to integrated schools simply to get a better education. The average Mississippian was convinced that sex was all "they" thought about. Social equality still meant what Thomas Nelson Page said in 1904: "To the ignorant and brutal young Negro, it signifies but one thing: the opportunity to enjoy, equally with the white man, the privilege of cohabiting with white women."

And the feeling was compounded by a constant, ceaseless fear of Negro rape. Visitors couldn't hope to understand how deeply this gnawed, for it stemmed from a combination of unique, mysterious forces: the dread of being overwhelmed, the sanctity of Southern Womanhood, whispered superstitions of Negro sexual prowess. Actually, there was little danger. As that astute observer William J. Cash remarked, a Southern white woman had less chance of being raped by a Negro than of being struck by light-

ning. Yet there were occasional cases, and the barest hint was
enough to send most Mississippians racing to man the barriers of
total segregation.

Statistics seemed to back up the white state of mind. The
Negroes did indeed have a far higher crime rate. Although they
were only 45% of the population by 1950, they committed 75%
of the state's crime. But was this a basic quality or a symptom of
something else? There was almost an invitation to lawlessness in a
legal system that saw a Negro in Sunflower County fire five shots
at another and get off with a $10 fine.

White Mississippians also had reason to worry about Negro
sexual customs. Some 25% of colored births were illegitimate;
the rate of venereal disease among Negroes was 15 times that
among whites. Yet here too the question arose, was this inherent
or more likely a matter of living conditions? After all, as State
Judge Tom Brady explained matters, "We have not and do not
punish the Negro—except in rare instances—for desertion, ille-
gitimacy or bigamy." With the brakes off, no wonder the girls'
basketball coach at a Calhoun County Negro high school once saw
his season ruined because the team was pregnant.

The whites also pointed out that Negro children did far worse
at school. In 1949, for instance, when a group of colored pupils
took the Metropolitan Achievement Test in Sunflower County,
they scored two full grades behind the white norms. But it happens
that most of the Negro children had no desks; many sat on the
floor; some had teachers who couldn't do fractions; and all belonged to a school system that the University of Mississippi's
Bureau of Educational Research labeled "a dreary spectacle."

Mississippi, of course, was not alone in this pattern of white
and Negro relationships. There were similarities in all the Southern
states, and, for that matter, the rest of the country too. Still, there
were also differences—differences that by 1950 made Mississippi a
special case.

One obvious difference lay in population. In 1950 Mississippi
was 45% Negro—the highest percentage in the country. True, the

figure was slipping—some 87,187 Negroes had left the state since 1940—but the percentage was still high compared to other states. Besides, in some parts of Mississippi the whites were far out-numbered. Tunica County, for instance, had 17,700 Negroes, only 3,900 whites. And there was always the past—those fearful days when a defeated, shattered, white minority lived in constant dread of an untrained but politically powerful Negro majority. Mississippians had long memories, and the specter of those times lingered on.

A more subtle but more important difference was the state's special brand of poverty. In 1950 Mississippi was easily the poorest in the Union. Her citizens had only half the per capita income enjoyed by the rest of the country. Both races suffered—in Issaquena County even the whites averaged only $967 a year. The state's Agricultural and Industrial Board worked hard to bring in new business, but its very sales pitch hinged on conditions remaining depressed. One brochure boasted, "There are available at least two applicants for each new job offered." The fight for jobs—the battle to hold the few advantages left—made the white people all the more determined to hold the line against any sign of Negro advance.

Still another distinction was the state's low level of education. Poor people can't afford the best schools, and Mississippi was no exception. In 1950 the state paid the lowest faculty salaries in the Southeast, and the ablest teachers naturally drifted elsewhere. Poverty also meant that many people couldn't afford to go to school at all—half the state's adults had only eight years' exposure. Nor was low Negro attendance by any means the whole explanation: the whites alone averaged less than ten years. The significance of all this emerged in many ways. Mississippi had the fewest number of patents for its population of any state in the Union . . . the fewest doctors and nurses . . . the next to smallest number of dentists . . . the poorest trained teachers. There was, in short, a striking lack of educated leadership.

Life in Mississippi also had a stagnant quality that made the state a special case. Jackson, Greenville, the Gulf Coast might be thriving, but their shiny motels were deceptive. Far more meaningful were the scores of sleepy little towns quietly withering away. In 1950 county seats like Mayersville, Carrollton and Pittsboro had fewer people than any time since 1900. Whole counties were fading away. Carroll, Jefferson, Claiborne, all had less population than in 1840. The downward trend had been going on for some time, but the new mechanical cotton picker gave it an extra shove. The machine was a godsend to the big plantations, but it doomed thousands of field hands, dirt farmers and the whole network of stores and suppliers that kept them going. Some ten people were leaving Mississippi for every one person coming in, and, still worse, those departing included 75% of the state's college graduates.

The strange emptiness of Mississippi gave the place an air of isolation that was another of its special qualities. Even Alaska had a greater percentage of its population in urban areas. There were no really large cities—in 1950 the capital, Jackson, was still under 100,000. Nor was there any of the culture that serves as a link with the outside world. Jackson's only bookstore was run by the Baptist Church and limited largely to religious topics. Elsewhere there wasn't even that—Oxford, the state's center of learning, had no regular bookstores at all. Nor were there adequate libraries to fill the gap. Twenty-seven of the state's counties had no library that met any standards whatsoever. Even the newsstands had little to offer; they rarely displayed the better-known national magazines, featured instead a host of titles devoted to lust and horror.

As a result, Mississippi inevitably took little interest in the rest of America, and by 1950 the rest of America took little interest in her. Poverty and isolation had done their work. In fact, the last major Presidential candidate who had bothered to visit the state was Henry Clay.

All this led to an enormously self-contained existence; and that, in turn, became one more difference that set Mississippi apart from the rest of the Union. In the words of a native, "Mississippi is not a state but a club." Everybody seemed to know everybody else. Doors always seemed open—all a visitor needed was a name that clicked. Personal relationships were the key to everything.

This small world gave Mississippians certain virtues fast disappearing from the rest of the world. People were immensely courteous to one another and never seemed particularly hurried. A man would go ten miles out of his way to show a stranger the right road. The smallest purchase wound up with a friendly clerk's "Come back and see us some time."

But by the same token, everybody knew exactly what everybody else was doing. A 70-mile drive through the Delta elicited the most minute details about the homes along the way: this man had a new brown dog . . . that man sold a field last week . . . the family over there was fighting with the insurance adjuster. It was impossible to take a step—or a stand—in Mississippi without the rest of the state instantly knowing about it.

The tendency to conform was enormous. Far more than elsewhere, men wore the same necktie (dark), drove the same cars (cream-colored), lived for the same football games (Ole Miss—LSU), and above all belonged to the same party (Democratic). The state's allegiance was never better expressed than in 1890, when Chancellor Edward Mayer of the University of Mississippi declared, "I have never failed to vote Democratic, I have never scratched a ticket, and I would not, no matter whom the party might nominate for its candidate."

The New Deal did indeed strain the allegiance, but characteristically Mississippi still conformed at the moment of truth—election day. When the state finally strayed from the fold in 1948, the rationalization developed that Mississippi was still holding to the true faith; it was the rest of the Democrats who had bolted away.

The more postwar America changed, the more Mississippi retreated into its own self-contained little world. By-passed by the march of events, the state saw little connection between itself and all the strange new things going on—the UN, Marshall Plan, NATO, welfare measures at home. All this meant only more centralized government, and the people were in no mood for that— states' rights were the very heart of the South's solution to the race problem. Mississippi became increasingly suspicious of "outside interference" and increasingly proud of its own way of life. Once again thoughts turned to the glorious past. . . .

"For any Southern boy fourteen years old," wrote Mississippi's own William Faulkner, "not once but whenever he wants it, there is the instant when it's still not two o'clock on that July afternoon in 1863, the brigades are in position behind the rail fence, the guns are laid and ready in the woods . . . and it's all in the balance, it hasn't happened yet."

It might only be added that in the Mississippi of 1950 the daydream was not limited to 14-year-old boys. Every age lived with the fantasy. The state officially observed Confederate Memorial Day, Lee's and Jefferson Davis' birthday . . . while studiously ignoring Lincoln and the national Memorial Day. Jackson boasted its Rebel Concrete Company, Rebel Garment Company, Rebel Roofing & Metal Company. Hattiesburg had its Rebel Theatre, Oxford its Rebel Cosmotology College. Schoolboys loved to dress up in Confederate uniforms . . . older men wistfully told how it all might have been different if only Pemberton had held at Champion Hill. ("It still breaks my heart when I think of it," one confessed.) Confederate flags hung from porches all over the state; and in case anyone ever needed reminding, there was always the reproachful gaze of the noble stone soldier who stood atop the Confederate monument in every courthouse square. . . .

> Lord God of hosts,
> Be with us yet,
> Lest we forget,
> Lest we forget.

So ran the lovingly carved inscription on the monument at Kosciusko, the quiet, pleasant seat of Attala County. The gray ranks were fading fast by the time these words were chiseled, but the inscription went on to promise that "the South will live forever in the glory of your world."

Kosciusko kept faith. In 1950 very little was going on, and the town seemed more than content to live with its memories. The county's population was falling—now down to the 1900 level— and the Negroes' share of 43% had remained fairly constant for 40 years. As people drifted from the marginal hills, Kosciusko itself tended to grow, but a glance at the listless figures lolling by the courthouse suggested anything but a boom town.

That June a 17-year-old Negro boy named J. H. Meredith completed the 11th grade at Kosciusko's Tipton High School and began to think about the rest of his education. Christened simply "J.H."—a device frequently used by Mississippi Negroes to keep whites from calling them only by first name—Meredith was one of ten children. His father, Moses Meredith, scratched out a living on an 84-acre cotton and corn farm not far from town. Moses was considered a "good" Negro—so "good," in fact, that he was one of 34 Negroes (out of 5,179 of voting age) that the county allowed to vote.

It was a relaxed family, and in many ways J.H. lived the typically relaxed life of a Negro child in rural Mississippi. Like the other boys, he sold grasshoppers to local fishermen for bait, belonged to a Scout troop and caddied at Kosciusko's golf club.

But there were differences too. For one thing, he didn't scare easily. He never worried about the thickets and dark hollows that often give pause to small boys at night. Also, he was strikingly independent. Growing up in the middle of a large family, he wasn't especially close to any of his brothers and sisters; going from the farm to school in town made him neither a city nor a country boy. He seemed something of a loner, and his father noticed that he read a lot.

Perhaps all this helped explain still another difference—from his earliest years young Meredith was exceptionally sensitive about his race. In a way this seemed odd, for as Mississippi towns went, Kosciusko was a "good" town for Negroes, and the Merediths themselves, owning their own farm, lived reasonably free of white pressures. Nevertheless, the feeling was there, and when the local white patriarch distributed pennies and nickels to the Negro children, J.H. would quietly turn away.

He experienced a far more searing incident when he was 15. Returning in 1948 from a trip to Detroit, the conductor made him change to the Jim Crow car when the train reached Memphis. Negroes had been doing this for over 50 years, but it was the first time for J.H., and he cried all the way home.

This kind of boy couldn't help but notice that the lines of segregation were even more firmly drawn at school. As always, everything was supposed to be "separate but equal," but, as always, the standard only got lip service. In 1950 Mississippi spent $78.70 a head teaching white children, $23.83 teaching Negroes; white classes ran around 26 children, Negro classes 34; white teachers averaged $1,865 a year, Negroes only $918. White students, though outnumbered by Negroes, even got 80% of the money for school busses. J. H. Meredith knew none of these statistics, but any sensitive schoolboy could see the difference. In 1950 he decided his prospects just weren't worth walking those four miles to Tipton High any longer.

That summer he went to live with his uncle in Florida and took senior year at Gibbs High School in St. Petersburg. Here he had an unpleasant surprise. Always one of the brightest boys back in Kosciusko, he suddenly found himself desperately trying to keep up. It seemed that a person's performance had a great deal to do with past training.

Back home after graduation, J.H. yearned to go to college, but he well knew that Mississippi's special brand of "separate but equal" applied here too. Alcorn, the most established of the Negro colleges, had just one Ph.D. on the entire faculty. While white students at the University of Mississippi enjoyed their new million-dollar library, Alcorn students huddled in overcoats in a crowded second-story room with no heat, little light and books stacked all over the floor. Only 15% of the state's appropriations for what it liked to call "institutions of higher learning" went to Negro colleges. In fact, the only statistical area where Negroes enjoyed an edge was in the matter of library use. At new, lively Jackson State books circulated at twice the rate they did at Ole Miss.

If the Negro colleges were discouraging, so was the future that awaited the graduates. They were prepared for practically nothing except teaching. Even here the level of training was too low to get a job anywhere outside the state system of public education. The effect was significant: the only "home-grown" class of Negro professionals was in the state's pay, completely at the mercy of the white politicians who held the purse strings.

Independent, race-conscious J. H. Meredith wanted none of it. Far better to get his military service out of the way; so on July 28, 1951 he entered the Air Force as a volunteer. His choice of branch was easy. It was common knowledge among draft-conscious Negroes that the Air Force gave them a better break. It was almost symbolic that now for the first time he decided to adopt a full name—the initials "J.H." were converted to "James Howard."

Years would pass before James Howard Meredith had to face the problem of being a Negro in Mississippi again. Meanwhile a great force was gathering momentum which would have infinite bearing not only on his own future but on that of every other Negro in America.

3

"We Shall Overcome"

Private James Howard Meredith was still in basic training at Sampson Air Force base when in the fall of 1951 another sensitive American Negro named Oliver Brown decided to do something about his daughter's education. The Browns lived in Topeka, Kansas, where the elementary schools were segregated, and eight-year-old Linda had to cross the railroad yards and take a bus 21 blocks for her classes, while the white school was an easy walk just five blocks away.

Along with a dozen other Negro parents, Oliver Brown sued to end Topeka's segregated school system. They argued, as other Negroes before, that this was discrimination and violated the Fourteenth Amendment, guaranteeing them "equal protection of the laws." The court disagreed. It followed, as other courts before, the line laid down in the *Plessy* case: segregation was legal as long as the facilities were "separate but equal." Since the Negro schools in Topeka were admittedly on a par with the white, Oliver Brown and his friends had no case.

They now appealed to the Supreme Court, but if precedent ruled the day, they had no chance here either, for in six consecutive cases since 1899 the Court had accepted the "separate but equal" yardstick. Then why do it? What made them think that the Supreme Court might change its position after all these years?

The answer lay in the new awakening of what had been for most of the past 75 years a slumbering giant—the American Negro. Since 1875 his dormancy had been more than a story of Southern repression and paternalism . . . more than a case of Northern hypocrisy and indifference. He had also retired as a matter of choice.

Booker T. Washington had pointed the way. As the racist fever mounted in the '90s, the great Negro educator urged his people to be patient. They should renounce any claims to social, political and economic equality . . . concentrate instead on a simple, useful role that would win white acceptance. "In all things that are purely social," Washington declared at Atlanta in 1895, "we can be as separate as the fingers, yet one as the hand in all things essential to national progress."

In this partnership the tasks assigned the Negro were mostly humble and manual: "The masses of us are to live by the production of our hands, and we shall prosper in proportion as we learn to dignify and glorify common labor." Later, after the Negro had proved his worth, he could go on to higher goals. But Washington soft-pedaled this at the moment—agitating for equality was "the extremest folly."

Called the "Atlanta compromise," Washington's overture was probably the best deal he could make at the time. With more than 90% of the nation's Negroes living in the rural South—where the slightest sign of resistance brought the fiercest retaliation—the practical course was to renounce any lofty ambitions. Moreover, Washington's views meshed perfectly with the current thinking of Northern philanthropists. A shower of Yankee dollars descended on "worthwhile" Negro projects like the vocational program at Washington's own Tuskegee Institute.

But the price was high. Accepting an inferior role meant more and more Negroes squeezed out of good jobs; and swallowing segregation eased the burden on a lot of white consciences. The very next year the Supreme Court issued its famous *Plessy* decision, approving the idea of "separate but equal." Then came a host of new Jim Crow rules, covering every conceivable activity—Louisiana segregated tent show ticket windows . . . Oklahoma, phone booths . . . Atlanta, even the Bible used in its courts.

Most important of all was the effect of the "Atlanta compromise" on the Negroes themselves. It was not a big step from giving up any role in public life to giving up any interest in it. Politics became "white folks' business"—40% of Birmingham's Negro teachers never even asked to vote. School dropouts increased; attendance fell: only 31% of the nation's Negro children were going to school by 1900—a lower figure than in 1880. In the words of their own spokesmen, the Negro people developed "a fatalistic indifference" . . . "a corroding sense of inferiority" . . . "a tacit acceptance of things as they were."

"Your race is adapted to be a race of farmers, first, last, and for all time," President William Howard Taft told a group of Negro students at Charlotte, North Carolina, in May 1909. Certainly the government acted that way—only 1,000 Negroes held federal jobs in 1900. Negro mail clerks gradually swelled the ranks, but the number of responsible openings actually shrank: Negro postmasters declined from 153 in 1910 to 78 in 1930.

Yet even when the Negro was most firmly "in his place," there always remained faint stirrings of protest. In 1903 a slight, nervous Negro sociologist named W. E. B. DuBois snorted at Booker T. Washington's faith in humble industry, wondered how any people could become great by going to vocational school alone. In 1905 DuBois joined some other Negroes at Niagara Falls, Canada (the hotel on the American side was segregated), and launched a program for full equality. In 1910—after a jarring race riot in Abraham Lincoln's own Springfield—these leaders joined a still larger group, both Negro and white. Together they formed a new organization, the National Association for the Advancement of Colored People, to work permanently for genuine equality.

And all the while there were other Negroes who kept quiet the way Dr. Washington wanted, but who inwardly seethed at wretched seats in the theater balcony . . . at "nigger wages" . . . or even at the humiliation of finding their first reader was a small picture book called *Little Black Sambo.*

But the mass of Negroes did remain inert, even content, and it required something far more forceful than splinter movements or hidden pangs of resentment to wake them up and change their ways. The harbinger came on June 28, 1914, when a bomb in distant Sarajevo killed an archduke, launched a war and stopped the surge of immigrants to America. These new arrivals had previously given the North a steady supply of good, cheap labor. Now the flow immediately slid from a million in 1914 to only 300,000 a year later. Northern industry began to look around for a new source of unskilled workers.

At the same time a series of triphammer blows hit the Negro in the South. The boll weevil was ravaging cotton. Many big planters were shifting to better land in the West. Unemployment ran high, with whites moving in on Negro jobs more vigorously than ever. A disastrous flood in the summer of 1915 was ironically capped by a ruinous drought the following year. All these things had happened before, but never so many at once.

The pull of the North and the push of the South had its effect. Negroes began to head for the new opportunities they heard were opening up. At first it was a barely perceptible trickle—just a few ragged families tumbling off the Jim Crow cars in Chicago or New York. But as word got back that indeed it was true—as Northern hiring agents made the circuit with tales of good jobs and high wages—the trickle became a stream . . . a river . . . a torrent. By 1917 some 500,000-750,000 Negroes had moved North—one-tenth of the nation's entire colored population.

The great migration, of course, brought release from the worst Jim Crow laws and with it, wider horizons. More important, it also brought positive gains. The new jobs typically paid four times as much as a field hand could earn back South. Above all, the move North turned into a move to the city, and in the great urban centers where he settled the Negro soon discovered that he was no longer a lonely isolated figure on the farm; he was now part of a bloc that could control votes and bring pressure.

All this was busily fermenting in 1917 when America's entry into the war gave a new impetus to the whole trend. "Make the world safe for democracy," Woodrow Wilson said, and the black man heard him along with the rest. Then came the draft— 400,000 Negroes in the armed services, 200,000 overseas, finding ever wider horizons, gaining ever more challenging ideas. And on the home front, shipyards, steel mills, defense plants beckoned still more Negroes from the South. By the war's end 15% of all U.S. Negroes now lived in the North.

The '20s saw a bitter reaction—race riots, intolerance, Klansmen riding again in the night—but these years also saw another new development that affected North and South alike. As the Negro moved off the farm into the city (and he was doing this all over the country), he was suddenly exposed to real education. Negro school attendance soared from 31% in 1900 to 60% in 1930. In 1915 there were only 64 public high schools for Negroes in the entire South; by 1935 there were 2,305. The effect was inevitable; years earlier Mississippi's Jim Vardaman had put his finger on it when he complained, "This education is ruining our Negroes. They're demanding equality."

Better education had another effect too. An ever-growing number of Negroes were getting jobs higher up the pay scale . . . beginning to make real money . . . building an important, potentially powerful business and professional class of their own. Some 30 successful Negro insurance companies were founded during this period. And all the time the great migration continued. During the '20s over 700,000 more quit the South; by 1930 some 20% of the nation's Negroes were now in the North.

And then the depression. In the South it hit cotton worst of all, for on top of the slump there were rising foreign production and the trend to rayon. By 1932 anyone growing cotton was making only 31% as much money as he made in 1929. The Negroes suffered most—they had the poorest land, and were at the bottom of the economic ladder anyhow. And this time there were no jobs waiting in the North. A forest of smokeless chimneys told the story. Half of all the Negro men in Philadelphia were unemployed.

At this desperate hour help came from an unexpected source. The Negroes were traditionally Republicans, and 1932 was no exception—75% voted for Hoover in Chicago, 63% in Detroit. Nor was there reason to expect much hope from the victorious Democratic candidate, Franklin D. Roosevelt. Certainly he had never shown much sensitivity on Negro problems. During the Washington race riots of 1919 he had jokingly written his old Harvard classmate, Joseph R. Hamlem, in Little Rock: "With your experience in handling Africans in Arkansas, I think you had better come up here and take charge of the police force."

Yet somewhere along the line a change had taken place in Roosevelt—perhaps due partly to shrewd politics, partly to a wife with a great social conscience, partly to the workings of his own impulsive heart. In any case, when the reporters assembled around FDR's desk at the very start of the new Administration, there among the others was Edgar G. Brown of the Chicago *Defender,* the first Negro correspondent ever admitted to a White House press conference.

It was symbolic. Negroes suddenly began getting attention. Secretary of the Interior Harold Ickes, once head of the Chicago NAACP, became a sort of coordinator on racial matters. The Administration was soon appointing Negroes to important jobs. The burgeoning New Deal agencies started paying attention to Negro problems and interests.

Not that it was all clover. The FHA not only approved restrictive covenants but even explained how to draw them up. The NRA froze wage differentials based on race—40 cents an hour was the pay set for a white steelworker in Pittsburgh, as against 27 cents for a Negro in Birmingham. The AAA crop reduction program threw thousands of Negroes off the farms, and its schedule of benefit payments seemed ludicrous: a typical plantation owner received $979 in annual payments, while his Negro tenant got only $11. Even the progressive TVA played favorites: its fertilizer program completely ignored Negro agricultural colleges.

But all this was nothing compared to the blessings. Down South the FSA taught small Negro farmers how to diversify, how to live off their land, even how to keep accounts. In the great urban centers the USHA gave the Negro his first taste of subsidized low-cost housing—41,000 units by 1941. The PWA poured money into Negro education—$3 million for Howard University alone. The WPA had over 237,000 Negroes on its payroll by 1941, and its adult education program taught 400,000 Negroes how to read and write.

Best of all was the new atmosphere. At last somebody really seemed to care. On February 19, 1934, a Mississippi Negro farmer named Sylvester Harris, facing a mortgage foreclosure, knew just what to do. Taking his last $10, he put through a call to the White House. He did not even consider it unusual when he was ultimately plugged through to the President himself. "A man is getting ready to take my land," he explained. "I want to know what to do and the papers say call you. . . ."

"Sylvester," Roosevelt quietly replied, "I'll investigate and you'll hear from me." A flurry of White House calls followed, and in due course Harris' farm was saved.

November 2, 1936, and the Negroes showed their gratitude. One after another Roosevelt won the "black belt" urban districts that had gone for Hoover in 1932. In Kansas City's Second Ward FDR's margin jumped from 41% to 61%; in Detroit's Third Ward, from 46% to 71%; in New Haven's 19th, from 39% to 61%.

The effect was not lost on the Democratic Party. In a close election states like Illinois, Michigan and New York could swing the victory; Chicago, Detroit and New York City could swing those states; and the local Negro population could swing those cities.

Nor was the point lost on the Negroes. There was suddenly a feeling of new power and importance. Maybe not yet in the South, but certainly in the North—in fact, in the country as a whole— they were at last a force to be taken into account. And adding to their pride in these days of fresh hope were exciting new Negro personalities: Jesse Owens, the great Olympic star . . . Joe Louis, the heavyweight champion of the world . . . A. Philip Randolph, rising to the top rank among America's labor leaders. Negroes like Robert C. Weaver began reaching the policymaking level of the federal government.

It was hard for the whites not to notice. In the paneled drawing rooms of the North rumors spread of "Eleanor Clubs" composed of Negro bus riders pledged to jostle at least one white passenger a day. In the South a wistful William Alexander Percy lamented, "The Negro is losing his most valuable weapon of defense—his good manners."

Pearl Harbor brought still another turning point. Oddly, its first effect was not to advance but to slow down the Negro awakening. The country's military leaders were traditionally conservative, tended to do things the usual way, and included an exceptionally large number of Southerners. Negro soldiers were used for only menial jobs and enjoyed no particular respect. As late as August 8, 1941, a Negro detachment marching along an Arizona highway was pushed off the road by the state police. When their white officer protested, the patrolman slapped him about and called him a "nigger lover."

The bombs of December 7 only froze these conditions. There was much talk about putting aside all other goals until the war was won—which, of course, meant any drive for equal rights. Entering the services, the Negro quickly found evidence of a world he had hoped he was escaping—no Negro Marines . . . no Negro

WAVES . . . and for a while no Negro pilots. In the mushrooming defense plants the Negro suddenly found all over again many of the obstacles he thought he had conquered. As late as June 1942 there were only 5,000 Negro aircraft plant workers—about 1% of the total.

The result was a bitterness far different from the reaction in 1917 when even the fiery W. E. B. DuBois had called for "closing the ranks." This time there had simply been too many advances ever to go back. And discrimination seemed especially ironic in this of all wars—with the chief target Hitler and his concept of the "master race." So the Negro declined to put aside his goals. Rather, he continued to press for better treatment in return for his all-out contribution. And the Administration responded—the FEPC, ever broader integration of the services.

Nor did peace mean any return to the past. Communism . . . the Cold War . . . establishment of the UN headquarters in New York . . . Korea . . . the emerging African nations all saw to that. In 1948 Harry Truman issued effective orders that permanently integrated the armed forces, and in countless other ways Washington responded to the dictates of foreign policy.

The Negro leaders pressed their advantage. By now they had far more savvy than before the war—the natural result of service abroad, the GI Bill of Rights, the ever-wider horizons opened up by television and automobiles. These leaders immediately saw the paradox of courting Negroes in Africa while suppressing them at home. They easily recognized the irony of the whole State Department trying to get a cup of coffee for a Negro diplomat on Route 40, while nobody lifted a finger for a Boston Negro in exactly the same fix. "The most wonderful thing that can happen today," Negro minister Gordon Taylor bitterly told author Louis Lomax, "is to be black in America as long as you're not an American."

All these feelings surged to the fore at the very time when the rural Southern Negro was once again facing a crisis. With the end of the war he found himself up against an agricultural revolution. New methods of scientific farming encouraged larger holdings and concentrated production on only the best land—displacing thousands of Negroes on marginal patches. The mechanical cotton picker was at last a reality too, and each one of these monstrous, clanking machines displaced 150 field hands.

At the same time the pull of the North was stronger than ever. Far from the postwar unemployment so direly predicted, both jobs and pay were soaring. By 1950 a typical Negro family made $3,243 a year in a Northern city compared to $763 on a Southern farm.

Word drifted back and the stampede was on. While the country's over-all Negro population went up two million during the '40s, the figure actually fell in seven Southern states. Alabama lost 202,000 . . . Georgia, 240,000 . . . Mississippi, a whopping 326,000. In Mississippi rural counties like Carroll and Alcorn lost a quarter of their Negroes in ten years.

The picture was, of course, exactly the opposite in the great Northern cities. In Cleveland the Negro population climbed from 84,504 to 217,000 . . . in Detroit, from 149,000 to 375,000 . . . in Philadelphia, from 250,880 to 456,000. Aided by the new network of postwar highways, the tide spread West too—the number of Negroes in Los Angeles, for instance, jumped from 63,774 to 275,000.

Even the Southern cities felt the impact. If the opportunities weren't quite so bright as in the North, at least a man could make more than three times as much as he did on the farm. And it was the chance to make money, rather than oppression, that was driving the Negro from his land. It was only after he got to town that he began to think of other things too. But then he did, and it was of no little importance that cities like Atlanta, Birmingham and Jackson also saw a great increase in their number of Negroes.

It all added up to an enormous shift in half a century. In 1900 two out of every three Negroes lived quietly and docilely on a

Southern farm. By 1950 only one out of six was still there; nearly all the rest were now crowded into teeming Southern towns or the great industrial cities of the North and West. They were highly restless and likely to grow more so.

For their power was steadily rising. Politically, the more they piled into the key Northern cities, the more their leverage grew. Economically, many were now reaching a point where they could start to swing some weight. By 1950 Negro businessmen represented real money—Durham's North Carolina Mutual Life Insurance Company boasted $50 million assets, Birmingham's A. G. Gaston was becoming one of the wealthiest men in Alabama. Expensive Negro homes dotted Atlanta's Collier Heights, Chicago's Hyde Park district, Los Angeles' Country Club Drive. More important, decent incomes were beginning to seep down to the ordinary ranks—some 12% of all Negroes were now holding white-collar jobs and the number of union members had doubled in ten years. Total Negro income now touched $11 billion a year—three times the prewar figure and worth as much as America's whole export business.

With better times went better education. In 1939 some 9,000 Mississippi Negroes went to public high school; by 1952 the figure was 27,000—an increase of 300%. College education soared too—Mississippi's Alcorn College had 173 students in 1944, 760 nine years later. By the early '50s some 8,000 Negroes were graduating from U.S. colleges every year.

By now the American Negro was a far cry from the submissive rural creature who bore segregation so easily at the turn of the century. The great migration North, two wars, new political power, more money and the rudiments of a good education had all done their work. He was now wide-awake. In the South the mass of Negroes were not yet on fire with any deep yearning for equality —but they had reached a highly combustible state. In the North there was still some indifference too—but much less so. And among a growing group of young Negroes—both North and

South—there was no apathy at all. There was only impatience. Armed with a new sense of self-respect and dignity, they were determined to win an equal share of everything the country had to offer.

There was no formal starting date for their drive. Soon after the war a wide variety of signs simply began to appear, showing that the time had come. In Columbia, Tennessee, one February day in 1946 a young Negro Navy veteran hurled a white TV repairman through a plate-glass window after the repairman reportedly slapped the Negro's mother. A white mob built up, but instead of hiding in their shacks, this time the local Negroes stood their ground and emerged from the ordeal with a new feeling of purpose.

Over much of the South Negroes were also beginning to vote in unprecedented numbers. In fact, the vote doubled in five years. Some of this was certainly due to the Supreme Court decision outlawing the "white primary," and the fast-vanishing poll tax also played a part. But there was more to it than that. The real answer lay in the mounting tide of protest and a new determination to act.

On the job front there was the same mood of rebellion in the air. In Charleston, South Carolina, Negro members of the Food and Tobacco Workers Association—feeling at last the strength that went with having a union—struck to raise their wages of 45 cents an hour. Marching on the picket line, they sang a haunting song they had picked up somewhere:

> The truth will make us free, the truth
>   will make us free,
> The truth will make us free some day.
> Oh, deep in my heart I do believe
> We shall overcome some day.

But it still seemed so slow. True, there were the great symbolic gains that turned out to be real breakthroughs: Jackie Robinson, the Bell Telephone Company's first Negro phone operators, a few others. But all too often these symbolic victories were only that and nothing more. In housing, the Supreme Court declared restrictive covenants were unenforceable, yet 231 out of 253 Chicago suburbs remained virtually segregated. The unions spoke piously against discrimination, yet even in the UAW, one of the most liberal, only 40% of the locals had any skilled Negro workers. The professions talked of more openings, yet only 200 Negro doctors, 150 Negro engineers entered practice every year. (In 1950, in fact, 22% of all Negro college graduates could only find laboring and service jobs.) Economists pointed out that the Negro-white income gap was closing, yet the fact remained that 40% of all Negro families still made less than $2,000 a year. The South was promising great things for Negro education, but in a candid moment the Speaker of the Georgia House of Representatives confessed, "Negro education in Georgia is a disgrace. What the Negro child gets in the sixth grade, the white child gets in the second grade."

In some areas the Negro was even losing ground. There was less room for expansion—the segregated suburbs now circling most cities served as a white wall penning minority groups into the heart of town. There was more Negro unemployment too, as automation began to squeeze out the unskilled jobs. Above all, segregation itself was spreading in some areas, as Southern whites countered the Negro advance. Passing through the Nashville airport in 1945, Negro journalist Carl Rowan saw no trace of separate washrooms; by his next visit in 1951 the "white" and "colored" signs were firmly posted.

"They like it better that way," Southern whites continued to say, and to a certain extent it was true. Many older Negroes in the cotton states were content as long as they had that kindly planter who looked after them when they were sick, broke or in jail. Others didn't care, they weren't going anywhere anyhow: only 2% of Mississippi's colored children ever finished high school;

only 20% of one Harlem district bothered to vote. Still others had made their peace. When the Rev. Vernon Johns was ordered off a Montgomery bus for refusing to sit in the back, he appealed to the other Negro passengers to follow him, but not a single one did. Instead, they later passed him the message, "You ought to knowed better."

But many of those docile faces were deceptive. As James Baldwin has explained, the Negro is "almost always acting," and much of his contentment was put on for the whites. Fired by the victories and frustrations of a changing world, he was more and more often seething inside. The Southern hosts who assured visitors that the Negroes really liked segregation ("My cook told me so") were much further from the truth than the others who confessed, "You never really know what they're thinking."

The younger Negroes—those born between the wars—didn't even bother to hide their feelings. They were mad at everybody —at the segregationists, at the ineffectual moderates, at their own rank and file. And especially at their leaders. It was with good reason that the rising Negro sociologist, Whitney Young, wryly observed, "Hurry up, there go our followers."

The Negro business leaders seemed unbearably cautious. They were to be the great future hope under Booker T. Washington's master plan, but it hadn't worked out that way. Instead, they ended up with a vested interest in a special Negro world apart from the rest of America—which was exactly what the young people were trying to escape.

The Negro press talked a good game in the North, but only to other Negroes, and in the end it too was based on the premise of a separate Negro life. In the South this press had additional difficulties, for it was nearly always hard up, and in a hostile community had to watch its step to stay alive.

Negro educators were even less likely to spout fire. Most were constantly under the thumb of some Southern state legislature. One false step—a questionable remark or some sign of student unrest—could mean no money, and maybe no job. Since there were no other openings for an educated Negro in the Deep South, most played ball with the state. As a Negro teacher in Mississippi put it, "If a college man gets out of line, he can't make a living."

The Negro clergy were most exasperating of all. They seemed such logical spokesmen for the rising tide of protest, yet most sounded not only passive but quaint. They saw the church as a way to escape the pains of the world, not as a moral force that could help heal them. When a Negro minister in Savannah was asked just before the war why he tried to discourage a voter registration drive, he explained, "All we preachers is supposed to do is to preach the Lord and Savior Jesus Christ and Him Crucified, and that's all."

Nor by 1950 did the aroused Negroes have much patience with the organizations trying to advance their cause. The interracial Urban League—orginally formed to help colored migrants find jobs and adjust to city life—seemed to dodge the main issue. It operated, to use the caustic words of an angry young Ralph Bunche, "within the genteel framework of conciliation." The Southern Regional Council was even more suspect. It was the only interracial group based in the South itself, and the courage of its white members was overlooked in the suspicion and scorn that greeted their caution. The National Association for the Advancement of Colored People was admittedly beyond suspicion (despite its interracial leadership at the top), but it was narrow and intellectual in its approach. Its main emphasis was on lobbying and filing suits. To the growing mass of restless Negroes these paper battles seemed mighty remote.

This was misleading. In its unexciting way, the NAACP was steadily laying a solid, indispensable foundation for a mass movement that could later take off in any direction. Its effective campaign against lynching, for instance, helped give the Southern Negro the physical safety he absolutely needed if he was going to do anything at all for himself. And by winning the so-called

Arkansas Riot Case in 1919, NAACP greatly strengthened the position of Negroes forced to defend themselves when physically attacked by whites. Other Supreme Court victories were one by one blasting some favorite segregationist devices—1915, the "grandfather clause" that erected special voting barriers against anyone whose grandfather hadn't voted . . . 1923, exclusion of Negroes from jury lists . . . 1944, the "white primary" . . . 1946, segregated interstate busses. True, after every defeat the segregationists usually came up with some new device (there was no limit to their ingenuity), but each time they were on a little bit more dubious legal grounds. And each time the next NAACP victory was that much easier and the day that much closer when ordinary Negroes might act on their own, feeling they could count on the federal government.

This quiet but effective battle was in full swing when a new young lawyer came to work for NAACP in 1936. Thurgood Marshall was only three years out of law school, but his tough quick mind soon put him in charge of the work. It proved a wise choice; before he was through, Marshall was to win 29 of the 32 cases he argued before the Supreme Court.

All the time the battle steadily advanced. When Marshall first came, NAACP's legal budget was perhaps $8000-$9000 a year, but the case load steadily grew—and with it, the need for money. By 1940 the great American game of tax-saving led NAACP to set up a separate organization to handle all this law work. Called the NAACP Legal Defense and Educational Fund, it seemed the only way to keep contributions for these courtroom battles deductible, since the lobbying phase of the organization's work clearly didn't qualify for tax relief.

The new organization had its work cut out for it. Under a strategy devised by Marshall's predecessor Charles H. Houston, NAACP was now cautiously attacking school segregation. Previously this had been left pretty much alone—first, because the South was so sensitive about it; second, because the Supreme Court itself had been so firm in following the doctrine of "separate but equal."

But times were changing. For one thing, the country's liberals had at last taken up the racial issue. This was partly due to the Negro's ever-growing strength in the great urban liberal centers, but an even more important reason was the emotional experience of the war. Nazi Germany put the racial issue forward in a way that couldn't be dodged, and America's liberals began doing some soul-searching of their own. In Congress the tide of civil rights bills rose from ten in 1937-38 to 72 in 1949-50. By 1949 some 70% of the faculty members in white Southern colleges favored admitting Negroes to graduate and professional schools. As always in American life, the Supreme Court began reflecting the mood of the times.

At the same moment the Negro was also picking up important new scientific backing. It had long been noted that colored IQs ran lower than white; in fact, this was often used as one more argument for segregation, since most people felt a person's IQ was something inherent and quite unrelated to influences like education or environment. But during the '30s and '40s a whole new school of social scientists took the opposite position. They marshalled reams of statistics to prove that the IQ is directly related to environment—hence the Negro's low intelligence score might well be due to his poor schooling, wretched housing and dreary prospects. One study showed that Negroes in the rural South averaged 25% lower scores than those in the border states. Another showed that Negro children who had just reached New York averaged only 72, but after seven to nine years in the city the figure jumped to 92. One survey even showed that Negroes in the most prosperous Northern states had a better average than whites in the poorest Southern states. Authorities like Clyde Kluckhohn and A. L. Kroeber turned out popular books spelling out their theories, and the Supreme Court's decisions began to suggest that some of the judges were reading them.

"The basic consideration," declared Chief Justice Hughes in a

1938 case rejecting Missouri's attempt to provide separate but equal education for Negro law students by paying their way to schools outside the state, "is what opportunities Missouri itself furnishes to white students and denies to Negroes solely upon the ground of color." It was a major departure to weigh an intangible like "opportunity"—more was to follow.

In 1950 the Court rejected Texas' attempt to solve the same problem by setting up a "separate but equal" law school for its Negro students. There were grounds enough simply to cite the far better plant at the state's white school, but the Court went much further:

> What is more important, the University of Texas Law School possesses to a far greater degree those qualities which are incapable of objective measurement, but which make for greatness in a law school. . . . Few students and no one who has practiced law would choose to study in an academic vacuum, removed from the interplay of ideas and exchange of views with which the law is concerned.

On the very same day the Court also rejected Oklahoma's policy of accepting Negroes to the state's graduate school but separating them from everyone else in class, cafeteria and library. Again, psychological intangibles ruled the day. Even if everything else was equal, the Court found missing "the intellectual commingling of students."

In all these cases the Supreme Court still accepted the idea of "separate but equal." But as the Justices thought of the problem more and more in psychological terms, they gradually broadened their definition of "equal" to a point where it was virtually impossible to be separate and equal at the same time. No wonder the South became increasingly exasperated. No wonder the NAACP suddenly saw the gate was now wide-open to scrapping the doctrine altogether.

Right after the 1950 cases, NAACP lawyers held a strategy

meeting in New York. Their decision: "a bold frontal attack," and at the public school level. And the attack was indeed "bold," for until now the target had been graduate schools and the battlefield mainly the border states. Yet when would there ever be a better time? The Court seemed willing; Truman liberalism offered a favorable Washington climate; and the Negroes themselves were never more aroused. It wasn't hard to encourage Negro parents in four different states and the District of Columbia to file separate suits.

So it happened that Oliver Brown and the other Topeka parents went to Court. So it happened that this case, and the four others like it, were eventually appealed to the Supreme Court. And so it happened that 56 years after some thought the issue was settled forever the Supreme Court was once again considering whether "separate but equal" treatment violated that provision in the Fourteenth Amendment that guaranteed equal protection of the laws to all persons in a State.

The battle lines were drawn in the fall of 1952 after the Court lumped all five cases together for purposes of argument: On the one side were Thurgood Marshall and his young NAACP staff; on the other, the best legal talent the South had to offer, led by the venerable John W. Davis. Next, the Justice Department jumped into the picture with an *amicus curiae* brief on behalf of the Negro cause, and the lines were drawn more sharply than ever.

At last the case came up in December 1952, but it proved only the start of months of mounting tension. In June 1953 the Court called for reargument . . . heard the case again that December . . . then settled down for months of meditation in the spring of 1954. Never did the lawyers play harder at their favorite guessing games: Would the liberal Black-Douglas bloc carry the day? Would Frankfurter's special brand of Harvard liberalism (so scorned by Yale's Douglas) follow along? Would Burton, the conservative Republican, pull for the status quo? Above all, what would Chief Justice

Warren do? As an Eisenhower appointee, he might be expected to follow a conservative course on domestic issues; on the other hand, there was always his moderate record as Governor of California. . . .

On Monday, May 17, 1954, the Court convened as usual to deliver its weekly batch of decisions. But this time something special seemed in the air. Justice Robert Jackson, recently down with a heart attack, came straight from his hospital bed: it was apparently important to present a united front. The reason soon became clear. At 12:52 P.M. Chief Justice Warren at last began reading the Court's decision in *Brown et al.* v. *Board of Education of Topeka.*

Warren first examined whether the Fourteenth Amendment was originally meant to outlaw segregated schools. Southern lawyers had offered strong arguments that this was never its intent, but the Court found the evidence "inconclusive." In any case, Warren said, it didn't really matter—times had changed. "In approaching this problem we cannot turn the clock back. . . . We must consider public education in the light of its full development and its present place in American life throughout the nation."

Having disposed of intent, the Court now shattered the bonds of precedent. True, six previous decisions had accepted the "separate but equal" rule in education—but here too times had changed. Whatever past legal authorities said, modern social and psychological experts held there could be no true equality where a racial minority was segregated. The Court had already leaned toward this view in the case of university students; it was all the more true when applied to schoolchildren:

> To separate them from others of similar age and qualifications solely because of their race generates a feeling of inferiority as to their status in the community that may affect their hearts and minds in a way unlikely ever to be undone. . . . We conclude that in the field of public education the doctrine of "separate but equal" has no place. Separate educational facilities are inherently unequal.

The decision was unanimous—and emphatic. It contained, in fact, only one small conciliatory gesture toward the Old South: because local conditions varied, the Court postponed granting immediate relief. It would take that up later. But from the moment Chief Justice Warren finished reading at exactly 1:20 P.M., a new and historic course was set. It was no longer lawful to keep Linda Brown and "others similarly situated" from going to a public school with white children simply because they happened to be Negroes.

"Affords all Americans an occasion for pride and gratification," rejoiced the Washington *Post*. "A monumental constructive stride in constitutional law and fundamental justice," rumbled the *New York Times*. "A black day of tragedy," mourned the Jackson, Mississippi, *Clarion-Ledger*. But whatever the reaction, the whole country recognized immediately that here was indeed a milestone —probably the most far-reaching Supreme Court decision in 100 years.

The men in America's armed services were no less interested. When Sergeant James H. Meredith came before an Air Force promotion board shortly afterward, the three colonels asked nothing about his qualifications—all they wanted to know was what he thought of the decision.

They came to the right man, if they really wanted an opinion. Meredith was as disturbed about race as ever; he poured out his thoughts. The colonels understood. They told him they were with him, but "the outcome will depend on you."

4

"You Are Obligated to Defy It"

"WELL, ARE WE GOING TO HAVE NIGGERS THIS FALL?" A PARENT asked a Cleveland, Mississippi, school official shortly after the Supreme Court's momentous 1954 decision. Not that soon, came the answer, but everyone would probably have to get used to it in four or five years.

The incident was typical of the mood that spring. As elsewhere in the South, the average Mississippian felt an initial flash of dismay . . . then struggled to adjust. A Brandon housewife mused that this was the penalty for holding the Negroes back "too long"; a Jackson mother said she didn't like it but was ready to obey. The head of a Delta school board, noticing whites and Negroes mingling together at a funeral, philosophized that school integration would probably work out too. As one Black Belt school superintendent put it, "What else can you expect in a Christian and democratic country?"

This attitude of regretful acceptance was helped by the fact that Negro-white relations were at their best in years. Mississippi hadn't changed its views on segregation, but good times, and a new generation coming to the fore, seemed to promise much better communication between the races. For the first time newspapers were criticizing the Bilbo-Vardaman school of race-hating politician. Negroes and whites were gingerly starting to work together, exploring possible desegregation of public washrooms and waiting rooms. In 1949 Sunflower County had even established an interracial committee to investigate the appalling condition of Negro schools.

In this climate responsible leadership might well give substance to the Court's decision. The average Mississippian believed in law and order despite Carl Rowan's scornful assertion that "Apparently a 'moderate' is any white Southerner who can prove that he hasn't lynched any crippled old Negro grandmothers during prayer-meeting hour." Real moderates were there, all right, but they were also people who deeply believed in segregation; to overcome their qualms, they needed all the encouragement they could get.

Instead, they got silence—not only in Mississippi but from Washington too. Interviewed on the Supreme Court decision, President Eisenhower gave a few cautious observations which many construed to mean he wished it hadn't happened. Nor was the national Democratic leadership any more outspoken. In Mississippi itself there was no comment from the church, the educators or the responsible press. And from the bar—where the leaders knew perfectly well that the Supreme Court, right or wrong, had the final say in interpreting the Constitution—not a word was heard.

Into this vacuum roared a cyclone—an ardent band of white supremacists whose sense of purpose was matched only by their skill. They knew exactly what they wanted, and as past masters at the art of state politics, they knew exactly the chords to strike that would best arouse the average frightened, isolated, white Mississippian.

"The South will not abide by nor obey this legislative decision by a political court," declared Senator James Eastland, wrapping himself in the mantle of Vardaman and Bilbo. "BLOODSTAINS ON WHITE MARBLE STEPS," proclaimed the lead editorial in the Jackson *Daily News*. "The Supreme Court drove a knife into the heart of the U.S. Constitution," thundered Congressman John Bell Williams, and he labeled the fateful day "Black Monday."

In a contest of mounting invective Mississippi's leaders outdid themselves in vilifying the Supreme Court. And, ironically, the Court played into their hands by delaying its final decree. The idea was to give the South a breathing spell, and even when the decision came in May '55, it was a mild decree entrusting the matter to the local federal courts, while merely urging "all deliberate speed." This was seized as a sign of weakness in Mississippi, and the torrent of abuse grew still stronger.

What was behind it all? Communism, cried the group. "It is a fact," Circuit Judge Tom Brady declared on one occasion, "that Communist sympathizers and left-wing organizers founded the NAACP and largely control it." As for the sociologists relied on so heavily by the Court, Senator Eastland said they were "agitators who are part and parcel of the Communist conspiracy to destroy our country." It made no difference that J. Edgar Hoover himself had cleared the NAACP, or that the Court's sociologists were among the best known in the country.

And why did the Communists want integration? *"The mongrelization of the white race,"* shouted the supremacists, once again sounding the alarm that for 90 years had rallied Mississippians to present a united front, whatever their daily differences. "If the blood of our white race should become corrupted and mingled with the blood of the African," Hugh V. Wall warned the Mississippi State Bar Association, "then the present greatness of the United States of America would be destroyed and all hope for the future would be gone forever."

Bad enough anywhere if you believed it, but all the worse in Mississippi, where the Negro was next to nothing, and the white woman next to a goddess. Judge Brady conveyed the mood well in a little book predictably called *Black Monday.* On the one hand, in the forward march of civilizations "the negroid man, like the modern lizard, evolved not." On the other, "The loveliest and the purest of God's creatures, the nearest thing to an angelic being that treads this terrestrial ball is a well-bred, cultured Southern white woman or her blue-eyed, golden-haired little girl."

Every white Mississippian understood. It was what he had been taught since childhood. It was why his father had been off in the night in the cross-burning days of the '20s . . . why his grandfather had risked so much in the thrilling years of redemption . . . why Jefferson Davis, Bedford Forrest and the whole pantheon of heroes had sacrificed everything for The Cause. In the end, when all the talk of socialism and tariff policy was done, this was what states' rights were all about. "We are up against enemies," warned the Jackson *Daily News,* "who would destroy our way of life and put an end to the traditions so precious to our people."

There was only one answer—defiance! And a steady tattoo began which mounted in fury with the years. "You are not required to obey any court which passes out such a ruling," Senator Eastland told a cheering audience in 1955. "In fact, you are obligated to defy it."

"We as Mississippians," Judge Brady told a group in 1959, "will not bow down to a court of nine old men whose hearts are as black as their robes."

"God forbid that we might be forced to resort to any extremities," declared Professor W. M. Casky in 1960, "but we are determined to maintain our traditional Southern way of life, which is our problem, because self-preservation is the first law of nature."

But words alone were not enough. If defiance was to be more than fist-shaking, there must be organization, and almost from the start the supremacists set about laying the groundwork. Mississippi had always been first in devising Southern racial "solutions" . . . now she was the first in 1954 to come up with a concrete program for thwarting the Supreme Court.

One day in early July 1954 a Delta planter named Robert Patterson sat with five other men in the little town of Indianola, deploring the Court's decision and what it would do to the South. There had been countless such discussions since the *Brown* case, but this time was different: a real plan of action emerged. They would form a "Citizens' Council"—the responsible people in the community would keep in touch and act together to stop any move toward desegregation. Better still, similar groups might be set up all over the state—perhaps the whole South—and by working together provide the kind of massive force that offered the only hope of blocking the federal government.

Excited by the possibilities, they held another meeting July 11 —this time attended by 14 leaders—and hammered out a simple, workable machinery. Each Council would be organized the same way: largely autonomous, with a minimum of central direction, and built around a few highly functional committees. It was a design perfectly suited to the Mississippi temperament. First of all, it was loosely organized—these fiercely independent people weren't fighting for states' rights just to give it all up at home. Second, everything depended not on an elaborate chain of command but rather on personal contact—the way business, politics, education and everything else was conducted in this most intimate and isolated of states. Finally and most important, the leadership was in the hands of the most responsible men in the community—far different from the Ku Klux Klan with its nightshirts and hocus-pocus that appealed to only the dregs. Mississippi had always been a land that looked up to its leaders—the brigadier in gray, the planter in the Big House, the bulky sheriff, the captain of the team. This time they were all there.

Missionaries fanned out all over the state. In less than six weeks Councils were operating in 17 counties . . . by October, in 20 counties . . . by November, in 30 counties. A central headquarters was established at Winona with the original spark plug, Robert Patterson, in charge. A blizzard of application forms blanketed the state, and by the 1954 fall elections the Council boasted over 25,000 single-minded, purposeful members.

The results were immediately apparent. A new constitutional amendment was up in November tightening qualifications so as to keep more Negroes from voting. At this time a prospective voter had to be able to read or interpret the state constitution—

good enough in 1890 when only 40 percent of the Negroes could read or write. But by 1954 over 90 percent were literate, and the old rule was no longer an effective barrier. Now the idea was to tighten the law by requiring voters to read *and* interpret the constitution, for a resourceful registrar could always reject anyone on the "interpretation" test. A similar proposal had been made in 1952 but was decisively beaten; then the old rule seemed good enough to keep things under control.

This time was different. In an all-out drive for the amendment, the new Citizens' Councils bombarded the mails, scattered leaflets, harangued meetings, pushed doorbells, used other forms of "persuasion" too. And the tighter qualifications won by a landslide— 75,488 to 15,718. Significantly, in Sunflower County, birthplace of the Councils, not one of the 114 registered Negroes even went to the polls.

This heady victory was almost immediately followed by a second triumph, when another constitutional amendment was proposed authorizing the legislature to close the public schools if necessary to prevent desegregation. Again the Councils moved into action; again the voters fell in line.

Fired by success, the Citizens' Councils rolled on—60,000 members by August 1955. By October there was an official paper too, edited by the organization's administrator, a quiet man with a calm smile named William J. Simmons. Well-born and pleasantly articulate, he pursued segregation as a career the way other men might choose medicine or follow the sea. Surrounded by Confederate bric-a-brac that seemed oddly out of place in the bright, trim offices of the Jackson Council, Simmons gradually became the closest thing there was to an official spokesman for the movement.

One question was politics. "The Citizens' Council," Simmons declared, "is definitely a nonpartisan organization and is not engaged in politics." Yet the organization's official circular stated that the Political and Elections Committee functioned to "screen all candidates," and Representative Wilma Sledge assured the state legislature that "Candidates for offices at all levels will be carefully screened by political committees."

Another question was pressure. "No," said Simmons, "there never has been any economic pressure by the Councils as such." Yet as Executive Secretary Patterson smoothly observed, "Of course we don't denounce individuals who use freedom of choice in their business arrangement."

Finally, there was the matter of outright force. Simmons and every other Council leader deplored the use of violence, yet increasingly their language couldn't help but have the opposite effect. Thus Judge Brady urged non-violence in *Black Monday,* then on the next page declared, "We have, through our forefathers, died before for our sacred principles. We can, if necessary, die again." Thus Representative Wilma Sledge stressed the Councils' reliance on "all legal means," then called for the support of "all who are willing to mutually pledge their lives, their fortunes and their honor to the preservation of an unsullied race."

Thanks to all this duality, it was never possible to pinpoint the Councils' exact role in a series of events that began happening almost as soon as they were formed. Was it the organization itself or merely individuals who happened to be members? Nobody knew. All anyone knew were the events themselves, but there was no doubt about these or their impact.

In Yazoo City the Citizens' Council ran a full-page ad in the local press carrying "an authentic list of the purported signers to an NAACP communication to our school board." Many of the signers found themselves out of work, until they saw the light and withdrew from the NAACP petition. One Negro plumbing contractor lost two construction jobs and couldn't even get supplies from his warehouse.

As always in Mississippi, racial friction soon spread to the area of Negro voting. In March 1955 the Belzoni Citizens' Council was reported to be behind a list of 94 registered Negroes being circulated to stores and banks. The Negroes named soon found they couldn't get any business done until they took themselves off the voting lists. Grocer Gus Courts refused to do this—and soon lost his store. After undertaker T. V. Johnson also proved stubborn, a mysterious circular appeared suggesting white farmers might help their tenants by guiding them elsewhere. Then on May 8 the Rev. George Washington Lee, who worked for Negro registration, was shot dead in his car.

The gunfire continued. In August 1955 Lamar Smith, another Negro voting leader, was shot down on the Brookhaven courthouse lawn. Later that month 14-year-old Emmett Till, visiting from Chicago, got his famous lesson in Delta manners—for treating a white woman to his South Side wolf whistle, he was kidnapped, shot and dumped into the Tallahatchie River. Then in November Gus Courts, still determined to vote, was gunned down in his new store in Belzoni. All these cases had one thing in common: no one was ever found guilty.

There were no firing squads for the white people of Mississippi, but there were still plenty of effective ways for dealing with any who cared to protest. When Hazel Brannon Smith, peppery editor of the Lexington *Advertiser*, criticized the local sheriff over the shooting of a Negro prisoner, she was promptly sued for libel. One of her witnesses, Dr. David Minter, got it next. He and Eugene Cox ran a co-op farm near Tchula; rumors spread that white and Negro tenants went swimming together; a mass meeting demanded them to leave; they left. After the Rev. Marsh Calloway protested against such tactics, he was fired from the Durant Presbyterian Church. Watching the storm brew, Greenville's liberal editor, Hodding Carter, wrote an article for *Look,* "A Wave of Terror Threatens the South"—and was promptly censored by the state legislature for "selling out the state for Yankee gold."

The storm was just too much. Mississippi's moderates shrank back from their gingerly laid plans for biracial cooperation—no more talk of a Negro policeman for Jackson, no more joint committees like the group that investigated Negro schools in Warren County. At the same time, the state's archsegregationists took new heart, became even bolder. Leaders who had reluctantly acknowledged the Supreme Court's authority now breathed defiance. That Cleveland school official who had quietly accepted desegregation in four or five years now shouted, "Never!"

For the Negro, it was disaster. Right after the Supreme Court decision, his hopes were high—when Governor White called a meeting in July '54 to win Negro support for continued segregation, those present voted 89 to 1 to defy him. Now the fun was over. By December 1955 they had withdrawn all six of the desegregation petitions that had been filed with various school boards. And the number of eligible Negro voters had fallen from 22,000 in 1952 to less than 12,000 in 1955.

Little wonder Senator Eastland outdid himself when he addressed the Citizens' Councils Convention in Jackson on December 1, 1955. Desegregation was dead, the Negro in his place, the Supreme Court put to rout. The Senator poured it on: "The Supreme Court of the United States in the false name of law and justice has perpetrated a monstrous crime . . . The anti-segregation decisions are dishonest decisions . . . The judges who rendered them violated their oaths of office. They have disgraced the high office which they hold . . . There is no law that a free people must submit to a flagrant invasion of their personal liberty."

But that very same day—Thursday, December 1, 1955—an utterly unexpected event was taking place 250 miles away which would change the whole course of events.

It was late afternoon in Montgomery, Alabama, when Mrs. Rosa Parks, a Negro seamstress in her 50s, boarded the Cleveland Avenue bus. Weary from a long day on her feet, she went to the Negro section in the rear and sank into a seat. Gradually the bus filled, and several stops later the driver ordered her to give her seat to a white man standing in the aisle. So far, nothing unusual— this was Montgomery—but the next thing that happened was highly unusual indeed: Mrs. Parks refused to move. She was promptly arrested.

Early next morning the phone rang in the parsonage of the Rev. Martin Luther King, Jr., the young Baptist minister of Montgomery's Dexter Avenue Church. It was a local Negro leader, E. D. Dixon, urging a bus boycott in retaliation for Mrs. Parks' arrest. At a meeting that evening the boycott was approved, and a committee set up to run it. Somewhat to his surprise and regret, Martin King found himself elected head.

After all, he was only 27. He had been in Montgomery less than a year and wanted badly to devote more time to his church. Nor was he the gregarious, committee-head type. On the contrary, he was a rather remote young man of black suits and a subdued sense of humor.

But integration ran in his veins. His minister father had once led Atlanta's NAACP, and King himself—like so many young Negroes born between the wars—had grown up full of the new thirst for equality. He had benefited too from the new trend toward good Negro education: far from the old-fashioned Baptist preacher full of fire, brimstone and little else, he was steeped in the teachings of Thoreau and Gandhi. He felt certain that their principles of nonviolence and passive resistance could be effectively applied as a Negro weapon.

But so far it had all been just intellectual exercise. Now suddenly he was called to test his theories in real life. How would Montgomery's Negroes respond to the dittoed circulars that were soon flowing through town? Theoretically they could swing a lot of weight—they made up 75% of the town's bus riders. And certainly the goal was modest enough—it didn't even call for desegregated seating, just courtesy and fair treatment. Still, Montgomery was a town where the Negroes "knew their place." Would they dare, would they really dare? Discussing it late Sunday evening, the night before the boycott, King and his wife Coretta decided they'd be happy if they got 60% cooperation.

At 5:30 next morning the Kings excitedly watched for the first bus of the day to pass their house. It was a good one to check, normally full of cooks and maids on their way to work. At 6:00 o'clock it rolled by—empty. Then the next—empty. And so on, all day long. The boycott was an incredible, near 100% success. For the first time, a whole Negro community in the Deep South steeled itself into taking strong, single-minded mass action.

Montgomery's white people charged a dark NAACP plot with Rosa Parks as the willing pawn. But there was no evidence of this, and Mrs. Parks was probably close to the truth when she explained, "I really don't know why I didn't move. I was just tired . . . my feet hurt." And like Mrs. Parks, the rest of Montgomery's Negroes also had simply reached the breaking point. After years of abuse, they too felt the great Negro awakening sweeping the country and just decided not to take it any longer.

Martin King understood, and that night at a great rally in the Holt Street Church he struck exactly the right note: "There comes a time," he said, "when people get tired. We are here this evening to say to those who have mistreated us so long that we are tired. . . ." He had a remarkable way of putting things just the way the Negro people felt, and he was never in better form than tonight. He made the boycott both a practical step for getting results and at the same time a thrilling new venture on the highest moral plane. He was a man of peace, but his final words had the ring of Churchill in 1940: "If you will protest courageously, and yet with dignity and Christian love, when the history books are written in future generations, the historians will have to pause and say, 'There lived a great people—a black people—who injected new meaning and dignity into the veins of civilization.'"

Bolstered by such visions, the Montgomery Negroes fought on. The city government of course counterattacked, using all the ingenious legal devices a Southern town can muster in meeting a racial problem. But this time the Negroes fought back with new ingenuity of their own. When they were cut off from all local sources of insurance for their emergency car pools, the Negroes insured with Lloyd's of London.

Meanwhile the Rosa Parks case worked its way through the federal court system. Finally on November 13, 1956—eleven months later—the Supreme Court of the United States declared that Montgomery's segregated bus system did indeed violate the Fourteenth Amendment, guaranteeing equal protection of the laws to all persons in a State.

So the boycott was won, and the victory came at just the right time. First, it happened at a moment when the American Negro—his hopes raised so high in 1954—was suffering the first pangs of new discouragement. Although the Supreme Court had banned segregated schools, it hadn't meant much—next year saw only 23 of 2,315,062 Negro children in the old Confederacy integrated into white schools. And in the Deep South not a Negro child had yet stepped over the threshold. Clearly, court orders would not be enough—here was a new approach.

Even more important, Montgomery answered a need that the NAACP, dedicated though it was, had failed to meet. It was still an intellectual movement; its victories were highly technical, invisible to most and participated in by only a brilliant few. That was no longer enough. With the great awakening, Negroes in all walks of life wanted to play a part. Mass action like Montgomery gave them all something to do.

The idea was soon spreading all through the South. Often the mere threat of mass action was enough—some 21 Southern bus lines desegregated without even a court order. To help guide the movement, a group of churchmen formed the Southern Christian Leadership Conference in 1957 with Martin Luther King at the helm, and the mere existence of this new, dynamic SCLC gave the older groups a shot in the arm. Under Roy Wilkins, the NAACP began to broaden its base. Wealthy Negroes, who had always withdrawn into a cloistered life of their own, began feeling they should be a part of this too. The Negro clergy—so long accustomed to preaching only about a better life some day—caught the high moral tone of Dr. King's message and plunged into the struggle. All over the country the Negro movement gained new fire.

Washington soon responded to the heat—in 1957 Congress passed the first civil rights law since Reconstruction days. While not as broad as its sponsors had hoped, it did allow the Justice Department to step into cases where local officials kept Negroes from voting. Until now the Department's only weapon in these cases had been three antiquated criminal statutes. This meant a jury trial—and in these cases everyone knew that a Southern jury automatically voted acquittal. Under the new law the government could file civil suits in a federal court—meaning no jury, a judge appointed by Washington and an infinitely better chance of winning the case. The Southern states bitterly denounced this new sign of "federal interference."

But this was nothing compared to what happened next. All that summer of 1957 trouble had been brewing in Little Rock, Arkansas. Complying with the Supreme Court's decision, the local school board had worked out a plan for gradual desegregation, starting that fall with nine Negroes in Central High. Sensing popular opposition—and perhaps a good political issue—Governor Orval Faubus called up the National Guard "to preserve order"— which in this case meant keeping the Negro children out of Central High.

The federal court, which had approved the school board's plan, ordered Faubus to cease his "defiance," and after a brief legal skirmish the Governor pulled out his Guard. But by now Little Rock was in an uproar. Die-hard segregationists swarmed in from the cotton country, and when the Negro pupils finally entered the school building on September 23, rioting erupted all over town. After a morning of chaos, a side door opened, the nine Negroes were removed, and once more Central High was white.

President Eisenhower felt no special love for the desegregation decision, but defying a federal court was another matter. Next day he sent the Army, and the nine Negro children finally entered the school to stay . . . but thanks only to the protection offered by a detachment of paratroopers under the command of a brigadier named Edwin A. Walker.

Shades of Sherman, Union bayonets, "the crime of Reconstruction" . . . the Deep South was appalled. And as always, the lonely, isolated people of Mississippi shuddered the most. All the old feelings came pounding back: the old fears, the old defiance, the old glory too. A local official in the town of Forest told the high school band to play "Dixie" from now on before football games—no more "Star-Spangled Banner."

Fortunately, the people were told, the nightmare of Little Rock couldn't happen here. Farsighted leaders had come up with a marvelous weapon called "interposition"—the theory that a state government can throw itself between an objectionable federal order and the state's own citizens. It was a theory that had been rejected as long ago as 1809, when a famous opinion by Chief Justice Marshall said that if the states could ignore the federal courts, "the Constitution itself becomes a mockery." Subsequent Supreme Court decisions agreed . . . Andrew Jackson further demolished the idea in the nullification crisis of 1832 . . . and the Civil War of course settled the issue for good.

None of this mattered that year in Mississippi. Legislative experts rooted around the law libraries, announced there was ample precedent for interposition—for instance, a long-forgotten land grant case in the 1870s when Iowa ignored a Supreme Court ruling and Washington never pressed the matter.

Such cases were enough. With a joyful whoop the legislature rammed through a resolution declaring that Mississippi was "sovereign" and that it had never "delegated to the federal government the right to educate and nurture its youth and its power and right of control over its schools." The law went on to announce that the Supreme Court's ruling was unconstitutional and "of no lawful effect within Mississippi."

The people roared approval, and if they seemed gullible bank-
ing their hopes on such a flimsy legal structure, it was quite under-
standable. The press, their leaders, all who had anything to do
with molding public opinion never told them about the other
side. The newspapers promised that interposition would work.
The politicians assured them that the whole country was rising
up behind them. "Organizations to resist are springing up all
over the United States," Senator Eastland told a wildly cheering
crowd at one Citizens' Council State Convention. "Mississippi is
the hard core of the resistance in the country. It is spreading from
here throughout the nation. It is growing very, very fast."

The educators too were now falling into line. Wholly dependent
on state aid, Mississippi's complex system of public colleges had
already learned to think right. When it was revealed that the Rev.
Alvin Kershaw, scheduled to speak at the University of
Mississippi's Religious Emphasis Week in 1956, had contributed
to the NAACP, the authorities canceled his appearance and set
up a screening commission to see that such misadventures didn't
happen again. Occasional professors jumped the traces—and a
smattering of independent schools like Millsaps still encouraged
discussion—but by 1957 most of the state's teachers had suc-
cumbed to what a teacher at Mississippi State called "intellectual
strait-jacketing."

Strict control continued all the way down the line. The February
1957 issue of the Citizens' Council paper recommended a reading
exercise for third- and fourth-graders that was to become something of a minor classic:

> Do you know that some people in our country want the Negroes
> to live with the white people? These people want us to be unhappy.
> They say we must go to school together. They say we must swim
> together and use the bathrooms together. We do not want to do
> these things.
>
> "Why do some people want us to live together?" you will ask.
> They want to make our country weak. If we are not happy, our

strong and free country will grow weak. Did you know our country will grow weak if we mix our races? It will.

The organized churches seemed no different. On paper, the Catholics and Episcopalians were committed to integration, but no one would ever guess it. The Baptists simply fed their flocks what they wanted to hear. The Methodists and Presbyterians cheerfully broke with their national bodies, stood firmly for segregation. "Bluebirds never mate with redbirds," the Rev. G. T. Gillespie assured the Presbyterian Synod in Jackson, drawing on an analogy that had proved useful in the 1870s.

To bolster this united front, the state legislature churned out an endless stream of helpful statutes. One obvious measure allowed the governor to close any school threatened with desegregation. Another established a State Sovereignty Commission. Its stated purpose was characteristically defiant: "to prohibit compliance with the integration decision."

Other measures showed a second but equally characteristic side of Mississippi—the state's passion for ingenious political devices. One law made it a crime for any organization to institute desegregation suits in the state courts, thus aiming a heavy blow at civil rights groups. Another abolished common law marriages, thus making many Negro children illegitimate at the stroke of a pen, and barring them from public schools on moral grounds. Still another law banned barratry. When puzzled lawyers rushed to their textbooks, they discovered that "barratry" meant encouraging legal quarrels. It also appeared that in the whole history of English common law there had been only one indictment for barratry since 1750; little matter, it just might be useful against the NAACP.

The results of all this were devastating for Mississippi's colored population. The number of Negro voters took another slide—down to only 8,000 by 1957. And even when a Negro managed to register, chances were he didn't vote. More and more were dissuaded, like James Harris of Yalobusha County who came home one evening and found this note tacked to his cabin door:

> You is getin to smart trin to vote. Mr. Harris. Have youre name took off them Bookes—Real soon like—an straiten yore friens.

Nor did the Negroes have any better luck cracking the school barrier. Two attempts—two disasters. In 1958 Clennon King, a Negro professor at Alcorn College, tried to enter the University of Mississippi summer session. He was promptly packed off to the insane asylum. King was indeed erratic, but certainly no lunatic and his fate seemed a cruel practical joke. ("Any nigger who tries to enter Ole Miss *must* be crazy.") The effect was not lost on the Negro community.

Next time the state's reaction was even more emphatic. In 1959 Negro Clyde Kennard, a former paratrooper and student at the University of Chicago, tried to transfer to Mississippi Southern College near his home in Hattiesburg. Emerging from a visit to the registrar, he was confronted by two officers at his parked car and arrested for "reckless driving"; next, some bottles of illegal whiskey were "found" in the car. While still trying to clear himself of these charges, Kennard was again arrested, this time for stealing chicken feed. He was quickly convicted and sent to prison for seven years. Even staunch segregationists suspected a frame-up, but once more the effect was not lost on the Negro community. There was little appetite left for crusading.

Although the chicken-feed episode came later, both Negroes were blocked during the shrewd administration of Governor J. P. Coleman. From the results, one might suppose he would be the toast of the state. Far from it. Coleman talked a good segregationist game, but so did everyone in Mississippi politics. A man's real position was judged not by his words but by small incidents, an unusual gesture, the company he kept, a dozen little things. These might seem meaningless to a stranger but made all the difference in the world to those who lived and died in the state. It was almost as though Mississippians had a built-in seismograph which could measure the subtlest distinction in the attitudes of their politicians, but which nevertheless determined whether a man was "safe" or not.

The seismograph showed that Coleman wasn't "safe." He went to a Citizens' Council rally during his campaign, but failed to appear at the Council's convention right afterward. He pushed through the State Sovereignty Commission, but he vetoed a bill that would have put any federal official in jail for five years for attempting to integrate schools, busses or public facilities. He talked states' rights, but he didn't back up Faubus. And worst of all: he signed the interposition law, but in an unguarded moment he called the weapon "legal poppycock."

The Citizens' Council decided that this sort of thing shouldn't happen again. In the 1959 election it ignored Coleman's choice, picked instead Ross Barnett, a loyal Council member who left no doubt where he stood. Barnett had little experience, but he was a highly successful damage suit lawyer—a superb man at handling a hill-country jury. That proved talent enough. With the Council's well-oiled machinery running in high gear, he sailed into office.

"If we start off with the self-evident proposition that the white and colored are different," Barnett explained to the people, "we will not experience any difficulty in reaching the conclusion that they are not and never can be equal." To drive home the point, 24 new segregation bills cascaded into the state legislature during the first ten weeks of Barnett's administration. In a rare internationally minded moment, the legislature even offered a resolution assuring the Union of South Africa that Mississippi was with her all the way.

Closer to home, another new law gave the Governor far greater control over the rating and selecting of textbooks for schools. There had been considerable worry about this problem ever since the Citizens' Council discovered three favorable pages on Negroes in the *World Book Encyclopedia.* Until now the Rating Committee had been appointed by the Superintendent of Education; henceforth the Governor himself would name the majority.

The reins were tightened on other officials too. Orders went out to the state librarians not to give the Civil Rights Commission any data on Negro facilities. Circuit clerks were advised to refuse any Justice Department request for registration figures.

The state government also moved closer to official intimidation. A new law threatened those who "falsely" testified before the FBI or the Civil Rights Commission with a streamlined perjury indictment; in these cases it wouldn't be necessary to have any corroborating witnesses or show that the false statement was material to anything. Another law required any voter applicant to have his name and address published in a local newspaper for two weeks—it took a brave Negro indeed to face that ordeal.

There was an enormous step-up in behind-the-scenes secret activity, most of it never emerging unless by accident. Late in 1960 an enterprising Memphis reporter sifting through records in the State Auditor's office, discovered that the State Sovereignty Commission was quietly paying the Citizens' Council $5,000 a month. Other warrants showed heavy expenditures to a Negro newspaper, which incidentally came out against integration. The editor said the checks were for subscriptions to Negro schools. Still another series of checks went to a Negro minister who declared, "There is nothing that has contributed as much to Negroes' success and welfare here in Mississippi as segregation."

Official espionage was now in fashion too. One blustery March day in 1961 a state legislator appeared on the University of Mississippi campus, declared that the Governor's office had information that Billy Barton, candidate for editor of the college paper next year, was really a secret member of the NAACP and had joined Atlanta sit-ins the previous summer. Frantic calls, and the State Sovereignty Commission produced a "confidential report." No one had ever checked it out, the contents proved totally false, but by that time the damage was done—a jittery student body preferred a "safer" editor to one the state had set out to get.

Espionage . . . irresponsible charges . . . intimidation . . . secret payments . . . official fingers in everything, down to a college newspaper—that was the state of Mississippi by 1961. In this atmosphere desegregationists were, of course, beyond the pale. They were not merely wrong, but wicked and sinful. No one was spared. The YMCA, the YWCA, Boy and Girl Scout camps were among the suspect organizations castigated by *The White Sentinel,* printed in Florida but widely distributed in Mississippi. "Their object," warned the *Sentinel,* "is to destroy the civilized world for Communism by mating your White Innocent with the loathsome negro."

Gradually, the moderates too were out. At first they were compared to oppressors and scalawags . . . then to Tories and Quislings . . . then to Communists and Marxists. Finally, no comparison at all was necessary. The very word "moderate" went into the Mississippi lexicon as a scathing denunciation. The whole concept was regarded with contempt. Ross Barnett congratulated the Citizens' Councils because they "do not pursue in any manner the avenue of moderation." When J. P. Coleman once sounded a note of caution, Judge Brady sneered at him as "Fair-minded Jim." The Durant Methodist Church canceled an invitation to a visiting minister because he said he approved hearing "both sides" of the segregation question.

Finally, the staunchest segregationists also began to fall under suspicion if they failed to support the all-out tactics of the Citizens' Councils. Later, even members of the State Sovereignty Commission came under a shadow. When publicity director Erle Johnston said he hoped whites and Negroes could work together to make segregation succeed, Citizens' Council Administrator William Simmons snorted that Johnston "sounds like he is ready to surrender."

It was a brave Mississippian who dared buck the tide, yet here and there a few were willing to pay the price. Citizens of Glendora openly collected funds for the family of Negro Clinton Melton, shot by a white after a minor squabble at a filling station. In Jackson a group of Negroes and whites quietly worshiped together every week. These bold souls were what Robert Penn Warren has called the South's "fifth column of decency."

But most responsible citizens—even those who thoroughly opposed the tactics of the extremists—simply kept quiet. Completely unorganized, they were terrorized into silence. The price was simply too steep for open disagreement: lost business, insults in the press, Citizens' Council vitriol, ostracism by friends, garbage on the front lawn. "I've learned to be ambivalent; oh, how I've learned to be ambivalent," sighed a Yazoo City housewife to a visitor.

So once again—as in 1866, 1875, 1890 and other years too—the decent, reasonable people of the state only appealed for more time. Even William Faulkner, who believed deeply in racial equality, begged for patience: "Let us sweat in our own fears for a little while."

But time had run out for that. Events that couldn't be controlled by any Mississippian, white or black, were taking over. On February 1, 1960, four Negro college boys had wandered into the Woolworth store in Greensboro, North Carolina. Almost on impulse, they sat down at the all-white lunch counter and asked for service. When refused, they stayed—day after day. It was such a simple idea, it immediately caught on. The Congress of Racial Equality, a small but lively civil rights group, was called on for organizing help, and CORE-inspired sit-ins were soon sweeping the South. They proved an incredible success—counters and dining rooms desegregated in some 112 Southern and border towns altogether.

A heady victory, and, even more important, a victory for the young. For it was students who started the sit-ins, carried forward the idea and won the triumphs that their stodgy elders had sought for years in vain. Soon little bands of students were organizing everywhere—the Baltimore Civic Interest Group, the Nashville Student Central Committee, a dozen splinter outfits. Martin King's SCLC watched and understood, helped launch a Student Non-Violent Coordinating Committee to provide central guidance. Irreverently dubbed "SNICK," it proved an immediate if impoverished success.

All through 1960 the students' drive gained momentum, and it was soon clear that they brought special assets to the battle, which would make a lot of difference over the months and years ahead. They had the rapport of undergraduates everywhere; this in turn meant good communications and a large turnout wherever needed. They also had the originality and resourcefulness of all students; they were good copy for the national press as the sit-ins were rapidly followed by swim-ins at white municipal pools, park-ins at shopping centers, even putt-ins at public golf courses.

Another student contribution was less immediately appreciated, but no less real. They caught the fancy of the older, conservative Negroes in a way the NAACP court victories could never hope to do. A man might feel that the vote was "white folks' business" or that his own children might indeed be happier in an all-Negro school, but the right to sit at a counter, use a library or go to the bathroom was different. As their young people marched on, even "good" Negroes began feeling a secret glow of pride.

But perhaps the students' greatest contribution was their bodies. As the Southern towns fought back with mobs and mass arrests, it took more than the fiercest resolve to carry on. But with the stamina and resilience that only youth enjoys, the students took their beating—clubs, dogs, fire hoses, cattle prods, endless days in filthy jails—and still came back for more.

They needed it all in the spring of 1961. That May CORE followed up the sit-in success with a loudly heralded Freedom Ride to test snack bars, rest and waiting rooms at bus stations throughout the South. It proved fairly easy going until May 14, when a slashed tire brought the big Greyhound to a stop near

Anniston, Alabama. A white gang swept forward with pipes and chains, and for a moment it looked like the end for the riders inside. Then suddenly there appeared at the door one of those rare, steadfast men for whom duty is so paramount that no other course even occurs to them. Eli Cowling of the Alabama highway police was probably as staunch a segregationist as any on the scene, but he was there to protect the riders. He stood off the mob alone until reinforcements arrived fifteen minutes later. In the end the bus was burned, but the riders were safe.

It was not that way in Birmingham, where a second bus arrived the same day. This time the police were conspicuously absent, and the crowd happily hunted down the riders as they tried to scurry for safety. It was Mother's Day, a police official was said to have explained, and the men were all visiting their mothers.

Worst of all was Montgomery on May 20. Again little protection; again the mob attacked, this time slashing and clubbing not only the riders but reporters, photographers, even a Justice Department observer. Now federal marshals poured in, followed by the National Guard. Order gradually returned, and, thanks to another thoroughly professional performance by the Alabama Highway Patrol, the Freedom Riders moved on to Mississippi.

Jackson's law enforcement machinery brooked no nonsense. The riders were swiftly arrested and bundled off to jail. Again the physical resources of the young proved a great asset—jail, in fact, became a badge of honor—but the price was high. The NAACP Legal Defense office rushed to the rescue, and before the rides were over it found that bail, fines and other legal expenses ran beyond $300,000.

It was probably inevitable that Roy Wilkins, the tall, urbane president of the NAACP parent organization, should ultimately explode that other groups "make the noise while NAACP pays the bills." With four organizations in the field, all drawing money from the same sources, rivalries were inevitable, and white segregationists took new heart watching the Negro groups snap at each other. An NAACP official called CORE members "a bunch of loonybirds." CORE people called NAACP "worn out." A top lawyer in NAACP's Legal Defense Fund shuddered at SNICK— "These wild kids will try anything." Sniping went on even in the family. Asked if he felt NAACP headquarters was asleep at the switch, Jersey City branch chief Raymond Brown cracked, "Hell, they don't even know where the switch is."

But the rivalries and bickering were nothing compared to the surge of enthusiasm that swept all the groups. If the NAACP had once been doctrinaire, it was soon launching youth councils and college chapters. Even the most conservative groups jumped into the fray. The Southern Regional Council began pumping out research to use in the fight; the Urban League got itself a new director, Whitney Young, who was soon demanding preferential treatment for Negroes to make up for lost time. The Negro elite were deeper in the struggle too, and more than ever the students were involved. As Ron Hill at North Carolina's Livingston College remarked, "Now you have CORE and SNICK chapters where you used to have just fraternities."

Washington—responsive as always—felt the pressure and passed the Civil Rights Act of 1960, strengthening the Justice Department's hand in Negro voting cases. The national magazines, intrigued by the sheer buoyancy of the Negro's battle, played up the sit-ins and Freedom Rides . . . further infuriating an already frightened, bewildered South. Northern students caught the new spirit too. "I didn't want to live on the Grand Concourse all my life," explained Terry Perlman, a 21-year-old Freedom Rider from the Bronx, emerging from 38 days in a Jackson jail.

"Outsiders," explained Ross Barnett, "are the cause of all the trouble." "It's the outsiders," added a Delta plantation supervisor, and picking two of those least responsible, he singled out "Adam Clayton Powell and that other fellow up there, Humphrey." How did Mississippi's Negroes feel? Everyone still agreed they weren't interested. And for confirmation the whites once again turned to their cooks and maids, their field hands and yard boys. As usual, these dutifully replied that it sure was so, Mississippi Negroes just wanted to be let alone.

There was a time when it might have been true. Mississippi Negroes, even more isolated than the state's whites from the mainstream of American life, were the last to know or care about the new movement. Most had long ago given up any hope for equality and took their lot as it came—and for many it was pleasant enough. The 1954 desegregation decision had stirred some interest, but the swift white crackdown convinced most that there was no chance. Montgomery also stirred a glimmer of interest, but again the crackdown and the Negroes got the point.

But now came the Freedom Riders, and for the first time real crusading Negroes were pouring into the state. Not just scholarly NAACP lawyers whom the local people could never hope to know, but young ministers, teachers, college kids full of contagious enthusiasm. True, some of the old uncles and aunties, watching the arrests from their porch rockers, once again decided that this was not for them. But many, many more caught the fever at last.

Tougaloo, a church college founded in Reconstruction days, became a center of integration excitement. Jackson State and Alcorn, the two main state-supported Negro colleges, were stirred too, despite the desperate efforts of their dutiful Negro officials to sidetrack the subject. And most significant of all, there was the surging interest at high school level. It was a revealing statistic that by 1961 over 81% of the state's Negro high school students were taking the course in American government—compared to only 35% of the white students.

So the demonstrations spread all that summer of 1961, often fanned by outside leaders but always built around a very real and rapidly growing Mississippi Negro movement. Jackson students staged a sit-in at the local library . . . a young veteran named

Charles McLaurin led another group boycotting the state fair . . . local freedom marchers erupted in little towns where no one ever dreamed there would be "trouble." Frightened whites were soon meeting together, and when a group of McComb demonstrators were hauled into court, the judge laid it squarely on the line: "Some of you are local residents, some of you are outsiders. Those of you who are local residents are like sheep being led to the slaughter. If you continue to follow the advice of outside agitators, you will be like sheep and be slaughtered."

There was plenty of evidence to drive home his words. Starting New Year's Day—when a pair of white men on a motor bike gunned down two Negroes in Greenville—the year 1961 blazed with violence. In May several white boys, riding in a convertible, lassoed nine-year-old Gloria Laverne Floyd and dragged her down a Jackson street. In September registration worker Herbert Lee was shot dead in the town of Liberty by State Representative E. H. Hurst—acting, the coroner's jury decided, in "self-defense." In October Negro motorist Eli Brumfield was shot to death by a policeman in McComb—again, a coroner's jury decided, in "self-defense." Altogether, the Southern Regional Council toted up 24 cases of beatings, whippings, clubbings and shootings this tormented year.

And through all too many of these cases ran a growing streak of cruelty and sadism on the part of the local police. They amused themselves by beating a 14-year-old boy . . . sicked dogs on demonstrators they had already arrested . . . mercilessly whipped their victims in the station house. It was a trend that would have dismayed thousands of decent Mississippians—had they only known. But with press, church and education now thoroughly stifled, there was no way of learning—or of doing anything even if one suspected.

So it went on, and in the dead of a quiet country night there came a time when one more Negro car screeched to a stop as the siren wailed behind. A curt voice ordered a woman in the car to get into the police cruiser immediately. "What are the charges?" the woman asked, and back came the answer that told perhaps more than the officer dreamed: "For being a nigger."

However, something better was needed in facing the rest of the world, and these years saw Mississippi's racists engage in a remarkable, all-out drive for respectability. They had never been bothered by suppression before, and in a way it was a tribute to the Negro movement's effectiveness that some explanation now seemed in order. The scholarship of segregation moved forward on many fronts. . . .

History was ransacked for quotes from great Americans. There were those remarks by Jefferson, clearly indicating that he did not think the Negro was mentally equal to the white . . . but no one mentioned that Jefferson added, "It would be hazardous to affirm that, equally cultivated for a few generations, he would not become so." Early Lincoln statements were produced in triumph, especially a speech in 1858 when he declared, "I am not now, nor ever have been in favor of making voters or jurors of negroes, nor of qualifying them to hold office." It was ignored that Lincoln steadily grew more liberal as the years passed. By 1864 he was writing Governor Hahn of Louisiana, "I hereby suggest for your private consideration whether some of the colored people may not be let in—as, for instance, the very intelligent and especially those who have fought gallantly in our ranks." By 1865 he wasn't even cautious. Speaking from the White House balcony three days before his death, he openly urged Negro suffrage for "the very intelligent and those who serve our cause as soldiers."

The pages of ancient history were studied with equal fervor. It was claimed that all the great civilizations were white, and all met their downfall when the Negro entered the picture. Egypt was a favorite example, ignoring the fact that the world's outstanding Egyptologists considered the Land of the Pharaohs an enormous melting pot with no interest in race whatsoever. Ancient history, in fact, proved such a booby trap that the argument was ultimately abandoned, except in the hills. Too much depended on a particular vantage point. As the Persian might have said of the Greek on the eve of Marathon, "What's *he* ever done?"

The Bible was a safer weapon, and it was sifted line by line for evidence that God liked his children segregated. The Rev. G. T. Gillespie thought he saw an important revelation in Lev. 19:19:

> According to the law delivered to Moses, the crossbreeding of diverse strains of cattle, the planting of mixed seeds, and the mixing of wool and linen in a garment were forbidden. We are not told the reasons for this curious law, but it seems impossible to escape the conclusion that if such intermixture of diverse elements in the lower orders of animal and plant life were unseemly and contrary to the Divine purpose, the same principle would apply with even greater force with respect to human relations.

In all this research the Biblical scholars said very little about the First and Second Commandments.

Medicine offered another whole field of study. Statistics were pulled together showing that the Negro was more prone to whooping cough, heart disease and lobar pneumonia—making integration clearly a health hazard. Nothing was said about the Negro being more resistant to measles, diphtheria, polio and cancer.

Special attention was given the Negro's skull. Scholars dusted off a 1909 study indicating that the average Negro brain weighed 100 grams less than the average white. Parlor anthropologists were soon explaining to one another that F. W. Vint's examination of the skulls of 100 Kenya tribesmen showed that the supragranular layer of the Negro cortex averaged 14% less thickness than the white. No one mentioned that most anthropologists link the size of a person's brain to his build . . . that Negro men have larger brains than white women . . . that Eskimos have the largest brains of all.

This interest in brains was, of course, just leading up to that favorite subject, the Negro IQ. Extensive research by Dr. Audrey M. Shuey showed that the Negro IQ ran 15% to 20% below the white, and the gap increased with age. Nor, the segregationists hastened to emphasize, was this just a matter of environment, motivation, all the usual integration arguments. On the contrary, there were the important tests conducted by Dr. H. A. Tanser on the Negro community in Kent County, Ontario. Here the Negroes enjoyed all the advantages of the whites, yet still lagged behind the white norm.

No one noted that these Kent County Negroes—for all their shortcomings—had about the same IQ as white Virginians, judging from similar tests. Nor did anyone ever mention the dramatically higher IQs that nearly always resulted when children —white or black—moved from country to town, from South to North, or from poor to good schools.

Little matter, the drive for respectability rushed ahead—a vast collection of figures and theories unearthed by school boards, bar associations, medical committees and retired professors in nearly every town of the old Confederacy. But that was just the trouble. To the North the overwhelmingly Southern origin of the materials made the whole campaign suspect. Gradually it became clear that if the drive for respectability was ever to succeed, one more ingredient was essential: a good Yankee to present the case.

He appeared in the person of Carleton Putnam, whose impeccable New England background included Israel Putnam and the glories of Bunker Hill. Putnam entered the scene in 1958 with a widely published letter to President Eisenhower attacking the integration decision. Next came a lively book in 1961 called *Race and Reason, a Yankee View*. Flatly asserting the Negro's inferiority in terms of Western civilization, Putnam seemed a godsend to the South's embattled spokesmen. "A dyed-in-the-wool Northerner," enthused editor Tom Waring of the Charleston *News-Courier*, "a Yankee in the true sense of the word."

Actually, Putnam's Yankee credentials were somewhat suspect. He had indeed been born in New York and gone to Princeton, but he had spent most of his later life as an airline executive in the South. As early as 1935 he listed his home as Memphis.

Twenty-five years later he had moved to Washington, but his days in the Delta had left their mark. The North he viewed bleakly as the center of what he called the "new immigration." The South, on the other hand, was the great defender of our cultural heritage, a bulwark against a host of national perils ranging from "the sordid content of literature and the drama" to "the disappearance of the servant class."

But if Putnam was a rather farfetched Yankee, he was useful in the South. He had much to offer as a talented voice for segregation. He wasn't just one more professor emeritus, puttering about some sleepy Southern campus—he was the brilliant, far-ranging businessman who had built Delta Air Lines. He was at home in Shepherd's Hotel . . . had a Columbia law degree . . . flew his own plane . . . could quote A. E. Housman . . . had written a splendid biography of Theodore Roosevelt's early years.

Putnam plunged into his new role with typical energy. There wasn't a trace of the defensive in his vigorous style; he clearly relished trading blows with the hallowed names of science. Scorned by the head of the anthropology department of an Ivy League university, he happily lashed back, "The sooner you are brought to the bar of public opinion to answer for this hoax, the better . . . you have undoubtedly intimidated for the time being a number of your colleagues, but your day of accounting may be closer than you think."

"Hoax," "intimidate"—Putnam's book was full of such allusions, and here lay his greatest appeal of all. He added a new note of conspiracy to the story. Not the usual Communist plot, but an intriguing tale of skulduggery on the campus. It all went back to Franz Boas, the famous Columbia anthropologist. Boas had gathered a band of immigrant scholars, the story ran, and filled them with "insidious propaganda." They then fanned out, capturing other universities until finally all were contaminated. Too late, decent scholars realized what had happened: they no longer dared speak out for fear of committing "academic suicide."

Putnam never explained how Boas achieved his mysterious hold over his colleagues . . . or how these newly arrived immigrants managed to "capture" whole universities . . . or how they were able to obtain such a life-and-death hold over educational funds . . . or how any amount of money could keep so many professors so silent for so long. After all, Boas had arrived at Columbia in 1896; but as late as 1961 the American Anthropological Association was still voting 192 to 0 that all races were inherently equal.

If there seemed a touch of fantasy in all this talk of dark conspiracy, it wasn't surprising. As the Deep South became more and more isolated in its position, the need for justification became all the greater. Any argument would do, and this in turn often led to a world of make-believe. Nowhere was this more true than in the most isolated state of all—sultry, volatile, brooding Mississippi.

The state's supremacists viewed the Mississippi Negro as the luckiest of God's children. Senator Eastland declared that the field for Negro advancement was "unlimited," yet there were still only 1 Negro dentist, 5 Negro lawyers and 60 Negro doctors in the state.

The world of fantasy spun on. More than ever rose the old cry of "Communist plot." The NAACP was at the heart of it all, and it did no good for an exasperated Negro to explain, "It's bad enough to be black without being black and red."

Against this threat, the white Mississippian saw himself more than ever as a patriot in the old American tradition. Senator Eastland's words conjured up visions of the Magna Carta and the Spirit of '76. The Citizens' Council paper declared that in his day Paul Revere was doubtless considered an extremist too.

More than that, the Mississippian also saw himself as a knight of old. For in the end his thoughts always drifted back to horrible visions of "mongrelization"—and there he stood, the only protector of the white woman's purity. In vain, Martin Luther King complained that he only wanted to be the white man's brother, not his brother-in-law. In vain, a Negro writing to *Life* wondered how, if he was so inferior, he could also be considered so irresistible to the white man's sister.

But contradictions, just as much as fantasies, were typical of the Mississippi mood. Nor did the visitor who triumphantly pointed them out really win any victory at all. Nobody cared. As always, logic didn't matter. It was perfectly all right to use one argument one day and a completely different one the next. Anything to hold the line.

So the same pamphlet referred to a Negro as an ungrateful neighbor on one page and an inferior creature three pages later. He was both a docile servant, destined by his very nature to wait on others, and also a bloodthirsty savage who had to be held down. One moment he was a splendid citizen happily forging ahead under segregation—the next he was an ignorant, slothful fellow who would never get anywhere and didn't deserve any rights.

But of all the contradictory positions taken by the people of Mississippi during these years, none was odder—or destined to have more far-reaching repercussions—than their stand on Negro education. On the one hand, they maintained ever more fervently that the Negro's mind was inherently inferior; on the other, they launched a massive, all-out drive to make the Negro schools equal to the white. If the Negro was so inferior, one might ask, why spend all that money on useless education? Vardaman had at least been consistent when he ranted against Negro schools.

Today's Mississippians reasoned differently. In 1953 the Supreme Court had not yet acted—"separate but equal" was still the rule—and the initial hope was to keep it that way by making a truly honest effort to approach the standard. The state first scrapped a tangle of some 2,000 separate school districts, boiling them down to 150 by 1961. This consolidation meant fewer schools but far better ones, and the Negroes gained the most since they had nothing to start with. Next, a new construction program provided $12 a white student, but $15 a Negro. New certification rules also helped Negro teachers; from now on, for instance, the state paid at least $3,175 for an M.A.—black or white. Finally came what Mississippi called its Minimum Foundation Program—a complicated formula designed to put all schools on the same basis as far as state funds were concerned. Under it, the Negro schools were soon getting 65% of the money.

The program was just moving into high gear when the Supreme Court scrapped "separate but equal." Logically, this should have meant the end of it, for Mississippi could ill afford to spend its low income on a doctrine declared unconstitutional. Actually, the opposite happened. Everyone was soon saying that it was the Court's decision—not "separate but equal"—that was unconstitutional, and, far from tapering off, the state charged ahead with more vigor than ever. From '56 to '61 nearly three out of every four new classrooms built were for Negroes only.

By 1961 the program had accomplished wonders. In eight years the number of one-teacher Negro schools was down from 1,077 to 47. The number of Negro children enjoying free bus service soared from 22,124 to 136,223. The number of Negro teachers with M.A. degrees rose from 66 to 489, while those with only high school education fell from 1,275 to 20. Starting almost from scratch, 80% of the Negro schools now offered plane geometry, 91% biology, 67% chemistry.

Trouble was, despite all this effort, Mississippi still spent less per pupil than any other state in the Union—$226 against a national average of $390—and most of this still ended up in the white schools. For the total outlay for education came from both state and local funds, and while the state's contribution did indeed favor the Negro schools, supplementary county levies were even more heavily weighted to favor the white. Hence in 1961 Coahoma County allotted $139.33 per pupil to white schools, $12.74 to Negro; Quitman $90.28 to white, $8.41 to Negro; Yazoo $245.55 to white, $2.92 to Negro.

Even where Negro schools were exceptionally favored, those shiny new façades often hid a multitude of sins. Over half the principals complained of inadequate lab equipment. McComb's Burglund High had a library of only 100 books for more than 600 students (the American Library Association recommends 6,000 to 10,000 for a school this size). In 1960 three districts didn't buy so much as a piece of chalk for their Negro schools. Even the exciting new bus service was woefully inadequate: two-thirds of the seven-year-olds had to leave home before 7:00 A.M. to get to school on time. Nor did higher salaries help poor teachers— some 1,170 still had no degree of any kind.

All these problems were accentuated at the Negro colleges— where good lab equipment was far more important, where a distinguished faculty really began to count. The striking new science building at Jackson State, for instance, virtually ignored the need for faculty research, and the head of the chemistry department could be found trying to do his experiments with some makeshift plumbing in a passageway. Most faculty members were young and poorly trained—at Alcorn 25% boasted only a B.A. Salaries were low (a Negro assistant professor got only $4,600 against an average $6,090 for the whole Southeast), and the turnover was frightening—over 50% of the Alcorn faculty left within four years.

The level of education showed it. There was no graduate work for Negroes, except a very limited M.S. program for high school principals at Jackson State. For most professional training, a Negro's only hope was to scratch for an out-of-state grant and leave Mississippi. As for undergraduate work, it was superficial and further handicapped because the students arrived so badly trained that their first year was largely spent teaching them things they should have learned at high school. No wonder they often knew little more by the time they got out. Some 95% emerged with degrees in teacher education, but many were scarcely prepared to do that. When one recent Jackson State graduate applied for a teaching job, it was found he couldn't even do common fractions —$\frac{1}{2} \times \frac{1}{12}$ was just too much for him.

No one understood these dreary prospects better than Staff Sergeant James H. Meredith when he left the Air Force in July 1960 and headed for home in Kosciusko. He now had a wife, a baby son, an honorable discharge and a handful of academic credits gathered here and there during his service, but basically he was still the same sensitive, race-conscious young man who had always worried about segregation.

In fact, he still worried so much that his last months in service had been something of a comedown. He got a nervous stomach, was often irritable and upset; his rating fell from "very good" to "good." When he took his problems to the hospital at his base in Japan, the psychiatric report noted: "Patient is extremely concerned with racial problems and his symptoms are intensified whenever there is a heightened tempo in the racial problems in the U.S. and Africa."

Then why go back to Mississippi? Meredith was never clear on that, but probably deep in his heart was the feeling that the way to beat segregation was not to move out but to face it. So back he came, yearning to take his part in the struggle. In doing so, he was wise enough not to think of himself as belonging to that growing band of well-polished, carefully picked Negroes now making their way into the white world. He was no Ralph Bunche, and he knew it. But that was just the point. The goal was not special treatment for the brilliant few, or even special treatment for anybody. (That annoyed him almost as much as discrimination.) All Meredith wanted was ordinary treatment for the ordinary Negro— the same chance as everybody else.

In education that meant a chance to go to the all-white University of Mississippi. There were eight publicly supported colleges in the state, but Ole Miss, as it was universally called, was easily the best. More than that, it was the best entree to law, politics, business, almost anything that mattered in the state. Any Ole Miss graduate was likely to use the contacts he made there for the rest of his life. As Meredith observed, "It's better than Harvard at teaching you how to use $2+2=4$ in Mississippi."

He had been thinking of applying there off and on for years. Now that he was back, the idea took fresh hold. And there was much going for him. He was comparatively old—at 29 he could face any reprisals better than a kid. He had picked up so many credits during his service years that a term or two should be enough to break the barrier, get his diploma, and be home free. Also, there were still some sympathetic people on the University faculty —most were cowed, but it was impossible to squelch a man like Jim Silver in the history department. Most important of all, Ole Miss was the only college in the state with even a faint trace of worldliness. Here alone he just might get by without blowing the place apart.

On the other hand, the University's elite status was also a drawback. Most white people would be indignant enough to see him anywhere—but Ole Miss might be the last straw. And there were his marks. No Mississippi college was very hard, but this was the toughest one—and Meredith couldn't forget marks like that "C" he pulled down in the politics course at Washburn. Finally, there was his personal situation. Here he was with a wife and a baby, just back from nine years in the service. Common sense seemed to call for a little more time to get his feet on the ground.

He ended up instead at Jackson State, the booming Negro college on the capital's outskirts. Entering in September 1960, he found the place riding the crest of Mississippi's all-out drive to achieve true "separate but equal" education, and on the surface, at least, it seemed a model of happy segregation. Underneath, it seethed with all the excited arguing that characterized the young Negro movement.

Meredith plunged into the life, and soon belonged to the Mississippi Improvement Association for Students, a militant Negro group that borrowed a page or two from the Citizens' Council's book. Among other things, the members were pledged to watch one another and report the slightest weakening in anybody's ardor for integration. Meredith was soon helping turn out their literature . . . and thought more than ever about cracking Ole Miss.

It was inevitable that sooner or later he would take his problem to the man who worked in the bare new building across Lynch Street from the campus gate. This was Medgar Evers, local field secretary of the NAACP and the heartbeat of any integration activity in the state of Mississippi. Evers was a wiry young man of immense energy, a quick smile and the most impressive set of teeth since Theodore Roosevelt. Sitting in his cluttered green office, practically welded to the telephone, he seemed in a million things at once, and delighted to be in them all. He was made of optimism, and he needed it.

Meredith first visited Evers one Sunday that fall. Initially it must have looked like a social call, for he came with his wife and baby boy. But the talk soon turned to Ole Miss, and Meredith poured out his thoughts on going there. If he applied and was turned down, could he count on NAACP support?

Evers said yes, he certainly could. Actually, he was going beyond his authority. Such decisions were made in New York by the NAACP Legal Defense and Educational Fund, a separate organization outside Evers' sphere. But again, optimism was what kept Medgar Evers going, and he felt no hesitation now.

In the end nothing happened this time. Meredith still felt he wasn't quite ready. So there were more weeks of debating, puzzling, wondering.

January 20, 1961, and his days of indecision came to an end. This was the day John F. Kennedy was inaugurated, and although Meredith belonged to no particular party, he always felt his chances lay with the liberal Democrats. Now, with the new Administration getting under way—with the excitement of the New Frontier in the air—he at last decided to act.

"Please send me an application for admission to your school," began the brief note he typed off on his Smith-Corona portable. There wasn't much time—February 6 was registration date for the next semester—so he also asked for a catalogue and any other material that might be "helpful." He said nothing about race.

"We are pleased to know of your interest," came Registrar Bob Ellis' cheerful reply. And he enclosed some forms which required, among other items, five character references from University alumni.

For Meredith, things were now getting complicated. How many Mississippi Negroes even knew an Ole Miss alumnus, much the less dared ask him for a character reference? With registration less than two weeks off, clearly the time had come to go back to Medgar Evers. Meredith now told him for the first time that he had actually applied, and it looked like there might be trouble. At the moment the difficulty was of course those character references. Since Ole Miss alumni were out of the question, they decided five responsible Mississippi Negroes would have to do.

January 31, and Meredith finally had his references in hand, his forms filled out. There was just one thing left. At the top of the form there was a space for the applicant's picture. Here he firmly stapled his photograph—a formal shot of a young man neatly dressed, wearing a polka-dotted tie, and unquestionably a Negro. Then he sealed the envelope and mailed it off.

5

"In the Eerie Atmosphere of Never-Never Land"

ONE LOOK AT THAT PICTURE, AND REGISTRAR ELLIS KNEW THAT the morning mail held more than its usual share of admissions problems. Gamely he read the covering letter. "I am an American-Mississippi-Negro citizen," James H. Meredith explained ever so carefully; and he trusted everything would be handled "in a manner that will be complimentary to the University."

It was a large order. All the fears and moods that were so true of the state as a whole were reflected in the University—and more so. Founded in 1848, Ole Miss—like the rest of the state—enjoyed a brief, glorious ante bellum fling. Its Yankee Chancellor, Frederick A. P. Barnard, dreamed of a Harvard-in-the-South and ordered the largest telescope in America. Then, as in the rest of the state, everything crashed with secession—the old empty observatory remains today a touching reminder of the glory that might have been.

During the war the students scattered, most to eternity. The University Greys proudly charged with Pickett at Gettysburg, fell by the score; none ever returned even for a reunion. After Appomattox Ole Miss, again like the rest of the state, struggled to recover but seemed numbed by nostalgia and poverty. In 1873 young men mooned over the lost cause and solaced themselves with orations on the nobility of women. Interest in scholarship vanished—in 1877 the librarian's job was turned over to the janitor.

Mississippi's red-neck revolution at the turn of the century caught the University too. The days of Vardaman and Bilbo saw its standards sink as never before. Chancellor Powers, who served off and on during these years, didn't even have a college degree. At one point the head of the philosophy department was a political crony who handled Bilbo's chores in the state Senate.

Ultimately reform triumphed, and in the '30s Ole Miss began a painful climb back to respectability. Yet even now the goal was decency and honor rather than academic standards. Intellectually, Ole Miss remained isolated and uninterested. As late as 1940 it couldn't raise $50,000 to match a foundation grant for its library.

Events took a new turn in 1946 with the arrival of Chancellor J. D. Williams, a young Kentuckian who had done a good job running a small college in West Virginia. Williams was no scholar, but he proved a fine administrator and a superb public relations man with a great knack of getting money from the state. New buildings sprouted everywhere: a respectable library . . . medical school . . . plans for the first atom smasher in the South. A far wider range of courses soon appeared in the catalogue; for the first time a student could take subjects like art, anthropology, classical civilization. By 1960 the University stood second in the South in Rhodes Scholarship winners. "It's perfectly possible," explained a nationally distinguished alumnus, "to get an excellent education at Ole Miss if you want it."

"If you want it"—that was the key. Despite the new buildings and courses, there remained no pressure, no real incentive. On the other hand, there were countless diversions: 25 elaborate fraternity and sorority houses . . . a glamorous football team . . . the liveliest campus politics east of Louisiana . . . all the happy folderol that went into launching, in a single four-year span, one Miss Dixie, a Maid of Cotton, four Miss Mississippis and two Miss Americas. Above all, there was an atmosphere of constant coming and going

—an amiable restlessness that saw carloads of students driving to Sardis to picnic, to Kiami's to bowl, and always to home for the weekend. Ole Miss remained a pleasant headquarters but scarcely a community of scholars. It was, as the expression went, "a suitcase school."

The University took a benign view of all this. Chancellor Williams pointed out to visitors that a cultural institution should be designed in terms of the culture it served. Hence it was all very well for a New York school to feature art and music, for that was what New York had to offer. But Mississippi was another matter. Here life was built around the outdoors, and different standards had to be applied. ("Why have an orchestra at Ole Miss—you can't get anybody to keep up with the violin.") In terms of the culture it served, the Chancellor felt, the University was nicely designed indeed.

The upshot of this philosophy was to nourish the beliefs and standards already held by those who went there—to make them, in effect, super-Mississippians. And all the more so since the idea persisted that the University was the key to many good things in the future. Ole Miss wasn't cheap—its tuition was very high for a state university—but parents skimped and saved to give their children this great opportunity. And the children understood; they happily accepted the place as a treat. "Everybody speaks," boasted the signs on the campus, and indeed it was so, for Ole Miss was very much a club. And given all of Mississippi's past, it was certainly not the kind of club that would cheerfully admit a Negro.

"For your information and guidance," ran the telegram Meredith received from the admissions office on February 4, "it has been found necessary to discontinue consideration of all applications received after January 25, 1961. Your application was received subsequent to such date and thus we must advise you not to appear for registration." The University later explained that the place was overcrowded, that similar wires had also gone to white students—yet the following semester it managed to fit 300-400 more students on the same campus.

Next, on February 7—just six days after the University received Meredith's application—the Board of Trustees suddenly tightened its regulations on transfer students. Previously anybody in good standing was allowed to transfer from one state school to another; from now on it would be "only when the previous program of the transferring college is acceptable to the receiving institution." The trustees later explained that this was just to improve academic standards—that it had nothing whatsoever to do with race—in fact, they had never discussed in any way the question of a Negro's wanting to go to Ole Miss.

If so, they must have been the only people left in the state not discussing it. Early the day before, as registration began, rumors swept the University that a Negro might turn up. Highway Patrol cars prowled every road leading to the campus. Plain-clothes men swarmed around the gym where registration was going on. Governor Barnett himself was said to be running the show, but he remained politely evasive: "It is for the best interest of the state for me not to make a comment."

On the 7th the Jackson papers bannered the news. Excitement increased as the students finished checking in. Gun-carrying police were now on hand too. Reports spread that the Negro was a Kosciusko boy trying to transfer from Jackson State, but it was hard to learn anything definite. Chancellor Williams was away, and everyone was referred to his assistant, Hugh Clegg, a deceptively roly-poly man who was actually an ex-FBI agent who once had traded shots with Dillinger. Clegg, it was reported, would say nothing except to "trusted members of the faculty."

Then suddenly it was all over. Registration closed at 4:30, the police left, the prowl cars vanished, and once again Ole Miss was the friendly place where "everybody speaks." With an almost audible sigh of relief the Jackson press reported that the Negro had meant no harm; it was understood he did it "more as a joke than a serious attempt."

Not exactly. About the time Meredith wrote the University, he also sent an appeal for help to the NAACP Legal Defense and Educational Fund in New York, and the tone was anything but jocular. "My long preserved ambition," he wrote,

> has been to break the monopoly on rights and privileges held by the Whites in the State of Mississippi. . . . I am making this move in, what I consider, the interest of and for the benefit of: (1) my country, (2) my race, (3) my family, and (4) myself. I am familiar with the probable difficulties involved in such a move as I am undertaking, and I am fully prepared to pursue it all the way to a degree from the University of Mississippi.

The appeal landed on the desk of Thurgood Marshall, still chief of the Legal Defense staff, and it posed a delicate problem. On the one hand, there was the NAACP's policy of taking any case that came along. Contrary to Southern white opinion, the organization did not hand-pick its clients. Some were indeed encouraged to come by NAACP field secretaries; other cases were brought up by cooperating lawyers; still others simply came "over the transom." But however they arrived, no one was ever turned down, unless for some obvious reason like a criminal record. The theory was that any rejected applicant would only go to someone else with less experience who might botch up the case, costing the NAACP only more work in the long run. On this theory, Meredith should be taken, especially since he came with the backing of Medgar Evers, who was thoroughly respected by the legal staff in New York.

On the other hand, this was Mississippi. There was a very real question at the NAACP whether they were ready yet to tackle a place that rough. It was all very well to say the policy was to take anybody, but perhaps this was different. After all, civil rights advocates had been known to die in Mississippi—should the NAACP take a case that might cost a man's life? And if so, was this particular man strong and hard enough to face the battle? It was the first time the organization had come face to face with these questions, for, again contrary to white Southern belief, there were not hordes of applicants waiting in the wings. Meredith was the only one. Was he tough enough?

One call to Meredith removed every doubt. Then and later he flared up so violently at any question of his perseverance that sometimes it was all New York could do to keep him from hanging up. It was immediately clear that if the NAACP didn't take the case, he would go some place else, and as always the organization didn't want that. Not only was there the fear of a botched-up job, but there was another factor—perhaps unconscious, certainly unspoken, but nonetheless real. The Negro movement was now in full blaze, and the NAACP could hardly afford the black eye of turning down a battle that some other civil rights group might triumphantly accept.

"I think it should go without saying that we are vitally interested in what you propose," Thurgood Marshall wrote Meredith on February 7, the day after their telephone talk. And he asked for a transcript of Meredith's record and the latest catalogue of the University.

Now to assign the case. Here too the NAACP legal office wasn't at all the way the white South pictured it. Instead of the vast, sinister, highly organized network generally depicted, it was really the smallest, most informal of places. Half a dozen crack young lawyers—white and Negro—tore into cases with the zest and verve of a college newspaper office. Assignments were usually handed out in the most haphazard way—"who you ran into in the hall or caught at coffee," according to one top official. This time, however, there was a careful matching of talent to problem. One of the best minds on the staff belonged to Constance Motley—a brilliant young Negro lawyer who approached every job with a blend of bristling sharpness and caustic humor that served her well in Southern courtrooms. She was good under fire . . . she knew Mississippi from working on voter and school salary cases . . . she had rammed through the Georgia and Florida university victories. Now she got the Meredith case.

His record was on her desk by the 16th, and a quick look dissolved any lingering doubts. Meredith wasn't brilliant, but he was good enough. His early marks were unimpressive, but he showed steady improvement, especially in those University of Maryland courses he took in Japan. By then he was taking tough subjects like Russian—he should certainly be able to get through Ole Miss. She wrote him to ask the University to consider his case a "continuing application."

Meredith did so when he next wrote Registrar Ellis on February 20. He also plied Ellis with a little soft soap: "Again I would like to express my gratitude for the respectable and humane manner in which you are handling this matter." All he got in return was a refund of his original $10 room deposit.

Three more letters got no answers at all, and finally on April 12 Mrs. Motley tried her hand at the game. She drafted a letter from Meredith to Dean A. B. Lewis of the College of Liberal Arts which for the first time laid the cards on the table: "I have concluded that Mr. Ellis has failed to act upon my application solely because of my race and color." The letter then asked Dean Lewis to look into the case and write back. Again, no answer.

Yet behind the scenes it appeared that Meredith was making an impression at least somewhere—if not at the University, perhaps in more political circles. The Negro grapevine warned him to stay away from his home town, Kosciusko—he was in danger of getting arrested.

May 9 brought an unexpected turn—Registrar Ellis' first letter since January. It assured Meredith that his case was getting careful consideration, but the University could give him only 48 hours' credit for his work at other colleges, instead of the 90 he sought. Was he still interested? Meredith said yes, he was.

A week later the University further tightened its admissions standards. From now on it would accept credits "only from institutions which are members of a regional accrediting association or a recognized professional accrediting association." It so happened that Meredith's college, Jackson State, was not a member of the Southern Association of Colleges and Secondary Schools, the main regional group.

Registrar Ellis now slammed the door. "The University," he wrote on May 25, "cannot recognize the transfer of credits from the institution which you are now attending since it is not a member of the Southern Association of Colleges and Secondary Schools. Our policy permits the transfer of credits only from member institutions of regional associations." And should Meredith remain unconvinced, there were other reasons too:

> Furthermore, students may not be accepted by the University from those institutions whose programs are not recognized.
>
> As I am sure you realize, your application does not meet other requirements for admission. Your letters of recommendation are not sufficient for either a resident or a non-resident applicant. I see no need for mentioning any other deficiencies.

With the NAACP handling the case, Meredith now went to court. Claiming that he was kept out solely because of race and color, on May 31 he sued the top University officials and the Board of Trustees of the Institutions of Higher Learning—the body that governed all seven of Mississippi's public colleges and universities. And since the first summer term would begin on June 8— just eight days off—lawyer Constance Motley also asked for a preliminary injunction. This would at least let Meredith start classes while the merits of the case were argued out.

Judge Sydney C. Mize, the courtly Mississippian in charge of dispensing federal justice in the suit, seemed to understand. He set a hearing for June 12 at Biloxi. Not too bad—that would still allow Meredith to turn up at school only four days late.

The case began on time. Things were proceeding smoothly, when at 3:30 P.M. Judge Mize suddenly stopped the trial. He explained that because of his crowded calendar he had set aside only one day for this, and the rest of the hearing would just have to wait until July 10. So went Meredith's chance of attending the University's first summer session.

But the new date wasn't too bad after all. It would still allow a week before the second summer term began on July 17—Meredith could start then instead. As matters turned out, however, it wasn't that easy. First, the case couldn't be heard on the 10th—Judge Mize discovered he had a calendar conflict. Then it couldn't be heard on the 11th either—Assistant Attorney General Dugas Shands got sick. Now it was reset for August 10 . . . and so went Meredith's chance of attending the University's second summer session.

When the hearing finally came off in August, Ole Miss moved swiftly to establish its defense: there was no segregation at the University. One paragraph in Registrar Ellis' formal answer set the tone: "Defendant was shocked, surprised and disappointed that the plaintiff would so rashly and so unjustifiably conclude that he, the defendant, had failed to act upon plaintiff's application solely because of plaintiff's race and color."

An incredulous Constance Motley asked him on the stand whether he had ever seen a Negro student at the University. "I have seen students with varying degrees of darkness of skin," Ellis answered thoughtfully, "but I can't tell you whether any of them were of the Negro race or not."

Asked if any of the reasons for rejecting Meredith had to do with race, Ellis replied, "Absolutely none." And did he ever take race into consideration in passing on applications? "No."

Then why was Meredith rejected? There seemed no end of reasons. Jackson State was not regionally accredited, as required by the Admissions Committee that May (just ten days before Ellis lowered the boom). . . . Nor was its program recognized as required by the Board of Trustees (just a week after Meredith's original application). . . . Nor did Meredith have any of the required letters from alumni. . . . Nor did he seem to be in good faith; look at the way he always wanted a return receipt for his registered letters to the University. And wouldn't a real scholar, faced with the loss of so many credits, simply go somewhere else?

Fresh facts, the University maintained, showed more than ever that the man was a bad risk. He said his home was Kosciusko in Attala County, yet he registered to vote at Jackson State in Hinds County—wasn't that a case of false registration? And look at his Air Force medical record. It showed that Meredith got easily upset, especially when the race issue came up, and had even been to the base psychiatrist. The diagnosis was one of those professional classics of ambiguity—"passive aggressive reaction"—but it all suggested trouble to Ole Miss. And, again, there was always that "rather insulting" suggestion that Ellis might be influenced by his race. "I definitely came to the conclusion," summed up the Registrar, "that a man who is ready to go off in all directions making charges of this serious nature is certainly not one who would be willing to abide by the regulations of the University and be an acceptable student."

It look Judge Mize 118 days to ponder this presentation (and so went Meredith's chances of attending the fall semester at the University), but there was no doubt in his mind when he finally gave his decision on December 12:

> The overwhelming weight of the testimony is that the plaintiff was not denied admission because of his color or race. The Registrar swore emphatically and unequivocably that the race of plaintiff or his color had nothing in the world to do with the action of the Registrar in denying his application. An examination of the entire testimony of the Registrar shows conclusively that he gave no consideration whatsoever to the race or the color of the plaintiff. . . .

"This case was tried below and argued here in the eerie atmosphere of never-never land," gasped the Fifth Circuit Court of Appeals, reviewing the case on January 12, 1962. Segregation in Mississippi schools and colleges, stressed the court, was a "plain fact known to everyone." It took judicial notice of the practice; it threw out the admissions rule requiring alumni recommendations; and it noted that since Judge Mize's decision the Southern Regional Association had accredited Jackson State. This new development knocked out the main reason Registrar Ellis originally gave for rejecting Meredith.

Despite all this, the appeals court affirmed Judge Mize's decision—not because it agreed, but because it wanted to get on with the case. After all, this was still just the opening skirmish— the motion for a preliminary injunction originally designed to let Meredith start college while the basic issue was thrashed out. That was seven months ago—three terms had passed since then— any further dickering over stopgap relief seemed ludicrous. So the Fifth Circuit simply let Judge Mize know how it felt and urged him to speed his trial on the merits of the case. This was now scheduled for January 15, and with the appeals court's views so emphatically spelled out, perhaps it would all be over in time for Meredith to start the winter term in February.

It worked out a little differently. When the trial finally got going on January 24 (after another week lost when Assistant Attorney General Shands fell sick again), Judge Mize ignored the Fifth Circuit's view that segregation in Mississippi was a "plain fact known to everyone." Instead, he carefully listened as a long stream of witnesses once again insisted that race didn't mean a thing at Ole Miss.

Constance Motley tried to pin them down. Asked if he had ever seen a Negro student at the University, Leston Lewis Love, Dean of Student Personnel, said he didn't really know "because I don't know the genealogical background of every person I meet." Asked if any had ever been admitted since his arrival in 1941, Vice Chancellor W. A. Bryant said he just couldn't tell—"I'm not an expert in the field of anthropology." Asked if he'd ever heard of a Negro there, Trustee Tally Riddell helpfully replied, "If you'll tell me what you mean by Negro, I'll try to answer it."

Again and again they stressed they had never discussed Meredith or Negro admissions generally at any faculty or trustees meeting. And certainly there were no instructions on the subject. "To the best of my knowledge," declared Chancellor Williams, "no official of the University—and that includes the Chancellor—has the authority to deny the application of a qualified applicant to the University of Mississippi on the basis of race or color."

Yet the University was never more certain that Meredith should be kept out. He was clearly a moral risk. In addition to the reasons offered at the last trial, there was now new evidence, involving those five recommendations he got from "responsible Negro citizens." It seemed that Assistant Attorney General Ed Cates had dropped over to Kosciusko recently and seen each of these people. After an interview at the bank before the local justice of the peace and a former member of the State Sovereignty Commission, four of the five withdrew their recommendations. They said they misunderstood . . . they thought Meredith only wanted a job . . . they never realized he was trying to go to Ole Miss. Now they were happy to sign a written retraction: "I could not now certify to his good moral character nor could I recommend him for admission to the University of Mississippi or any other college."

It was all very clear to Registrar Ellis: "This fellow is a troublemaker." Once again he assured the court, "Meredith's race or color has had no influence on the decisions which I have taken."

And it was equally clear to Judge Mize. Delivering his decision on February 3, he declared: "The proof shows, and I find as a fact, that the University is not a racially segregated institution. . . . Plaintiff was not denied admission because of his race." The judge did concede that segregation was practiced before the Supreme Court decision, but afterward all that had changed. There was no custom or policy now which kept qualified Negroes from entering the University.

"This about-face policy," the Fifth Circuit acidly remarked, reversing Judge Mize on June 25, "news of which may startle some people in Mississippi, could have been accomplished only by telepathic communication among the University's administrators, the Board of Trustees of State Institutions of Higher Learning." Or so it would seem, since nearly everyone denied discussing the subject. With this withering deduction, the court once again took judicial notice that the place was segregated—"what everybody knows the court must know."

The decision then tossed out each of the reasons given by the University for rejecting Meredith: Alumni letters were an unfair device. . . . Jackson State no longer lacked accreditation. . . . Meredith's service record was sound enough to win a Good Conduct Medal. . . . His so-called false voter registration was a frivolous charge. . . . The retraction by his character witnesses meant nothing under the circumstances. . . . His emotional troubles merely showed the kind of Negro who might be expected to try to crack Ole Miss: "a man with a mission and with a nervous stomach."

The conclusion was inevitable: "We find that James Meredith's application for transfer to the University of Mississippi was turned down solely because he was a Negro."

By now it was the summer of 1962—Meredith had missed two more semesters—but it no longer made so much difference. Originally time had seemed all-important, for fear Meredith would graduate from Jackson State before he could get to Ole Miss. But during the winter Constance Motley, on the appeals court's advice, had worked out a neat formula to avoid this danger: Meredith would only take courses that didn't lead to graduation. So all spring he had casually puttered away on an academic treadmill while the Fifth Circuit took its time for a thorough review.

Now at last the job was done, the case reversed, and Judge Mize told to issue the injunction that would let Meredith in. The Fifth Circuit's formal order, or mandate, was issued July 17, and that seemed the end of the battle. Mississippi would of course appeal to the Supreme Court, but few doubted the outcome, and meanwhile Judge Mize would do as ordered. For Meredith, it looked like a happy ending. No more waiting, no more useless courses, no more bullying like the time when Shands questioned him on stealing government property simply because he had used a few sheets of paper left over from Air Force days in typing up some of his letters.

For Constance Motley too the days of worrying at last seemed over. No more postponed hearings . . . no more denied motions . . . no more jousting with Assistant Attorney General Charles Clark over how to pronounce "Negro" . . . no more stale sandwiches simply because there wasn't any place a Negro lawyer could get lunch near the courthouse.

But July 18 brought a brand-new development. The Fifth Circuit's orders were suddenly suspended—in lawyer's language, "stayed"—by Judge Ben Cameron, who was a member of the court but hadn't sat on the case. This was totally unprecedented. Like other courts, the Fifth Circuit divided its work among panels chosen from its nine judges, and occasionally a panel member might issue a stay to allow time for an appeal to the Supreme Court; but never before had a stay been granted by a judge who hadn't studied the record, listened to the arguments or discussed the facts in a judicial conference. Whatever the propriety, the stay was issued, and was worded to run until the Supreme Court finally disposed of the case. Naturally, Judge Mize would respect it as coming from a superior court.

The rest of the judges, Constance Motley, her NAACP staff were all taken completely by surprise. Actually, they might have predicted it. Judge Cameron was not only an outspoken segregationist from Meridian, but he frankly considered that he represented Mississippi—and privately said so.

July 27, and the Fifth Circuit showed it could break precedent too. That day it vacated Judge Cameron's stay, recalled its earlier orders to Judge Mize, and issued a new mandate spelling out exactly what the District Court's injunction was to say. Then to make doubly sure, on July 28 it issued an injunction of its own. Rarely, if ever, had an appeals court dived so deeply into the mechanics of a case. It was practically acting as a District Court.

Now it was Mississippi's turn to gulp. But here too the action might have been predicted, for the Meredith case panel included two jurists who had always shown vigor and fire in pushing the Supreme Court's desegregation orders. Judge John Minor Wisdom was a most urbane and literate New Orleanean; Judge John R. Brown a peppery Texan transplanted from Nebraska. Neither was the type that shrank from a battle.

Judge Cameron too had a zest for combat, and he reacted in character. He issued two more stays suspending the new appeals court orders. The Fifth Circuit accepted the challenge and on August 4 vacated Cameron's latest stays.

August 6, Cameron issued his fourth stay, and this time the Fifth Circuit gave up. Clearly the game could go on forever, and there just wasn't time for that. Still another semester was coming up at Ole Miss, and while Meredith now knew how to tread water very well, there were signs that the constant delays and harassments were at last wearing him down.

The NAACP had one last card to play. It appealed directly to the Supreme Court to stop Cameron, vacate his stays, confirm the Fifth Circuit's directives and order Meredith admitted to school. At the moment the Court was in recess, but Justice Black was on hand, assigned to take care of any routine Fifth Circuit business, and the NAACP felt this was the sort of situation where he could act alone. But even if he could—then what? How could any directive be carried out? What new time-killing device would emerge in Mississippi?

It became increasingly clear that if these questions would ever be answered with finality—if Meredith would ever really get into Ole Miss—it would take more than the growing momentum of the Negro movement, more than the NAACP's legal skills, more even than the blessing of the federal courts. Some wholly new force must appear, lending new authority, prestige and resources to the struggle.

6

"You've Just Got to Keep Going Back"

"YOUR PREDECESSOR NEVER BROUGHT A CIVIL RIGHTS CASE IN Mississippi," Senator James Eastland playfully reminded the new Attorney General, Robert F. Kennedy, as the New Frontier took the reins of government in January 1961. Only joking, perhaps, but in many ways Senator Eastland could hardly have said a worse thing.

Above all, Robert Kennedy was competitive—eagerly rising to almost any challenge. He had always been that way—scrapping to make the 1948 Harvard football team . . . relentlessly pursuing Jimmy Hoffa . . . matching anything brother Teddy did at skin-diving . . . learning to read as fast as Jack . . . stepping on sacred toes at the 1960 Los Angeles convention.

He played to win, and it followed that results were what counted. It was the effective man, regardless of other qualities, who won that darting smile, the caustic crack that was really a compliment in disguise. By the same token, woe to the man who failed to produce. For him there was only impatience, scornful silence, or a cutting remark which, coming from a younger to an older person, often seemed needlessly harsh.

He would have been a simpler case if it hadn't been for that strong streak of idealism. Some people misinterpreted it as prudishness; actually it was more like the muscular Christianity of the turn-of-the-century years. It emerged in his love of family . . . in his personal integrity . . . in unswerving loyalty . . . in the ease with which he applied "right" and "wrong" labels to the things that concerned him. It was a trait that burst out in his righteous indignation at the height of the 1960 campaign, when Martin Luther King was arrested during an Atlanta sit-in and sentenced to four months' hard labor ostensibly for driving without a Georgia license.

"Four months for a traffic violation?" Kennedy exploded in his typical way of cramming a lot of feeling into very few words. His reaction was typical too. While Nixon, eying the Southern white vote, remained silent—and JFK, sensing the human equation, contacted Mrs. King—Robert Kennedy phoned the judge. It was his natural instinct to go straight to the heart of the matter, and second nature to get there by telephone, always an indispensable instrument in the Kennedy way of doing things. Within hours King was free on bail.

Good politics of course—no one knows how many Negroes shifted to JFK as a result; there's even reason to believe they swung the election. Yet people are what politics are all about, and in this case it's fair to say the political decision went hand in glove with the Kennedy conscience.

It didn't always work out so smoothly. Sometimes idealism and pragmatism collided head on, and then Kennedy's passion for the workable might well triumph—as in his 1961 support of broader federal wire-tapping powers. Or perhaps some well-meaning idealist might propose what Kennedy considered a hopelessly impractical approach to a problem. Then once again would come that burst of impatience . . . once again the curt brush-off . . . once again the impression that here indeed was a hard, insensitive young man.

He might have been pretty impossible to live and work with, without a warmer side. But that was there too, adding still another complex ingredient. Hence he might be tough, but he could also be gentle to a point of tenderness—like the time he spent hours picking tar from the wings of a fallen starling. And if he often brooded, he also had a brand of animal spirits.

Most important was his remarkable technique of mixing hard work and stylish play. It was, in fact, often impossible to tell where one stopped and the other began. At the office the toughest problem might be suddenly interrupted by a few moments of the sophisticated banter that was a hallmark of any Kennedy staff. By the pool at his country home Hickory Hill, he could draft a statement, hug his daughter Kerry, take a call on the white poolside phone, and slam a few balls into the tennis backboard—all without seeming to change gears at all. Moving so easily from work to play, and back again, he got an immense amount done, seemed nearly always fresh and relaxed, and gave those who worked closely with him an intoxicating feeling of being part of a very exciting world. It was fun to work for Bob (never Bobby on the job), and that made up for the frantic pace.

Such was the man who, on January 21, 1961, moved into the Justice Department. Lithe, tousled and seeming even younger than his 35 years, he established himself in Room 5115, the baronial office of the Attorney General of the United States. Rolling up his shirt sleeves, opening his collar, sliding down in the big leather chair almost to the point of invisibility, he looked at first glance like a kid who had slipped into his father's office while the old man was out. But that was only at first glance. . . .

The new tempo was the most noticeable thing. Traditionally the Justice Department, like all great government establishments, more or less ran itself. Even when the Attorney General was the most conscientious of men, it didn't much matter on most things whether he was there or not. The Civil Service regulars ran their little principalities pretty much the way they liked. And most of the political appointees nominally in charge—the various Assistant Attorney Generals—were perfectly happy to leave it that way. In the absence of a headline-making antitrust suit or such, top policies, administrative procedures, motor pools and coffee breaks all lumbered on alike, following lines set long ago for reasons long forgotten. Bureaucracy stood ever on guard, ready to challenge anyone who dared change the system.

It was the kind of bait Robert Kennedy couldn't resist. If the Attorney General was meant to remain pretty much in splendid isolation, then this one would roam the corridors. Soon he was jostling routine, poking his head into offices, asking people what they did. And one of his first discoveries proved jarring indeed to that idealistic streak of his: although the Department was the acknowledged guardian of the nation's civil rights, only ten of its 950 lawyers happened to be Negroes.

Something was done about that, and other things too, for it was no great exaggeration when the President called his brother "the best man in the United States on planning, getting the right people to work, and seeing that the job was done." There were occasional bleats of anguish when some jealously guarded preserve was pried loose, but most of the Justice Department's 31,700 employees caught the new excitement in the air and responded with enthusiasm . . . even with gratitude. Lights burned late; the underground garage began to fill on Saturday; telephones and intercoms multiplied.

A whole new set of young faces soon appeared. For the first time in years the agile figures breezing down the corridors seemed in keeping with the vigorous WPA murals left over from another, equally lively era. Byron White, the new Deputy Attorney General, trailed a dazzling career in such varied roles as Rhodes Scholar, Marine staff officer, Supreme Court law clerk and leading ground gainer in the National Professional Football League. Lou Oberdorfer, the tax chief, combined the soft voice of an Alabaman with the hard mind of a crack Washington tax lawyer. Bill Orrick, who headed the Civil Division, was a joyously energetic soul who rolled his sleeves even higher than the Attorney General. Press chief Ed Guthman was a Pulitzer Prize winner whose glasses, usually perched on the top of his head, almost told the time—the higher they were, the later the hour.

Whatever their specific assignment, they were expected to do more than that. A cardinal point of RFK's administrative philosophy was that a man should be good at anything, and he used his top aides as a sort of task force whose combined strength could be brought to bear on any problem confronting the Department. And more than that. As the President's brother and closest confidant, Robert Kennedy's activities ranged far beyond those of an ordinary Attorney General, and here too he considered his staff as a weapon to be used on any problem he tackled—whether at home or abroad. No wonder these bright young men (they averaged under 40) had the feeling that they were an integral part of not merely the Justice Department but the Administration itself.

And no wonder morale was so high. Much has been said about the sacrifices made by those who give up lucrative private jobs for government service—and it is true. But there are also compensations. Few of these 38-year-old junior law partners and associate professors had ever seen such trappings before—the paneled offices, the limousines, the big staffs, the private elevators and, above all, the excitement of being really "in" at the top of government.

Predictably, they thrived on Kennedy's patented formula of hard work in relaxed surroundings. They might drive their wives crazy keeping supper hot, but at the end of day they could usually be found sprawled over their red leather chairs, happily engaged in some bull session. Twice a week they lunched together in the Attorney General's posh private dining room—*they belonged*. Just like the chief they taped their children's drawings to their office walls, and proudly they added the waggishly inscribed photos he gave them in a mild spoof on one of Washington's oldest customs.

Nowhere did spirits soar higher than in the Civil Rights Division. Long a departmental stepchild, it boasted only five lawyers as late as Little Rock. In 1960—the year of the sit-ins—its budget was actually lower than the previous year. Everything changed with the New Frontier; from the start Robert Kennedy gave the Division the greatest share of his time and energy.

It was more than a shift in departmental policy; it was the heart of the Administration's whole strategy on civil rights. President Kennedy was sympathetic, but he also had a legislative program to get through Congress. This program couldn't pass without the support of important Southern committee chairmen, and they couldn't be won with another civil rights bill coming up. Yet something had to be done—both because he believed in it and because his powerful Negro supporters were clamoring for action.

The solution was to forego any new bills for the moment and push harder with the powers the Administration already had. There was the appointment power—Thurgood Marshall, for one, was named a Circuit Court judge. There was the power over government contracts—a new committee under Vice President Johnson became the first really effective watchdog on job discrimination. There was the commerce power—the ICC issued orders banning segregation on interstate bus travel. And above all, there was the Justice Department's power under the existing civil rights laws— within weeks Robert Kennedy was beefing up the staff for this work.

True, the 1957 and 1960 laws applied only to voting abuses, but there was the growing feeling that here might lie the key to everything. As the President told Martin Luther King, "Once you get the ballot and the Negroes are educated to its use, all other things will fall into place."

The person assigned to get this done was a taciturn young man named Burke Marshall. As the new Assistant Attorney General for Civil Rights, Marshall had been recruited by Kennedy talent scouts from the crack Washington law firm of Covington & Burling. Great at bringing opposite points of view together, he had all the patience his boss lacked. He also had a dry wit, a quiet manner and a devastating sense of logic—perhaps best illustrated by the famous time he went sailing and lost one of his socks overboard. After mournfully contemplating his plight for a moment, Marshall silently took off his other sock and dropped it overboard too.

If Marshall lacked patience on any count, it was with the Eisenhower philosophy that laws can't change the hearts of men. "But laws *can* change the hearts of men," he would say, a touch of exasperation creeping into his soft, nasal voice. As he saw it, the whole point of any law was to set desirable standards which might otherwise be ignored if men were left to do what they wanted. It was the law that set the climate that made change possible, he stressed, and just as important was its enforcement: "Knowledge that the law is going to be enforced is vital. Very often that knowledge alone makes conciliation possible."

And so it happened that when Burke Marshall had his own little colloquy with Mississippi's Senator Eastland at his confirmation hearing on March 2, 1961, he softly assured the Senator, "I would expect to file suits in some cases where the investigation started without a specific complaint." And he left no doubt that this included Mississippi too.

Exactly one month later two shoddy male figures blinked at the bright April glare that bathed the streets of Hattiesburg, seat of Forrest County and principal town of southeastern Mississippi. Both men seemed rather far down on their luck—their frayed shirts, rumpled khakis and scuffed shoes suggested a pair of unemployed hands from some lumber camp nearby. Actually, they were attorneys from the Civil Rights Division of the Department of Justice, and they had come down to Forrest County to see what was really going on.

For John Doar, 30-year-old leader of the pair, this masquerade was the product of long frustration. No New Frontiersman, he was an idealistic young Republican who had left a thriving small-town practice in Wisconsin and joined the Civil Rights Division in the dying days of the Eisenhower Administration. "I like trial work and knew this would be tough trial work," he later explained, but it's doubtful even he appreciated how resourcefully tough Mississippi could be.

He soon found out when the Department, gingerly trying out the new Civil Rights Act, politely asked to see the Forrest County registration records in August 1960. Registrar Theron C. Lynd requested 90 days to think the matter over, and the delaying action was on. After five months' parrying, the Department finally went to court for the records in January 1961. But Judge W. Harold Cox was a good Mississippian too, and the only result was ten more weeks of silence.

Meanwhile the Kennedy Administration came in, and Burke Marshall took over his new job. Casting one of his hard, quiet looks at John Doar, he quickly decided to keep Doar as his top aide. Swiftly they converted their stately three-room suite into a virtual command post. Maps of the South blossomed on the walls, colored pins showing the progress of battle in every state—airport facilities under investigation . . . school districts being desegregated . . . counties where voting suits had been filed. There were no pins yet in Mississippi, but other signs suggested the state was no longer neglected. Charts of estimated registration figures littered the tables; large-scale maps of various counties leaned against the chairs and walls. Among them was a big blow-up of Forrest County.

By April John Doar was convinced that new tactics were needed here. Clearly they were getting nowhere writing letters and filing papers. Forrest County could play that game forever. The only solution, he decided, was to go there and operate on the spot. And that meant working clandestinely, since Mississippi now openly regarded the Justice Department as "the enemy." Hence with Marshall's blessing, Doar dug out his old clothes, recruited Justice Attorney Bob Owen as a companion and headed for Hattiesburg.

So now they were on the spot, dressed in their worst and wondering what to do next. They knew nobody, had no appointments, knew next to nothing about the town. But they did have large-scale maps, showing not only roads but even individual houses. Picking a likely route, they headed toward the Negro section on Mobile Street and began knocking on doors.

By coincidence, on a hot afternoon that same week in Hattiesburg Mrs. Addie Burger left her neat frame house on Manning Street and went to the Forrest County courthouse near the center of town. Entering Registrar Lynd's office, she said she wanted to register to vote. The clerk gave her an application form, also a small card containing a section of the Mississippi state constitution for her to copy and interpret. The section was § 211—an enormously complicated provision dealing with that special phenomenon of Mississippi real estate called Sixteenth Section Lands.

Mrs. Burger was, of course, a Negro. Yet she wasn't especially upset and even felt she had a lot going for her. After all, she had taught school for 26 years, ran a social study class at Rowan High, boasted a B.S. degree, and was winding up her M.A. at New York University. She felt she handed in an adequate job.

Several days later she returned to see if she passed, but only Mr. Lynd could say and he was out. After several more days she finally caught him at the office, and it didn't take him long to tell her that she had failed. She tried to find out why, but without any luck. Lynd simply got up and strolled off into another room.

It was an old story, judging from the statements and testimony later given by the Negro applicants. "What do you boys want?" Theron Lynd liked to say when they managed to catch him at the courthouse. Then the game would begin. Until 1961 he simply turned them away—he wasn't set up yet, or he had to go out, or he didn't have the time. But late that January (just after the Justice Department went to court for his records) he began to test anybody, white or black. Word flashed through the Negro community, but those who rushed to the courthouse soon learned their problems weren't over. A truckload of Hercules Powder workers found that (unlike the whites) they could only be tested one at a time . . . and that seemed to take forever. Hollis Barnes was simply told his education wasn't good enough to take the test. Science teacher David Roberson could hardly be told that: he was bound for Cornell on a National Science Foundation grant. So he found himself interpreting § 273 of the state constitution—a tangled, 155-word sentence specifying the procedure for adopting a constitutional amendment.

Whatever their adventures, they all ended up the same way— still nonvoters. As of April 1961, not a single new Negro voter had been added to the rolls during Lynd's two years in office. Somewhere along the line he had accepted two transfers from other counties, but beyond these—nothing. The Registrar's office remained an impregnable wall between the Negro and the ballot.

Those turned down were never told why, giving them a chance to do things differently next time. On the other hand, they were never mistreated, giving them some tangible, dramatic grounds for raising an uproar. They just marched up the courthouse stairs, and then marched down again—empty-handed, completely baffled and ever more discouraged.

It was the story not only in Forrest County, but over much of Mississippi. For most Negroes were kept from voting not through brutality, but through something far more subtle. The deputy who beat Wallace Davis in Rankin County—the official who pistol-whipped John Hardy in Walthall County—were actually the exceptions. Mississippi's real answer to Negro voting was not a courthouse bully, but a massive recalcitrance that was all the more difficult to surmount because it was so formless, so intangible, so hard to get at. It didn't smash the Negro; it simply wore him down, tired him out, drained his energy until he finally stopped trying altogether.

Clearly a handful of Negroes, however dedicated, were no match for this resistance. It could only be overcome by a force equally massive, equally resourceful, equally relentless. . . .

Down the dusty black-top roads—along Scooba Street, out by Palmers Crossing, everywhere—John Doar and Bob Owen continued knocking on doors. Carefully they introduced themselves, sat in neat if threadbare front rooms, and listened to as much as Hattiesburg's Negroes might dare tell such a disreputable-looking pair of white visitors. Soon they had enough to start sending names to the FBI, and Bureau men began fanning over the county—a well-groomed contrast to the camouflaged Justice attorneys.

May 9, and the FBI reported it had now interviewed 54 Negroes who had tried in vain to register since 1949; the roster included ten college graduates. Also interviewed were six curiosities—Forrest County Negroes who had actually been allowed to vote. One of them, it turned out, had tried 50 times before he finally wore down some long-departed registrar. Studying the figures, Doar guessed that of the county's 7,495 Negroes of voting age, perhaps 25 were registered. It proved one of the few times he ever underestimated Mississippi's resourcefulness: as a matter of fact only 14 Negroes could vote in Forrest County.

July 6, and John Doar was at last ready to move. That day the Justice Department went to the federal District Court and moved to enjoin Registrar Theron C. Lynd from discriminating against Negroes. Considered together with a second suit brought against another county that day, a shattering precedent had been set. No longer could Senator Eastland playfully boast that the Department had never brought a voting case in Mississippi.

With the die cast, Justice investigators once again swarmed over Forrest County. And this time they discarded their old clothes, wore instead their best. They were now openly representing the power and authority of the federal government; they could no longer afford to look furtive. And this was especially important in winning the Negroes' confidence. For their role had changed too: it was one thing to confide in a federal investigator behind a closed front door; now they were being asked to testify in open court.

Mrs. Edna Carter wasn't sure she wanted any part of it, as she sat talking to Justice Attorney Arvid Sather in her trim little house off Scooba Street. She had a college degree, read the latest news magazines, would have easily qualified to vote almost anywhere, and had vainly tried three times in Hattiesburg. Yet suddenly her desire was gone, and she felt only a gnawing fear.

The government man earnestly persisted, and as he talked Mrs. Carter's husband drifted in from the next room. She looked up helplessly, seeking some word that might help. Finally he told her that it was really up to her, but one thing seemed clear: this was not agitating, or trying to get other people to vote; it was merely asserting a right that already belonged to her as a citizen. As for himself, he added, he felt they had been sitting on the fence long enough and the time had come to take a stand, even if it meant getting fired. The room fell silent for a moment; then Mrs. Carter said she would like to testify.

Meanwhile Registrar Lynd carried on as usual. Take science teacher David Roberson's account of what next happened to him: September 28, Lynd convinced Roberson that there wasn't enough time to try again that day . . . October 2, Lynd was out when Roberson came back . . . October 12, Roberson finally got his chance—only to learn he failed several days later. Why? Lynd just "walked out."

If the Registrar seemed oblivious to the Justice Department's onslaught, he had good reason to be. Everything was going smoothly in Mississippi. The state's lawyers—past masters at the delaying game—were filing motions to strike, motions for a more definite statement, motions for absolutely anything that might hold up the proceedings a little longer. Judge Cox, the loyal Mississippian who would handle the case, was most sympathetic. He agreed with the defense that before the federal government could see the Registrar's records, it must back up its charges with fuller details—but this, of course, was exactly why the government needed the records. In short, the very information the court demanded was the same information it refused to let the government have.

All this could go on forever—which was, of course, just what Mississippi wanted. For its basic strategy was the one that had worked in the days of Reconstruction: be stubborn enough, and the federal government would tire of the game; hold out long enough, and Washington would go away.

But this time Washington didn't go away. John Doar and his men simply plunged into Forrest County with more ardor than ever. But ardor alone was not enough to meet the next problem they faced. Both the state and Judge Cox were still insisting that the federal government back up its charges with fuller details. It was not enough to show that Negroes had a tough time voting; it must be shown they had a tougher time than the whites. John Doar was sure the Registrar's records would quickly bring this out, but again Judge Cox wouldn't let him see the records. Some other way had to be found to build up a file of white experiences.

As so often in the past, the solution turned on infinite patience and devotion to detail. Federal investigators pored over the files of the Hattiesburg *American,* copying down recent High School graduating classes—a likely source of new voters. Justice Attorney Gordon Martin visited a local Catholic priest, got from him another useful list of young white people. At the end of the day the task force spent more hours, matching and sifting the data, gradually building a master list of 800 names. Then 15 FBI men fanned out over the county, interviewing everyone listed. From their reports, a final list was drawn, and once again the Justice lawyers went into action, interviewing every prospect.

It wasn't always easy. As a Civil Rights Division attorney drew from Marcia Rae Wright, one of the new white voters, her account of how easily she registered, her father grew so upset by the interview that he finally seized her certificate to vote and crumpled it up. But Miss Wright clearly had a mind of her own—she calmly retrieved the wad and ironed it out for the government to use.

Her cooperation was typical of a surprisingly large number of these young people. Some were reluctant, to be sure, and others talked simply because they were uneducated people awed by the trappings of law—but many, many more spoke up simply because they felt they should. Once again, as so often in the past, hardened official investigators found that the decency in people runs deep indeed—if only there's someone willing to bring it out.

Gradually the stories unfolded, vividly pointing up the advantages enjoyed by the whites. Charles Still, Jr. told how he registered in 1960 without filling out any form at all—he just signed the big book. Harmon Gary Stewart did get a form, but a girl in the office filled it out for him. John D. Bennett had to take the constitutional interpretation test—but Section 118 was a brief sentence about the governor getting a fixed salary. James Bennett got perhaps the best break of all: the clerk pointed out for him an ingeniously camouflaged signature line at the very end of the form. It appeared to be merely part of a special oath for ministers, but actually it applied to everybody, and anyone who failed to sign it could be instantly rejected.

"Swarms of federal government employees, they go in the nighttime to see them, everybody in the nighttime under cover of night, without a moon. . . ." Such was the agonized picture painted by Lynd's lawyer, M. M. Roberts, when Judge Cox finally heard the case on March 5, 1962. And indeed it must have seemed so, for these painstaking federal men were everywhere . . . no lead seemed too small to run down . . . no detail too time-consuming to follow up. It was, in short, John Doar's massive answer to the massive resistance of Mississippi.

Even so, Doar had anything but an easy time in court. Lynd, a man of imposing bulk, proved hard to budge indeed. He stoutly denied race had anything to do with his practices; otherwise he was remarkably vague. Did he require that all applicants, both black and white, know their voting precinct? "Well, I wouldn't say that I required it, and I wouldn't say that I didn't require it."

Only when dealing with the constitutional interpretation test did Doar seem to make any real headway. As he brought out that the janitor of the Hercules Powder Company had to interpret § 112 —an enormously intricate provision dealing with uniform taxation

—Judge Cox's eyes suddenly sparkled with curiosity. The defense lawyers roared objections to such testimony, but this time the judge overruled them: "I wanted to see what he would say because the Supreme Court of Mississippi has had some trouble with this section."

But this small triumph was more than offset when Doar finally moved for a preliminary injunction, citing (among other reasons) Lynd's practice of letting his women clerks help with the whites but never with the Negroes. Judge Cox lost little time setting him straight on this point: "I think the colored people brought that on themselves. I am thoroughly familiar with the conduct of some of our colored gentry, and I am not surprised at Mr. Lynd's reaction to what he stated into the record. I think there is a clear justification for what he did. You people up North don't understand what he is talking about. I don't expect you to. But I do, I know exactly what he was talking about, and I think he did just exactly right in taking those things on himself."

Odd language for a federal judge in a federal court, but it certainly foretold the outcome. Judge Cox refused to grant the Justice Department's motion for a preliminary injunction, ordering Lynd to stop discriminating against Negroes. But he didn't deny the motion either. He just sat on it. To the exasperated Justice lawyers this was the last straw—it had all the effect of a denial, yet technically there was no formal denial to appeal.

Desperately the Justice Department went to the appeals court anyhow, and in another of its imaginative if somewhat free-wheeling decisions the Fifth Circuit agreed that the situation was indeed "appealable" . . . then went on to issue its own temporary injunction against Lynd. This not only ordered him to stop discriminating, but also instructed him to give Negroes the same kind of assistance he had been giving whites, and to test Negroes with the same sections of the constitution that he used for whites at the time of the trial.

At 12 noon, April 18, the court's order was personally served on Theron C. Lynd. By 4:30 P.M. the young Negro science teacher

David Roberson was already back, hoping the new ruling might at last see him through. Breathlessly he handed in his form . . . then learned it was the same old story. Lynd just told him he didn't make it. Why? begged Roberson; but as always, Lynd politely declined to tell him.

Day after day it was the same story, occasionally spiced with a bit of suspense. When the Rev. James Chandler, the elderly Negro minister at Mt. Carmel Baptist Church, handed in his form on April 23, Lynd studied it slowly . . . suggested a minor correction . . . then, of all things, entered Chandler's name in the registration book. But next moment, as the minister later told it, Lynd said he noticed just one little error after all. Chandler got the form back, hastily changed his name from "James C. Chandler" to "James Cleveland Chandler," and prayerfully handed it in again. No, said Lynd, that wasn't it; and with that, he carefully crossed Chandler's name out of the book.

But very few things in Mississippi are predictable, and on April 26—to the astonishment of practically everyone—the Rev. Chandler actually passed his test and was enrolled in the big book. He thus became the fifteenth Negro registered in Forrest County . . . the first new Negro voter in eight years . . . the first ever accepted by Theron C. Lynd.

It was not good enough for John Doar. One new Negro voter might be cause for celebration along Mobile Street, but Doar thought much more about the 26 who had failed in the single week since the Fifth Circuit ordered Lynd to mend his ways. In the last analysis it looked like the same old waiting game: hold out long enough and the federals would get tired and go away.

But Doar was more determined than ever. If it was a matter of outlasting the other fellow, he could play that game too. Moreover, he now had a valuable new weapon. Judge Cox may not have been very "friendly" (to use that revealing expression of lawyers), but at least he finally allowed the Justice Department to examine Lynd's records. This opened up a mountain of new evidence, and John Doar made the most of it.

Once again the secret was patience and infinite attention to detail. Investigators sifted through hundreds of forms, looking for signs of discrimination. They noticed, for instance, that 19 Negro applications rejected since April 18 were satisfactory except for minor technical errors, or missing the trick signature line. Lynd had given the Negroes no help on all this—had he ever helped the whites? If so, here was a violation of the Fifth Circuit's order.

So the staff turned to the white applications, and interesting clues began to emerge. Form 5556 was filled out in blue ink, but an error on Question 12 was crossed out in black ink like that in the Registrar's office. Form 5632 had a suggestive check mark by the trick signature line . . . 118 out of 305 white applications had these check marks altogether.

The investigators also spent a lot of time examining the constitutional interpretation tests given to Negroes since the date of the injunction. Did they get sections different from those given to whites at the time of the trial? If so, here was another violation of the court's order. To get the facts, the Justice men had to make point-by-point comparisons of 33 Negro applications with 281 white. But again, the paper work paid off: it turned out that two out of three Negroes got sections never given to a white.

"You don't know what the United States Government by the Civil Rights Division will do for one Negro voter against a million white through this business!" exclaimed Lynd's lawyer, M. M. Roberts, as the Justice Department moved on April 30 to cite the Registrar for contempt of court. The Fifth Circuit listened, and on May 1 ordered Lynd to answer the charge.

He didn't seem especially upset by this turn of events. That same day he rejected Negro Jackson Gibson, after giving him Section 17 to interpret—another clause that had never been given to any white. May 11, and he once again turned down science teacher David Roberson for trifling errors in filling out the form. June 4, and he again turned down Roberson on a minor technicality, but this time the young scientist was spared the frustration of hearing about it; before he could learn the result, he had to get back to Cornell to finish up his M.A.

Nevertheless, there were signs that the Justice Department's relentless pressure was not going entirely unnoticed. Lynd registered seven more Negroes by June 18. Even more significant, he began toughening the standards for whites. In fact, after June 21 64% of the white applications were rejected—an unheard-of high.

That still wasn't good enough for John Doar. The Fifth Circuit's injunction said that Negro standards should be as easy as white, not that white should be as strict as Negro. Any other course would only freeze the white advantage for a generation. So the Civil Rights Division worked on. The latest request to the FBI listed 29 questions to be asked 111 different people—3,219 answers altogether to be correlated with the data already gathered. And all the while, the research staff continued to sift the registration records.

They were no longer looking for a few witnesses of high principle; now they were searching for uneducated whites who probably had received favored treatment. These could then be subpoenaed, if necessary, to testify. The best prospects, the staff felt, could quickly be pinpointed by the worst spelling and handwriting. Applicant No. 5926, for instance, said a good citizen should "help and promotion eduaction and welfale for ouer young people." Here clearly was someone to look up.

"They're murdering us with those white voters!" a good Mississippian confided to a visitor as the Justice Department's strategy unfolded. And it was so. When the contempt case came to trial that September, nothing was more impressive than the bales of evidence John Doar trundled in—showing again and again the special consideration given a number of nearly illiterate white registrants of Forrest County. The judges took nearly a year to do it, but finally on July 15, 1963, the Fifth Circuit ruled that Registrar Theron C. Lynd was indeed guilty of civil contempt of court.

Meanwhile, what was being accomplished? On the eve of the contempt trial—more than 13 months after the federal attack began—a grand total of nine Negroes had been added to the voting lists. Some 7,486 others were still waiting in the wings. Considering all the time, work and manpower invested, the results seemed very small.

And this was just one county—a county only 25 per cent Negro, with no ante bellum tradition and no special reputation for violence. Would the Justice Department invest this kind of time and energy everywhere in Mississippi? What about the 13 counties where no Negroes could vote at all? What about Clarke County, where they wouldn't even register the man they named the Negro school after? What about Sunflower County, where Senator Eastland himself lived?

"To Burke Marshall—This is the way I looked when you told me you were bringing a voting suit in Senator Eastland's home county," ran the playful inscription on an exceptionally gloomy shot of the Attorney General that found its way to the head of the Civil Rights Division. And it was true. For Marshall remained more than ever convinced that laws *can* change the hearts of men, provided they are enforced and people know they will be enforced. And that meant everywhere, including Eastland's county.

So the charts and battle pins only multiplied, and Burke Marshall's big office looked more like a command post than ever. In just two years target areas increased from a dozen to over 80. The Election Section had photographed over 300,000 documents; investigations were under way in 60 counties; 33 suits had been filed in 5 Southern states—and "untouchable" Mississippi led the list with 11.

Things had come a long way since John Doar first pulled on

his old khakis. Where once the very thought of a federal man aroused cackles and guffaws among the courthouse loafers, now his mere appearance had an electric effect.

"He don't give a flip nor a flap-doodle for Forrest County!" exploded one of Lynd's lawyers at the first hearing before Judge Cox. "He's not interested in the people of Forrest County except for a few Negroes!" It was the anguished cry of an expert who had at last met his match at Mississippi's waiting game. For there seemed no limit to John Doar's patience and persistence. He would answer motions as fast as his opponents could cook them up. He would listen politely while the judge criticized his evidence, then go out and get another truckload. He would take his defeats— and next day start all over again.

"You've just got to keep going back," Doar would explain, and this was the heart of his approach. No one was better aware of Mississippi's reliance on the "Second Reconstruction"—the theory that it was really just like 1875 again, that the federal government would go away if only the state held out long enough. And to Doar the answer was an emphatic demonstration that this simply wasn't so. Be patient, understanding—get to know the people and their problems—but, above all, keep going back until the law is accepted.

And this meant not only in voting but in other areas too. It meant endless visits to stationmasters and airport managers to see that they really did comply with the federal rulings ending segregation of terminals. It meant John Doar's being at the McComb bus station that November day in 1962 when the showdown came over whether the town would or would not obey the ICC order to desegregate the waiting room. An ugly crowd marched around the dirty pink building, but Mayor C. H. Douglas belonged to that band of officials who put law and order ahead of their own personal beliefs, and the law was obeyed. Yet one wonders what would have happened without the presence of Justice Department men to encourage, persuade and, above all, show that Washington really meant business.

It would be easy to overstate such accomplishments. Actually, the McComb station was soon resegregated in an informal sort of way. But at least the signs were gone, there was no longer any official sanction, and, above all, the federal authority had been acknowledged.

The first chip had been made, and a gradual but steady process of chipping away was an important part of what John Doar had in mind when he patiently explained, "You've just got to keep going back."

Schools presented a special problem. Here the Civil Rights Division couldn't "keep going back" in the ordinary sense, for there was no federal statute or regulation giving Washington the opening it needed to take the initiative. There was only the Supreme Court decision in the *Brown* case, and the initiative was entirely up to private parties acting under it. They must sue in federal court first, and the most the Justice Department could formally do was to see that any favorable court decision was enforced.

Yet there was a vast informal area where the philosophy of persistence could still be applied. The Civil Rights Division could and did work steadily behind the scenes, lending its good offices, helping negotiate school desegregation plans. Dallas, Memphis, Atlanta all saw this type of activity.

And where there was no "dialogue," as the New Frontiersmen liked to say, the Division could at least keep on top of things. So Burke Marshall made a fetish of knowing everything possible about all school desegregation cases coming up: where they were . . . who was involved . . . when they were likely to come to a boil. Above all, the Justice high command wanted no part of what they called "another Little Rock"—which they considered an inexcusable mess, where Eisenhower's use of troops was made necessary only because no one had done enough planning.

In Mississippi Marshall's approach meant knowing everything possible about the Meredith case from the very start. Only two days after the suit was filed, he asked the NAACP for a copy of the complaint. Then all during the legal cat-and-mouse game that followed, the Civil Rights Division's research staff carefully compiled neat blue binders of everything it could get on the case. By June 1962 Marshall was in close touch with his contacts on the campus. August, and matters were clearly coming to a boil: on the 21st the NAACP reminded the Department that Ole Miss would reopen exactly one month from that day. Meanwhile the bizarre duel between Judge Cameron and the rest of the Fifth Circuit was racing to a climax. When the NAACP finally turned to the Supreme Court after Cameron had issued his fourth stay blocking his colleagues' orders to admit Meredith, the Justice Department sensed that its days of watchful waiting were over.

August 22, and the phone rang in the Justice Department office of Solicitor General Archibald Cox. It was John F. Davis, Clerk of the Supreme Court, and he wanted an *amicus curiae* memorandum giving the Department's views on Judge Cameron's power to issue his stays, and on Justice Black's power, acting alone in the case, to set them aside.

As in so many legal questions, it was not all open-and-shut. In the American system it has always been recognized that a judge can issue a stay, giving a losing defendant enough time to appeal, where he might otherwise suffer irreparable harm if the judgment were immediately carried out. But, the Justice Department felt, Judge Cameron didn't measure up to accepted practice. First, he was too late—the appeals court had already issued its mandate; once issued, no judge on the court had any further power to act, unless the mandate were recalled.

In any event, Judge Cameron was not intimately familiar with the case, and the law had long stressed that complete knowledge was all-important in granting stays. Nor was it likely that the decision would be reviewed—another element that should be present in granting a stay. Here the only issue before the Supreme Court was a question of fact—was Meredith kept out of Ole Miss because he was a Negro?—and the Fifth Circuit had already said yes. Normally the high court took the lower court's word on factual issues.

Moreover, even if the Supreme Court did review the case (however unlikely), the University wouldn't suffer any irreparable harm in the absence of a stay. As the Fifth Circuit acidly noted, "Other Southern universities are not shriveling up because of the admission of Negroes." Meredith, on the other hand, might suffer great harm if a stay were granted. He had already missed seven terms, and any additional time lost would be irretrievable. At some point an endlessly delayed education was bound to lose its value.

Finally, there was another point, perhaps more important than all the rest. If Judge Cameron could issue these stays, it meant that a single judge could reverse the action of his own court. To the attorneys of the Justice Department this seemed absurd.

As for Justice Black's power, acting alone, to set aside Judge Cameron's stays, this too was complicated. In the past individual Justices had occasionally *granted* stays, but had never vacated them. Was this essentially the same thing? The Justice Department felt it was: if an individual Justice could grant a stay, common sense said he could vacate one. Moreover, this was no matter of law to be decided by the Court sitting as a whole—it wouldn't affect the ultimate outcome in any way—rather it was one of those routine matters arising in the course of a case which individual Justices customarily handled while the Court was in recess. Since Black was the Justice assigned to the Fifth Circuit for such problems, he was the proper man to act now.

Only one question remained—not asked by the Clerk of the Supreme Court, but no less important to ponder. Even if Black did have the power to act, should he do so? Whatever his authority, he would certainly be breaking new ground in vacating Cameron's stays, and there was much to be said for breaking as little new ground as possible. Mississippi already felt much abused; if possible, it was important to give her leaders no new chance to claim she had been short-changed.

And this was especially true if the same results could be achieved by waiting only a little longer. True, Meredith had already waited twenty months, but the October session of the Supreme Court would soon be at hand and presumably the Court would quickly dispose of the case. Were these few extra days worth so much to Meredith that they offset the value of letting Mississippi be turned down by the whole Supreme Court?

But would the delay really be just a few extra days? Those closest to the case feared not. If Meredith missed the start of one more term, what next? Could he then be rejected for coming too late to register, starting a whole new round of hearings? In short, who knew what new device might then be concocted by an ingenious defense? And even with someone as tenacious as Meredith, there comes a time when a man has had enough. Certainly this was the heart of Mississippi's strategy in seeking the stays—as frankly revealed by the knowledgeable *Clarion-Ledger*—and it was very much on the mind of the staff in the Civil Rights Division.

August 31, the Justice Department submitted its memo to the Court. Predictably, it called Judge Cameron's stays "null and void," pointing out that he "simply assumed power to frustrate the decision of his own court." It was perfectly proper, the memo continued, for Justice Black to act alone in setting aside these stays, and it urged him to do so as fast as possible.

"Like a jackass looking up at the sky and braying at a great American eagle as it soars above," was the way Mississippi Attorney General Joe Patterson described the Justice memo attacking Cameron's actions. Brave words, but there was far more to it than that. Previously—despite Mississippi's suspicions—the Department had been no more than a sympathetic observer, lending encouragement to the NAACP by its obvious interest. Now for the first time, Justice was squarely in the case, and the tone of the memo suggested the depth of its concern: this was no formal statement of a legal position; it was a powerful brief urging Meredith's immediate admission.

Justice Black was quickly convinced. On September 10 he set aside Cameron's stays and ordered the University to admit Meredith immediately. It was true, Black conceded, that the case was up for certiorari, but it certainly didn't have very bright prospects. Under the circumstances, admitting Meredith couldn't work any great hardship on the University, while keeping him out could well cause Meredith injury.

As to his right to act alone in making the decision, Black observed, "Although convinced that I have the power to act alone in this matter, I have submitted it to each of my Brethren, and I am authorized to state that each of them agrees that the case is properly before this Court, that I have power to act, and that under the circumstances I should exercise that power as I have done here."

In explaining this, Justice Black's purpose was to leave no room for doubt. He wanted to show he had been extra careful, that he had gone out of his way to make doubly sure he had the power to act. It apparently never occurred to him that it could be interpreted the other way—that it might be considered an unconscious admission that he was not so sure after all, and that in trying to brace up his position he had followed a rather informal procedure.

In any case, Judge Mize got the intended point. He was as much the segregationist as ever, but he was also a federal judge and the Supreme Court had spoken. On September 13 he issued a sweeping injunction, ordering the University not to block Meredith's admission, not to interfere with his attendance, and not to discriminate against him "in any way whatsoever because of his race."

"This is the end of the road for the University," NAACP's Constance Motley happily told the press. Judge Mize agreed: at his last meeting with Mrs. Motley he said he felt the excitement would die down now that all legal remedies were exhausted. Meredith himself was confident too. The day after Black's decree he wired

Registrar Ellis that he was coming, and he even sent Mrs. Motley a copy of his schedule, which included a helpful course called "The Old South."

But it wasn't that simple. There were other factors to take into account besides a neat, orderly sequence of court decisions. There was the accumulation of a hundred years of bittersweet regret. There was poverty—and the ignorance and prejudice it bred. There was the fear that stemmed from lonely isolation. There was the bankrupt leadership that came out of all these things. There was, in short, the legacy of a past that would not die; and this, rather than court decisions, would determine what happened next.

7

"Ross's Standin' Like Gibraltar; He Shall Never Falter"

"WE WILL NOT SURRENDER TO THE EVIL AND ILLEGAL FORCES of tyranny," Governor Ross Barnett solemnly promised the people of Mississippi on a state-wide telecast the night of September 13. To the Governor it was all very clear. The Tenth Amendment of the Constitution reserved to the states all powers not specifically delegated to the federal government; control over education wasn't one of these delegated powers; therefore it must belong to the states, and no federal court could tell Ole Miss that it had to admit Negro James H. Meredith.

It never seemed to bother Barnett that the Constitution did not stop at the Tenth Amendment . . . that in the Meredith case the court felt the overriding provision was the Fourteenth Amendment, guaranteeing equal protection of the laws to all persons in a State. As far as the Governor was concerned, the whole business remained an outrageous power grab: "We must either submit to the unlawful dictates of the federal government or stand up like men and tell them 'NEVER!' "

For him it was "never," and he called on others to join him. "Every public official, including myself, should be prepared to make the choice tonight whether he is willing to go to jail, if necessary, to keep faith with the people who have placed their welfare in his hands. . . . We will not drink from the cup of genocide."

But what to do? At this point Barnett offered a thought which would have startled listeners in almost any other part of the country: "Mississippi, as a Sovereign State, has the right under the federal Constitution to determine for itself what the federal Constitution has reserved to it." And with that he once again dusted off the old Southern remedy of interposition—the idea that a state can protect its citizens by throwing itself between them and an unpopular federal decree. It was a doctrine that had been rejected by the Supreme Court as recently as 1960, but tonight it was "historic and time recognized."

With that the Governor produced a formal, sealed proclamation, suitably embellished with "whereases," and solemnly ordered his official family "to interpose the State Sovereignty and themselves between the people of the State and any body-politic seeking to usurp such power."

He wound up in a blaze of defiance. Twice in the speech Barnett had referred to resisting by "legal and constitutional" means, but now this touch of restraint was lost. He begged the people to "hold fast against this grave threat to our liberties." He urged them to "stand together, hand in hand, mind to mind, unyielding and unafraid." He conjured up visions of Valley Forge, Shiloh, Vicksburg, the Argonne, Guadalcanal and Heartbreak Ridge—"The burning question in the minds of all Americans today is whether, in this crisis, we will exhibit the same courage, the same devotion to deathless principle. . . ."

Oddly enough, these flaming words came from the most amiable of men. Ross Robert Barnett was a simple, kindly person who knew what it was to come up the hard way. Born in the little hill town of Standing Pine, he was the youngest of an impoverished Confederate veteran's ten children. As a boy, he plowed and sawed wood for 6 cents an hour. Hard work led ultimately to a $100,000-a-year practice, but he never forgot his homespun background.

"Just kick open the door and ask for old Ross," he'd say. And everybody did. Young lawyers were always welcome in his firm's law library. After he became Governor, job seekers swarmed over his office; at one point the line stretched 40 yards down the hall. Nor was the kindness segregated: always a soft touch, he was happy to lend $1,100 to Negro Dorsie Moore, a bird dog trainer whom he liked.

But this didn't mean he was any less firm on segregation in other respects. He not only believed in white supremacy, but preached it with a sort of Bible-pounding evangelistic fervor that could startle a visitor. "When God made the Universe, He put the races apart—the white man in Europe, the red in Asia, the black in Africa. They were meant to stay apart. Every time the races have mixed there's been nothing but trouble. Take Egypt. They had the greatest civilization in the world, a marvelous white civilization. Then along down the Nile came some of those black Nubians. First thing you know they began to mix—then they went to school together, to dances together. Look at them now."

Unlike Vardaman and Bilbo, whose racism always smacked of cynicism, Ross Barnett obviously meant every word, and his fervor came home to the struggling, uneducated white farmers of Mississippi's hill country, with their strong fundamentalist leanings. It also struck a chord with the Citizens' Council; hence their support and his easy victory in the 1959 campaign for Governor. Now they were the group closest to him—especially the fire-breathing faction of the Jackson Council: men like Bill Simmons, the group's administrative head; M. Ney Williams, Jr., a politically inclined anesthesiologist; Fred Beard, who ran stations WJDX and WLBT; Gene Wirth, city editor of the *Clarion-Ledger;* and Judge Russel Moore, who urged a go-to-jail-first policy three months before Barnett's speech.

All this is not to say that others weren't close to Barnett too. But some of them, while strong segregationists and states' rights men, were much more cautious in their approach to the problem. Men like John Satterfield, a smooth past president of the American

Bar Association, and Tom Watkins, a dynamic attorney whose offices in Jackson could well have been found in any urban center. These and others whirled about the Capitol, or dropped by the gracious ante bellum mansion that served as the Governor's residence. It was an atmosphere of pressure and maneuvering, for if Barnett had a reputation for amiability, he also had one for vacillation. Even James Jackson Kilpatrick, the highly sympathetic editor of the Richmond *News Leader,* conceded, "Governor Barnett leaves an impression of mildness, uncertainty and pathos." And one state Senator, who was close to the Governor and supported him straight down the line, nevertheless found him "a real weather vane—so much depends on who's seen him last."

Justice Black's ruling found all these factions tugging and pulling Barnett at once. At a series of talks on the night of the decision he was told by leading lawyers that Mississippi had reached the end of the road, that there was nothing left except compliance. But others urged him to "make his mark, stand by his principles." In the end the Governor chose the route of defiance, the line urged by the toughest faction of the Citizens' Council.

But despite his defiance he was still the same Barnett—still the same friendly, nonviolent, rural politician. Nor did it occur to him that his words might set people off. Warnings of "shame and ruin" and appeals to "sacred honor" were an old story on the stump circuit, and it seemed no great leap from the county fair to the cathode tube. "Didn't say anything I don't say all the time," he later told a visitor. "Just like the things in my campaign speeches. No reason why anybody should think I meant violence."

But whatever he intended, the inevitable effect of such words *was* to encourage violence—given the climate of the times. For seven years the people of Mississippi had heard nothing but hell-raising rhetoric. "There is no law that a free people must submit to a flagrant violation of their personal liberty," Senator Eastland assured them in 1955. "You've got to elect public officials who are

willing to defy federal injunctions and uphold the Constitution,"
Judge Moore was telling them in 1962.

This steady tattoo was bound to have its effect; by now the state's
temper was combustible indeed. Ross Barnett may have acted unconsciously, but he certainly applied the spark; others—perhaps less
innocently—were more than ready to fan the flames.

"PLACE ASSURED IN HISTORY FOR FEARLESS ROSS BARNETT,"
thundered the *Clarion-Ledger* on September 15. As usual, an
editorial paid lip service to restraint, but this mild rejoinder was
lost in the bombast of headlines, columns and wildly slanted news
stories. "The humble plowboy from Standing Pine," intoned Gene
Wirth, "fearless in his refusal to yield principle to compromise,
stands assuredly today on the blazing pages of American history
awaiting a challenger to his order to resist."

That same day the "humble plowboy" returned a long-distance
call to RE 7-8200, Washington, D.C. It turned out to be Attorney
General Robert F. Kennedy, who briskly explained that he wanted
to discuss "some of the details of how to work this thing out with
this fellow coming in on Thursday." They both agreed there must
be no violence. Then Kennedy ran through the procedure as he
saw it: on September 20 Meredith would turn up for registration
with a couple of marshals . . . he would be turned down . . .
Justice would take it to court . . . the court would probably order
registration . . . "then we will litigate."

"That will take about a year," Barnett observed placidly.
Kennedy brushed this aside, and the Governor didn't pursue the
point. Yet it told a lot . . . suggesting how little the two men were
in true communication. To Kennedy the Governor had been told
exactly what he was going to do; now he could move on to a
quick, orderly solution. To Ross Barnett everything was just beginning.

In Washington the wheels began turning at the Justice Department. Predictably, it moved into the Meredith case in the patented

Kennedy way—very little paper work and a great many small, informal discussions.

First, as the storm brewed in August and promised to be more than a Civil Rights Division headache, there were a growing number of conversations between Kennedy, Burke Marshall and Nick Katzenbach, who had become Deputy Attorney General when Byron White moved on to the Supreme Court. Gradually, as the crisis grew, these talks increased, and more people were brought in. As always, it didn't matter what they normally did; a good man should be useful anywhere. Louis Oberdorfer might run the Department's Tax Division, but he was also from the South and had a lot to contribute here—he put aside his taxes for a while. By September 15—the day of Kennedy's talk with Barnett —the top half-dozen men in the Department were spending practically all their time on the Meredith case.

To them all only one thing was crystal-clear: they didn't want to use troops. For one thing, the Kennedy Administration had made so much of Little Rock that it would be a political black eye, to say the least. But more important, the immensely moralistic Robert Kennedy was plainly repelled by the idea of using American soldiers against American civilians. Besides, in his simplified world of black and white, the federal government was so obviously "right" that a peaceful solution couldn't help being found. Katzenbach was equally against troops, though an entirely different kind of person. A warmly humanistic law professor from the University of Chicago, he was about as far removed from the military mind as a man could get. He took a positive zest in working things out with people, and soldiers were the last thing that would occur to him as the best remedy for anything.

Happily there seemed a perfect solution. During the Freedom Rider troubles at Montgomery in 1961 the Justice Department had escaped using troops by calling on some 300 U.S. marshals to maintain federal authority. In a limited way marshals had always been used to carry out federal court orders, but this was the first time they had been employed on a large scale, and it worked perfectly. True, for them to be really effective, the local law enforcement people had to cooperate, but in Alabama the state police were a highly disciplined organization, and when the Freedom Riders moved on to Mississippi, Colonel T. B. Birdsong's Highway Patrol took over the escort duty with clocklike precision.

Everything worked so well that the Justice Department decided this was the solution for any major civil rights crisis. While the force of regular U.S. marshals was small, they could be increased to as many as 500 by deputizing men in federal agencies like the Border Patrol and the Bureau of Prisons. Accordingly, studies were made indicating just how many marshals might be needed in any situation, where they could be drawn from, how they would be serviced and so forth. Riot control courses had been given to selected regulars since 1958; training for those to be deputized was far more sketchy, but in the Border Patrol considerable thought was given to selecting the men who might be most suitable for riot work.

Now the Justice Department made use of all this preparation. By early September the selected marshals had been alerted and were standing by. In New Orleans a big rangy Border Patrolman named Charles Chamblee got the word on September 14 and the following day headed for Memphis, the designated rendezvous. In Miami, Detroit, Waco, all over the country, other men began heading for Memphis too. In Washington all this meant the addition of a new man to the closely knit Justice Department task force: Chief U.S. Marshal James Joseph Patrick McShane—an ex-New York police officer of compact stature and immense Irish charm, who could perhaps best be described as a sort of tough elf.

By now that key weapon in any Kennedy operation, the telephone, was hard at work. There were calls to the FAA to line up planes . . . calls to business leaders with Mississippi outlets to bring pressure on their local contacts . . . calls to the FCC for communications and monitoring equipment . . . calls to Mississippi lawyers remembered from the days of private practice . . . calls to old classmates now living in the state.

The resources that the federal government can bring to bear on any crisis are enormous, and in Mississippi the University was already feeling the pressure. After all, it was not Barnett but the University officials and trustees who were the defendants in this case . . . they were the ones who had to answer in court. Yet they also had to answer to the state, and the Governor left no doubt what *he* wanted. This might not have proved so much a quandary in other states, where the federal authority was recognized as paramount, but this was Mississippi, where the opposite was the case. Moreover, there were the raw realities of the situation: whatever Washington's authority, the money to keep the University going—the power even to keep it open—came from the state Capitol.

On September 14 the trustees held a turbulent meeting in Jackson. A small but vocal minority argued that Ole Miss had reached the end of the road, might as well give in. But most felt they had to back the Governor. Still it was not decisive; so Barnett himself came to the next meeting on the 17th to bolster their spirits. "BOARD MEMBER SAYS HE'D GO TO JAIL TO KEEP INTEGRITY," crowed the *Clarion-Ledger* next morning, but on close reading it turned out that Trustee Vernon Holmes' defiance contained a large loophole: "I am not willing to go to jail if it will accomplish nothing."

Up at Oxford Chancellor Williams and his staff were just as much on the spot. Stripped by the trustees of any further decisions on Meredith, they still faced the problem of preserving Ole Miss's standing in this pressure-cooker atmosphere. The students were growing ever more restive, and the situation seemed to demand a ringing appeal for order—but in Mississippi this ringing appeal for order was tantamount to treason. What could be done?

There was no easy answer. People accustomed to privately endowed institutions tend to forget that the head of a state university may have much less leeway. Sometimes his choice is not between a cautious stand and a ringing stand for academic freedom. It may be a choice between a cautious stand and losing next year's appropriation . . . or being replaced by some lackey who will do the legislators' bidding and undo a lifetime of constructive work. Yet something had to be done, and so Chancellor Williams marched forth, a little like a man walking out on very thin ice. At some point the ice had to break—how far was it safe to go?

The Chancellor, as it turned out, wasn't willing to go very far. During all these days he issued no public statement to the student body calling for order and obedience. Instead, he and Dean Love followed a policy of speaking quietly to fraternity presidents, class officers and other campus leaders. These were urged to circulate among the student body, spreading the word to behave.

Maybe this was all he could do after all. The powerful *Clarion-Ledger* was already applying a little strong-arm journalism. On September 16 the paper told how Williams had warned campus leaders that any demonstrating student might be expelled. Another story in the same issue then hinted at the dire fate awaiting an unnamed "Ole Miss official" who was threatening to expel demonstrators. "It was said," the paper added darkly, "the Governor will watch with a jaundiced eye any attempt to apply punitive action against Mississippi patriots."

So the University remained discreetly silent, as did every other responsible voice in the state. Even those trustees who felt Barnett was hopelessly wrong decided they couldn't buck the tide. As one put it, "The board had to put its foot in the jailhouse door and let the court take the blame." The Ole Miss alumni, hearing that Barnett planned to close the University, hastily slapped together a Steering Committee—but only to keep the place open. Not a word was said about compliance, or even law and order. Political leaders long suspected of moderation, kept quiet . . . or obediently toed the line. Former Governor Coleman, forgetting that he had once called interposition "legal poppycock," was one of the first to back Barnett's stand, as the State House of Representatives howled through a rousing vote of confidence on September 18.

That same day the Justice Department—convinced that the state would never obey the court's orders without more active federal intervention—went to both the U.S. District Court and the Fifth Circuit, seeking the right formally to enter the case. It was an important move, for up to now this had always been technically a private affair—just an individual named Meredith, represented by the NAACP, suing a state university. If the Justice application was now granted, Mississippi would for the first time be up against not only Meredith and the NAACP but the whole federal government as an active party in the case.

At the District Court Judge Mize promptly turned down the Justice request, but there was no such trouble at the far more friendly Fifth Circuit. Judges Brown, Wisdom and Bell came through with everything Justice wanted. A sweeping order allowed the federal government not only to file a brief but to participate in the proceedings too. Most important, it even allowed the Department to initiate various steps, seek injunctions and prosecute for contempt of court. It could, in short, do anything necessary "to preserve the due administration of justice and the integrity of the judicial processes of the United States."

A cry of bitter anger rose in Mississippi. "It is a sad commentary," mourned State Attorney General Joe Patterson, "when the U.S. Attorney General permits his office to become general counsel for the NAACP, Martin Luther King, and other racial agitators and troublemakers." To many devotees of states' rights it was far worse than that: it was another dangerous encroachment on local government. The Fifth Circuit, they claimed, had gone far beyond its authority in giving Justice such a free hand. It had brushed aside an order of the District Court. It was acting like a District Court itself, although Congress had limited its role to appeals. It was letting the federal government start suits in the appeals court, when the law clearly said it could only do this in District Courts.

Worst of all, it was guilty of sheer hypocrisy. During the debates over the 1957 Civil Rights bill Congress had long argued whether the Justice Department should be allowed to initiate school cases. In the end the provision was stricken from the bill, and the government's powers were limited to voting suits. Now here was the Fifth Circuit letting the Department slip in the side door. Under the court's sweeping injunction, Justice could apparently launch proceedings whenever it felt the need—all this in a school case against the express wishes of Congress!

The Fifth Circuit's answer was simple: the court had a right to do whatever seemed necessary to carry out its decrees. Formally, it later explained, "This was not the government instituting a suit or intervening on behalf of private litigants to vindicate the civil rights of private suitors. It was the sovereign intervening in the sovereign's court to uphold and maintain the sovereign's rule of law. Congress never meant to withhold that power." Informally, one of the judges later put it more succinctly: "If the court hadn't acted as emphatically as possible, the whole business would have shown that you can stall off enforcement of the law any time you act enough like a bastard."

At the moment it made little difference. The people of Mississippi were in no mood for legal debate. "There must be no surrender," cried State Senator E. C. Henry, sounding the far more popular note of defiance. "ON YOUR GUARD—COMMIES USING NEGRO AS TOOL," the September 18 Jackson *Daily News* front page busily fanned the flames of race hate. "Little Brother," sneered columnist Tom Ethridge in the September 19 *Clarion-Ledger*, "has evidently concluded that the South must be forced to abandon its customs and traditions in deference to 'world opinion' —especially that of Asiatic cow-worshippers and African semi-savages not far removed from cannibalism."

And over the air a WLBT-WJDX editorial exhorted the University trustees to stand firm for the honor of the state: "These men are to be envied by all—for the heroic opportunity that comes to a man only once in his lifetime whereby he can, if necessary, sacrifice his life for his State and, in turn, save his country."

Nor was it all just frothing and ranting. With Meredith due on September 20, the state courts and legislature began taking hard, concrete measures to hurl back the federals. On the 19th, Chancery Court Judge L. B. Porter hit everyone in sight (including Meredith, Ole Miss, Kennedy and the FBI) with a sweeping injunction against "doing anything intended to enroll and register the Negro, James Meredith, as a student at the University of Mississippi." To be doubly safe, another state court in Lafayette County was preparing to issue a second injunction. And in Jackson still another judge ordered Meredith to stand trial on the 20th for false voter registration. This was based on the old charge that in registering he had not properly named the county where he really lived. It didn't matter that the Fifth Circuit had long ago rejected this charge as "frivolous."

But this alone was not enough. Even if convicted and jailed, it seemed possible that anyone as persistent as Meredith might try again as soon as he got out. So the legislature sailed into action on the afternoon of September 19. In seven minutes the Senate unanimously passed S.B. 1501—a peice of statecraft which said that no one convicted of a crime could go to a state college or university. More than that, it was a criminal offense even to apply when charged with a crime of moral turpitude. Certain crimes were specifically excepted from the act—little things like manslaughter committed by a drunken driver—but it clearly covered Meredith.

The House quickly approved 130-2, but the bill seemed a travesty to Representative Karl Wiesenburg, the scrappy Pascagoula lawyer whom nobody pushed around. To delay passage, he moved for reconsideration—a parliamentary device that would postpone final approval till the following day. With an angry roar, the legislature voted to adjourn until one minute after midnight. Back in session on the dot, they immediately tabled Wiesenburg's motion, and the bill sailed on through. Rushed to Barnett, the Governor signed it in the predawn hours of September 20.

The defenses were now set. When Meredith arrived later in the day, the state could not only get him on the false registration charge but arrest him under the new law too. It was a piece of teamwork that seemed to bear out perfectly Ross Barnett's latest pledge, "I will stand steadfast all the way down the line."

Meanwhile an interesting event took place that seemed oddly counter to all this elaborate strategy. At 2:00 P.M. on Wednesday, the 19th, Mississippi Attorney General Joe Patterson got a call from Burke Marshall, who was worried about Meredith's safety. Acting under instructions from the Governor, Patterson agreed that the state would provide protection when Meredith appeared to register the following day—despite all the new laws and preparations.

But by evening the wind was blowing from a different direction. The Governor now told Patterson that Meredith would be arrested when his car reached Batesville. Patterson announced he was willing to do almost anything to keep Meredith out of Ole Miss, "but I would not sacrifice my personal and professional integrity and would not be a party to going back on our agreement."

It must have been a hard night for Patterson. By 7:50 next morning he was on the phone with Burke Marshall. He quickly explained he could no longer keep his agreement that Meredith would be protected. Since he had given his word, he wanted to be sure Marshall knew.

Marshall took the cue. He immediately called his best personal contact in Jackson, the Governor's confidant Tom Watkins, whom Marshall had known from his days in private practice. No one was a better Mississippian than Tom Watkins—no one a stauncher segregationist or more loyal to Barnett—but he was also an immensely responsible man, with a sharp, penetrating mind. He understood the problem perfectly as Marshall sought his help in getting the agreement back on the rails. Serious trouble, Marshall stressed, could easily erupt if some local sheriff tried to seize Meredith from the federal officers accompanying him. The agreement was the best hope of avoiding violence.

There was no time to lose, for signs were multiplying that Mississippi was now proceeding swiftly with its plans for arrest. Right on schedule Justice of the Peace Homer Edgeworth tried Meredith in Jackson for false voter registration. The defendant wasn't present, so it took only ten minutes to try, convict and sentence him to a $100 fine and a year in jail. This ritual completed, Edgeworth ordered Meredith seized.

The Civil Rights Division did what it could to meet this threat, although there was little reason to suppose Mississippi would respect any federal countermeasures. Once again Justice lawyers rushed to the friendly Fifth Circuit in New Orleans, and the court sprayed injunctions against every obstruction in sight. With the same objective, other Department attorneys headed for the federal District Court in Meridian, as did NAACP lawyer Constance Motley.

At Meridian Judge Mize readily signed the injunction designed to block Meredith's arrest. He might be a good Mississippian, but the state was going too far. Still, it wasn't easy, and as he handed Mrs. Motley her set of the papers, he sighed that he hoped he would have no more desegregation cases—he was getting too old and only wanted to play with his grandchildren.

By 10:30 A.M.—12:30 Washington time—Burke Marshall's behind-the-scenes maneuvering began to show promise. Joe Patterson was on the phone again, this time speaking to both Marshall and Kennedy. With him was Tom Watkins, who had just come from the Governor's office with fresh assurance that Meredith wouldn't be arrested. Patterson said he'd advise all state law officers to obey. Later he reported back that he personally had phoned the District Attorney at Oxford to keep the sheriff in line, and the Governor's office had followed through with the other sheriffs. There should be no hitch. Kennedy settled back in relief, for Meredith should be starting soon.

At the University excitement was mounting. With tempers running high, it was arranged for Meredith to appear at a remote building called the Continuation Center; but few students knew that, and hundreds milled aimlessly around the center of the campus. Television cameramen appeared and tried to work up a demonstration. The crowd was only too willing to oblige. A surging mob of students paraded up and down, singing "Glory, Glory, Segregation."

Then a group of boys dashed for the flagpole carrying a Confederate banner, and with a wild Rebel yell began hauling down the American flag. It was halfway down before Grey Jackson, the dynamic vice president of the senior class, rushed up and stopped the show. A hush fell over the crowd. Hardly realizing it, they had come to the very brink of rebellion, and only a cool head had pulled them back again. Overwhelmed by the meaning of what they had almost done, the students now fell silent and drifted uneasily off. Even with the state in its present mood, it would take still more to whip basically decent boys to a point where they would really try insurrection.

In Jackson the trustees were working against time. They had argued the previous evening long past midnight . . . Tally Riddell, one of the few holding out for compliance with the federal court orders, grew so upset he suffered a heart attack. Reassembling early on the 20th, a minority still felt defiance was madness, but the majority remained behind the Governor. Even so, few were looking forward to going to jail as recommended by Barnett, and as the morning wore on they began searching for some out. Most leaned to an escape that had been brewing all week: make the Governor himself Registrar for the day and let him do what he wanted. Then if anybody had to go to jail, he could be the one.

They had still reached no final decision at lunch break, when word suddenly arrived that Meredith was about to start and Barnett was already en route to the "front." That settled it. No more time for debating. Reconvening at 2:15 P.M., they quickly appointed the Governor "with the full power, authority, right and discretion of this Board to act upon all matters pertaining to or concerned with the registration or non-registration, and/or attendance or non-attendance of James H. Meredith at the University of Mississippi."

Many insiders would later claim that the Governor really rigged his own selection. Barnett himself always denied it. He conceded he felt the University officials were weakening—that a substitute Registrar was needed—but he insisted he didn't want the job and suggested three other names instead: Lieutenant Governor Paul Johnson, Ney Williams or Gene Wirth. "But they chose me."

In the last analysis it doesn't matter whose idea it was. There really was no other choice, given the route the board decided to take. As one trustee later remarked with a candor that never emerged at the time, "It *had* to be Barnett. He was the only person who could possibly carry off the idea of interposition. The whole theory, poor as it was, depended on the Governor throwing *himself* in front of the federal authority."

As the distinguished substitute Registrar flew toward Oxford, a new development exploded at the Justice Department. The FBI flashed word that Oxford's Sheriff Joe Ford planned to arrest Meredith after all. Earlier the sheriff had indeed been told not to do so, but within the past 35 minutes he had received new orders to go ahead. Kennedy called Joe Patterson and broke the news.

"Oh, my gosh!" gasped Patterson. Then he rushed off to check with Colonel Birdsong of the Highway Patrol, while Kennedy himself tried to track down the Governor. Barnett was reached shortly after he landed at Oxford, and was smoothly reassuring: of course Meredith wouldn't be arrested. So once again the deal was back on the rails, but by now there had been so many twists and turns no one was very sure what would happen.

Well, they'd soon know. It was now three o'clock, and Meredith was just leaving Memphis in an unmarked Border Patrol car, accompanied by Justice Attorney St. John Barrett, Chief U.S. Marshal McShane and two deputies. As they crossed the state line, driver Charles Chamblee noticed the magnolia-festooned billboard, "Welcome to Mississippi."

"Do you think they mean us?" he asked Meredith.

"No, I'm afraid they don't." Meredith was never much at small talk.

By now Governor Barnett was already at the University, waiting in a small anteroom at the Continuation Center. It was here he officially learned what he already suspected—the trustees had made him the Registrar. At 4:30 the Meredith party arrived unmolested and entered the Center's brightly lit auditorium. Most of the green seats had been removed, but down front were two tables put together with chairs on either side. Meredith sat down with Barrett and the marshals on one side. Next Barnett entered and sat down with Ellis on the other side of the table. An uneasy pause, then Ellis read a statement announcing that the trustees had taken away his authority and given it to the Governor. He now left the table, leaving Barnett facing the little group alone.

"Is there anything further?" boomed the Governor. Silence, then he repeated it twice again. At last Meredith got the point, stood up and said quietly, "I want to register." Barnett then dramatically unrolled a long proclamation, complete with gold seal, and read the predictable contents. Using his police powers as Governor, as well as his newly acquired academic powers as Registrar, he formally refused to admit Meredith to the University. Finishing, he handed over the proclamation with a flourish, "Take it and abide by it." Meredith said nothing, but thought to himself it was a great performance—something like the movie he once saw when Charlton Heston played Andrew Jackson.

Outside, 2,000 students now jammed the grove in front of the Center. A wall of Highway Patrolmen held them back, but there was really no trouble—just an air of hushed excitement as they waited for the outcome. Suddenly word flashed that Barnett had "won"; then Meredith emerged, heading back for his car with Barrett and McShane. A great mutter went up, and when the car drove off, the crowd surged against the police lines in frustrated rage. As a senior later put it, "You had to see him right there to really feel sick."

So Meredith got back to Memphis unharmed and unarrested, but that was about all. It was clearly Ross Barnett's day, and that night WRBC ("This is Rebel") never blared "Dixie" more loudly. What a contrast to New York, the Jackson *Daily News* editorialized, "the land of the fleeced and the home of the depraved." Mississippi must never give in: "The price of appeasement is too high. The wages of surrender are too bloody to be given consideration."

The Justice Department remained unruffled, but admittedly the time had come for a little more firmness. At 8:00 P.M. on the 20th Chancellor Williams, Dean Lewis and Registrar Ellis were all hit with contempt-of-court charges. They were ordered to appear in federal court at 1:30 P.M. the following day . . . the hearing to be held before Judge Mize in Meridian—175 miles away.

"You just don't do that to three distinguished citizens!" exclaimed a lawyer deeply involved in the case. Normally five days' notice was allowed in such a case; here the contempt petition itself only arrived at 8:15 on the morning of the trial. To the Mississippi bar it seemed one more example of federal tyranny . . . of Kennedy ruthlessness.

Early on the 21st a group of defense lawyers huddled in downtown Jackson, trying to decide what to do. As they talked, Governor Barnett strolled in, and all looked up for the strategy that would win the day. But the Governor was interested only in keeping Meredith out and once again urged Williams to stand firm. If he went to jail, Barnett added brightly, he'd see that Williams' salary was doubled. "The Chancellor's teeth practically fell on the floor," reported an observer. Clearly hurt, Williams said nothing and the subject was dropped.

Someone asked the Governor how he planned to invoke interposition—but he brushed this off, saying everyone knew it wouldn't work. For the first time it dawned on one of those present that Barnett really had no plans at all—that he was simply playing the whole crisis by ear.

For the moment it didn't matter. At Meridian that afternoon Judge Mize was most accommodating. He quickly cleared the three University officials of contempt, holding that they had been relieved of all authority "to register or not to register Meredith" when the trustees put the whole decision in Barnett's hands. And since the trustees were not before the Court, there was no need to examine their conduct in the matter. So far, everyone remained in the clear.

The Justice Department was already on its way to the more friendly Fifth Circuit. On this same Friday in New Orleans the appeals court ordered the trustees themselves to appear at 11:00 A.M., Monday, the 24th, to face similar charges of contempt. And Saturday afternoon the three University officials were added to the case.

Once again the byword was speed, and the Mississippi lawyers seethed with indignation. This time they didn't get the contempt petitions until 5:00 P.M., Sunday—not even enough time to get their briefs typed up. And in the case of Williams and his colleagues it seemed especially unfair—they had already been cleared by Judge Mize. Little matter, said the Fifth Circuit; this was a different court and a different charge. As for undue speed, the appeals court couldn't have been less sympathetic. Formally, it explained, "The Court has moved as expeditiously as it has been possible because . . . a case involving a right, if there be a right, to obtain a college education expires of its own term within a reasonably short time." Informally, one of the judges later added with more than a touch of acid, "They would have been ready if it was a mortgage case."

So at 11:00 A.M., Monday, September 24, the trustees and top officials of Ole Miss stood before the Fifth Circuit in New Orleans, looking like accused truants hauled before some angry headmaster. Again precedent went by the boards. Instead of the usual panel of three judges, the entire court heard the case. Instead of using the measured language of the bench, the judges tore into the defendants—Judge Joseph C. Hutcheson flatly accused them of "monkey business."

Most important, instead of confining itself to the lawyers' briefs, the Fifth Circuit took testimony like any trial court. This was, of course, the inevitable result of the court's earlier precedent-smashing action in issuing its own injunction, yet the step was no less unusual. It added to the bitterness of a Mississippi that already felt it was getting a raw deal. As for the court, it simply felt that its orders had been scorned, dodged and ignored long enough. Now its patience was exhausted. As one of the bench later remarked, "Judges are human too."

The outcome was predictable. After a six-hour hearing the Fifth Circuit unanimously found that the trustees had willfully and intentionally violated the court's orders. It was no excuse that they had turned over their responsibilities to Barnett—that was just ducking their duty. But they could still get off if they now agreed to comply.

It took the trustees just thirty minutes to say yes. Going to jail was all very glorious, but that assumed it might accomplish something (and that they wouldn't stay in too long), but this wasn't the case here. Ever since that eye-opening meeting on the 21st, they knew very well that the Governor had no solution at all— that, in fact, he was just pointing an empty gun. Yes, announced Board Chairman Thomas Tubb, the board would comply; it would register Meredith by 4:00 P.M., tomorrow, Tuesday the 25th.

"We trust that the people will understand," began the timid

communiqué issued that night by the beleaguered trustees. The people didn't. Never dreaming that the Governor had no plans, they were only angry at what seemed a cowardly capitulation. What a miserable contrast, they felt, to a leader like Ross Barnett, who this very day issued another of his ringing proclamations— this time ordering jail for any federals who dared hold a state official for defying court orders. "If there are any yellow-livered appeasers in the crowd," roared the Fayette *Chronicle,* "get out of Mississippi!"

Barnett himself seemed to thrive on the adulation. If he had done much to stir up the crowds, their response couldn't help but be stirring to him. For years he had known more than his share of ridicule; suddenly he was everybody's hero. It was only human to try and live up to those new editorials.

On the phone with Robert Kennedy that night much of the Governor's old courtliness seemed gone. He was "shocked" by the trustees' surrender. He was bitter about Washington's lack of respect for Mississippi courts. Kennedy brushed it all off: Meredith was coming to register the following day, and all he wanted to know was whether Mississippi could provide adequate protection. Barnett said only that he'd study it out.

Next morning, the 25th, found Kennedy again on the wire— and the Governor no more accommodating. When the Attorney General pointed out that the federal court had ordered Meredith in, Barnett merely replied that the state court had ordered him out. There wasn't the faintest suggestion that the federal court orders might be paramount. On the contrary: "Mississippi ought to be recognized like any other courts. . . . I consider the Mississippi courts as high as any other court and a lot more capable."

It did no good for Kennedy to stress his duty to see that federal court orders were enforced. "Our courts have acted too," Barnett reiterated, "and our legislature has acted too. I am going to obey the laws of Mississippi." As for the U.S. Constitution: "The Constitution is the law of the land but not what some court says."

At this point came one of those rare occasions when Robert Kennedy allowed a phone call to stray into generalities. The result saw the conversation quickly slip to the college-bull-session level, but it did provide a unique glimpse of Ross Barnett's concept of the federal union and Mississippi's role in it.

"Governor," Kennedy observed, "you are a part of the United States."

"We have been a part of the United States, but I don't know whether we are or not."

"Are you getting out of the Union?"

"It looks like we're being kicked around—like we don't belong to it."

Back to specifics again, Kennedy finally ended the talk with a typically crisp wrap-up: "My job is to enforce the laws of the United States—I intend to fulfill it."

At 3:25 that afternoon a green twin-engine Cessna touched down at Jackson's municipal airport. It belonged to the Border Patrol, and from it emerged James Meredith, Jim McShane and, for the first time in this crisis, the gangling figure of John Doar— the man who believed that in Mississippi "you've just got to keep going back."

This time he was armed with more than persistence. Among the papers he carried was a sweeping temporary restraining order just issued by the Fifth Circuit, designed to overcome Barnett's defiance. It marked a new departure. Until now the Justice Department had tried to avoid bringing the Governor's name into the proceedings. Sticking to the University avoided the ultimate showdown. No longer—the new order specifically named Barnett. It forbade him from blocking Meredith's registration by any means . . . thus setting the stage for a direct confrontation between federal and state power. Armed with this new weapon, the Meredith party climbed into their car and headed for downtown Jackson.

At the 15-story Woolfolk State Office Building, which housed the trustees' headquarters, excitement was boiling. Word had long ago spread that this was where Meredith would next try to register, and by now the place was half-fortress and half-carnival. Pretty clerks and stenographers jammed the windows, waving at the Highway Patrol cars below, or at the growing crowd across the street on the grassy slope that led up to the limestone Capitol.

Around noon a big cheer went up as the Governor, hatless but neat in his dark gray suit, crossed over from the Capitol. He ambled into the building, went straight to the trustees' office on the tenth floor. Legislators followed . . . then trustees . . . then Registrar Ellis . . . then radio and TV men, until they packed the little reception room so tightly the checkerboard floor was lost from view. Occasionally a blonde in red fought through the mob to the Coke machine down the hall, returning with emergency rations for the defenders inside.

All through the early afternoon they restlessly waited, as the Meredith party—in the federal building a few blocks away— pondered its strategy. McShane wanted to get Ellis over if possible, but that proved out of the question. The heart of Mississippi's defense was to keep the capitulating Registrar from getting near the prospective student, and Ellis soon found himself virtually in protective custody.

At 4:34 P.M. a green Border Patrol sedan suddenly eased up to the Woolfolk Building. The crowd was now 2,000, and as they spied Meredith—already sporting the casual plaid jacket of an undergraduate—they let out a roar of rage and hate. He didn't even blink. Led by Doar, the party identified itself to a sentry at the door and swept through the surging, booing lobby.

At the tenth floor, now led by Colonel Birdsong, they pushed down the corridor through another crowd of jeering people. At Room 1007, the offices of the trustees, the door opened. There in the threshold stood Ross Barnett, literally interposing himself between the federal government and the state—or at least the state as represented by a room full of hooting legislators and office girls jumping on chairs and desks.

Floodlights blazed, the TV cameras rolled, the room fell silent and the show was on. The Governor politely announced he was glad to see Doar and McShane again. At this point the Chief Marshal blurted, "I have some papers," and Doar tried to hand Barnett a packet containing the Fifth Circuit's latest batch of orders. The Governor would have none of it. Doar then explained the appeals court's new restraining order and said in his matter-of-fact Western drawl, "We'd like to get on now, Governor, with the business of registering Mr. Meredith."

This was the signal for Barnett to read his latest proclamation—declaring that under his police powers he was "finally" denying Meredith admission to the University. As he finished, the crowd in the street—huddled around dozens of transistor radios—let out a Rebel yell that could easily be heard by the group on the tenth floor.

John Doar carefully spelled out his mission once more; Barnett remained unmoved. Still trying, Doar again held out the Fifth Circuit's orders. But now the legislators on the chairs and desks had had enough. "No! No!" they shouted, then turning on the federal party: "Get going! Get going!"

It was clearly no use. Meredith and the Justice men headed back for the street as the crowd in the halls let out another salvo of catcalls and Governor Barnett called after them pleasantly, "Come to see us at the Mansion."

On the street there was an angry surge forward when Meredith reappeared, but the group reached the sedan safely with the help of 40 Highway Patrolmen in Confederate gray. As the car sped off, the mob chanted after it, "Communists . . . Go home, nigger!"

From a tenth-story window Ross Barnett gave an appreciative wave, answered by a final roar of triumph from below. Then he too left the building—his big day marred only by the mild indignity of getting stuck in the elevator on the way down.

"The most brilliant piece of statesmanship ever displayed in Mississippi," declared State Senator Bill Jones of Brookhaven, as the legislature gathered that evening to assess the day's events. The rococo halls echoed with new cries of defiance, as the lawmakers drew fresh encouragement from this sweetest victory yet. Senator Hayden Campbell of Jackson stormed against opening doors to "murder and rape." Senator E. K. Collins of Laurel called for the same sacrifices the state had displayed in World War II: "We must win this fight, regardless of the cost in time, effort, money and in human lives."

At the very hour Senator Collins was speaking, the Fifth Circuit in New Orleans issued new orders summoning Ross Barnett to appear Friday, the 28th, and "show cause" why he shouldn't be held for contempt of court. Who cared? Mississippi vacillated wildly when depicting the federal government: sometimes it was a ruthless enemy who would stop at nothing; other times, an ineffectual booby long overdue for a smashing come-uppance. Now the Jackson papers easily swung from "the ruthless, Negro-loving Kennedys" and quickly found an anonymous observer who assured readers, "The Justice Department is down to its last-ditch measures now."

Perhaps this feeling accounted for Barnett's jaunty mood at 7:25 that evening when he again was on the phone with Robert Kennedy. He cheerfully reported that all had gone smoothly, that he had again turned down Meredith. Back came that smooth, flat Boston voice, announcing that Meredith was starting classes next morning anyhow.

Barnett gasped that he was astounded, didn't know what he would do. Kennedy, now coaxing, suggested they try it for six months and see how it went. The Governor wanted no part of that, adding . . . almost pleading: "It's best for him not to go to Ole Miss."

"But he likes Ole Miss," came the bland rejoinder.

A little later Kennedy was again on the wire, this time to announce that Meredith would be arriving in Oxford at ten o'clock next morning. A deflated Barnett said all right, but (back to an old line) why not keep him away altogether? Once again Kennedy patiently explained his position: he was just doing his job. Barnett remained unconvinced; in fact, he felt Kennedy owed it to the American people to tell the Supreme Court justices that the *Brown* case was not the law of the land. "When they don't follow the Constitution—it's so plain and unmistakable—I consider the law of the land instead."

The time had come when Kennedy felt he wasn't getting anywhere, and he now broke off the conversation. Meredith, he repeated, would be coming at 10:00 A.M.; the phone clicked and he was gone.

But behind the scenes other calls were being made. That same evening Burke Marshall phoned Tom Watkins in Jackson. Watkins, well aware of the heat on Barnett, could only warn that any desegregation would have to come forcibly.

Marshall still didn't give up. The following morning, the 26th, he again called Watkins, who by now was in New York on legal business. Once more he urged Watkins to try to change the Governor's course, pointing out that in the end Mississippi couldn't win. Watkins knew this, but he also knew the super-heated atmosphere in Jackson. Groping for some solution, he finally suggested that on the coming effort the federals should gently attempt to push the Governor aside. Using "the mildest kind of force" might give Barnett the out he needed, because he could then say Washington had "forcibly" brought about desegregation.

Marshall quickly passed the suggestion along to John Doar in Memphis, who was about to start down with Meredith for Oxford. Doar was highly dubious, but he'd try it. They'd see. . . .

At 9:29 A.M. the Border Patrol's Cessna dropped down from a leaden sky at Oxford's compact little airport. The familiar figures of Meredith, McShane and Doar emerged—the federal men huddling briefly with a waiting Highway Patrol inspector. Yes, the officer said, he had orders to escort them. Fifteen minutes later they were off—a highway patrol car leading, next Meredith's car,

then another carrying more marshals, and finally two more Highway Patrol cars guarding the rear.

The little convoy wormed through the town and then out University Avenue toward the campus. At South Fifth Street—about
two blocks from the entrance—they suddenly met the defenders
of the sovereign state of Mississippi. Deployed in a line across
the road were 20 unarmed state troopers; behind them another
line of county sheriffs; and finally a roadblock of three patrol cars
—a last-ditch barrier if all else failed.

The car leading the convoy turned into a side street and stopped.
The others did too . . . everybody piled out . . . and McShane ran
up to the officer leading them: "I thought you were taking us up
to the University grounds."

"My instructions were to take you as far as here, and I have
done that."

McShane now headed for the defense line, and as he approached, Lieutenant Governor Paul Johnson emerged from the
ranks. Low clouds had kept Ross Barnett from flying up, but the
Lieutenant Governor was clearly up to the occasion. He moved
like a general to the front of his forces.

"I would like to read this proclamation," Johnson announced
after McShane had explained why he was there. The gist was
thoroughly familiar: the state was interposing its powers, with
Johnson representing the Governor, "acting in his stead, by his
direction, and under his instructions." Finishing, he presented the
document to Meredith—one more addition to the Negro's ever-
mounting collection of official state papers.

John Doar now stepped forward, called attention to the Fifth
Circuit's latest orders, and tried unsuccessfully to give Johnson
copies. McShane then went back to the point of the visit: "Governor, I think it's my duty to try to go through and get Mr. Meredith
in there."

"You are not going in."

"I'm sorry, Governor, that I have to do this, but I'm going in."

Tipped off that a mild show of force might bring results, McShane then placed his arm on Johnson's arm; their bodies met ever so slightly. Whatever the effect might have been on Barnett, on Johnson it produced nothing. The Lieutenant Governor held firm: "You are not going in."

McShane now tried to get around Johnson, calling on one trooper after another to let him by. Not a man budged; not a man spoke a word.

John Doar began noting names on the state troopers' metal tags. The rest of the federal party seemed transfixed. Few were aware of the strategy being tried; most just wondered how far McShane could go without starting another Civil War. Marshal Cecil Miller moved closer to protect Meredith if violence broke. Meredith himself stood almost at attention. Border Patrolman Charles Chamblee studied the line of troopers—they all looked tough and mean. Finally, he picked out a big, burly one as the man he'd take on if it really came to blows.

But it didn't. Satisfied that he had tried "force"—and it didn't work—McShane now drew back. Then after another warning to Johnson, Doar decided to call it a day. The federals climbed into their cars and turned back for the airport, as the troopers exploded into yells and cheers for Paul Johnson.

"Lt. Governor Paul Johnson's name was added to the honor roll of defenders of the state's rights of Mississippi when the Fifth Circuit ordered him to show cause why he should not be cited for contempt of court," rhapsodized the *Clarion-Ledger* the following morning—and it was true. The Fifth Circuit had indeed added Johnson's name to the summons already issued against Barnett, but hysteria had now reached a point where contempt of a federal court was not a stigma but the highest peak of glory a public servant could achieve in Mississippi.

Nor did a man have to be governor to display his contempt for federal authority. When Marshal Henry Rowe tried to leave the contempt summons by Paul Johnson's locked door, a Highway

Patrolman threatened to have him arrested for littering. Abashed, the marshal went away, and the state roared with delight.

Now fantasy took over . . . the long-lost past galloped back. On the 27th a young man in the uniform of a Confederate lieutenant general strode through the state Capitol, and the rotunda rocked with cheers. Angry citizens called the State Historical Society demanding that the conciliatory statements by L. Q. C. Lamar and Robert E. Lee be erased from the walls of the Old Capitol. Automobile aerials blossomed with the Stars and Bars. The radio seemed to be playing "Dixie" all day long.

Best of all, this time they would win! Those occasional Cassandras who still warned that interposition wouldn't work were told to look at the facts. Three times Meredith had appeared; three times he had been rejected; three times the federals had been sent skulking away. Each new rejection fanned the flames, proved Ross Barnett more right than ever. "No man or woman in a lifetime has ever had the opportunity to witness the courage, the determination of such a great Governor," cried State Senator Bill Jones— and who could doubt the appraisal? As the Indianola *Enterprise-Tocsin*'s columnist put it on September 27, the Governor had "sculptured his shrine in American history."

Meanwhile, more behind-the-scenes phone calls. Right after Paul Johnson's rebuff, a puzzled Burke Marshall had once again contacted Tom Watkins. Not enough "force," diagnosed Watkins with his shrewd grasp of conditions in Mississippi. He then suggested that the marshals wear side arms next time, and much of the evening was spent trying to thrash something out along these lines.

Early next morning, the 27th, Watkins called Kennedy himself and formalized the state's proposition: if the marshals came and drew their guns, Barnett would step aside and let them on the campus. Kennedy wanted to make sure this had the Governor's approval. Assured that it did, he still asked for more confirmation.

Watkins was soon on the phone again: Yes, Barnett himself

would call directly. Meanwhile Kennedy had decided the proposal might be too dangerous as sketched out. He now said only one marshal would draw a gun. Not enough, said Watkins. A bizarre haggle developed, as Kennedy next offered one marshal pulling his pistol, the rest putting hands on holsters. The refinements were getting too much. Watkins begged off; these points should be worked out with the Governor.

What had happened? Notherners like to explain any Southern political phenomenon as the workings of the "power structure," and it would later be said that Mississippi's power structure finally blew the whistle. Fearing the effect of Barnett's policies on the state, and especially the University (the theory ran), the ruling clique called off the Governor and he dutifully obliged.

It wasn't that simple. There is indeed an inner circle in Mississippi, but it isn't so powerful as social historians like to think; and in this case much of it was as defiant as the Governor. But other factors were at work, and their combination couldn't help but have a powerful effect on his thinking. First, Barnett was listening more closely to his more conservative, cautious advisers. It was not so much that they were finally winning his ear—they always had that—rather, it was a case of the firebrands losing his ear.

Partly, this was simply a matter of geography: some of the biggest fanatics were off "at the front" in Oxford, 170 miles away. But more important was the fact that their arguments weren't coming true. They said Washington was just bluffing—but each federal move had been a little firmer, a little tougher. They said the Administration couldn't buck the public uproar—yet hundreds of marshals were now assembling in Memphis. They said "the Kennedys" would never risk the fall elections: close races in Texas and Alabama ruled out the use of troops—yet this very day RFK was getting in touch with the Pentagon. It took a long while, but Ross Barnett was at last getting to know his Kennedys.

Another big factor was also working to influence Barnett: his contempt trial was coming up the following day. He had talked a brave game about going to jail before giving in, but the closer it got, the less attractive it looked. And there was also the fine to consider. It could be colossal . . . and personal. The legislature was going to do its best to protect him, but leading lawyers privately conceded that the countermeasures wouldn't hold up in court.

Finally, there was the question of violence. By the 27th Barnett clearly realized that the state was perilously close to explosion. He didn't concede for a moment that he was in any way responsible; nevertheless, the hard facts remained. There was Collins in the Senate calling for victory "regardless of the cost in human life" . . . there was the bloodthirsty press . . . there was the response. "If standing for this means the sacrifice of my life," ran one of the thousands of letters now pouring in, "then I say that I only regret that I have only one life to give. I am at your service."

This was chilling. Whatever else Ross Barnett was, he remained a nonviolent man. Within the small white world he knew, he was still a warmhearted, if evasive, figure who didn't like physical force and genuinely recoiled from the thought of bloodshed.

So something had to be done. But what? It was no easy task to garb defeat in the guise of defiance. Yet things had gone too far for ordinary backtracking. A hundred years of build-up—capped by these last days of feverish rhetoric—had done their work. The state's people were out of control; they would never swallow mere compliance, and certainly Barnett's own career would be smashed beyond recovery. Something better had to be found . . . something that would combine compliance with the grandeur of resistance . . . something that would somehow convey the picture of a still-sovereign state bowing only before the overwhelming force of another power. And so it came to pass—in the form of the elaborate charade outlined by Watkins.

Why should Kennedy string along? He certainly had his misgivings. There was something rather queasy about the whole idea;

and besides, the play-acting was bound to seem ludicrous—and dangerous—to his practical nature. Yet there was another side. Quiet negotiations had worked well during the Freedom Rider crisis; now they again seemed the obvious way to start. Both Kennedy and his staff always clung to the idea that Justice should work through the Governor as long as possible—"It just seemed the right thing to do." If this was what he wanted, they should do their best to help him.

Kennedy, always down to earth, also turned the problem around: what would happen if they didn't play along? He decided if Washington then used troops, "Barnett could go before the people saying he had promised protection, but the federal government had brushed it aside and ruthlessly invaded the state with an army." Actually, this was impossible. Given the political realities of Mississippi, Barnett was in no position to tell the people that he had made any deals at all. But again, one hundred years of no communication had done their work. If the Governor was slow in getting to know his Kennedys, RFK was no faster in understanding how things worked in Mississippi.

But overriding all other factors was Washington's ardent desire to avoid using troops. This always remained paramount with both Kennedy and Katzenbach; so when the Governor's feeler arrived— with assurances that it would solve everything—it was just too much to resist.

Now that they were in it, they spent an anxious morning waiting for Barnett to confirm. Finally at 2:50 P.M. Washington time, an impatient Kennedy tracked down the Governor at Oxford. RFK tried out his modified version, with only McShane waving a gun, but Barnett refused. All right, Kennedy capitulated, *all* the marshals would draw their guns.

"Everyone pull your guns and point at them and we will stand aside and you will go right through," said the Governor, satisfied at last. Lieutenant Governor Johnson now came on the wire and explained how he was going to disperse the local sheriffs not in

on the act. Kennedy went over the plan with him too, then tried
to get a more definite assurance that the state would preserve law
and order. He hung up finally convinced that both Barnett and
Johnson would do their best.

But a tiger released from the cage is not so easily put back in.
Two thousand people—students, farmers, self-appointed vigilantes
—now swarmed around University Avenue, many armed with
clubs and pipes. Paul Johnson cruised up and down in a patrol
car, earnestly calling over a loudspeaker, "Return, return to the
campus . . . I'm pleading with you for your own safety . . . someone might easily get killed . . . you must stay out of the line of fire."

Nobody budged.

Rumors soon spread that the marshals would be carrying riot
sticks and tear gas. Judge Russel Moore, serving Barnett as a sort
of campus coordinator, knew just what to do. He broke out the
Highway Patrol's helmets, sticks and gas masks. Now the troopers
stood in a grim line across the avenue at Fifth Street—they looked
ready for anything and spoiling for a fight.

But the biggest problem was the hundreds of sheriffs, town
cops and hastily mobilized deputies. They had been summoned by
a telephone relay which the Sheriffs Association, acting "on
orders," apparently launched early in the day. This quickly spread
word through the state that officers were needed in Oxford. Now
east on Highway 6, south along 7, in fact from every direction, the
familiar white cruisers were rolling, converging on the University.
Some were dedicated lawmen, others less so—which Barnett soon
discovered as he circulated among these men, trying to get them to
disperse or at least put their guns away.

"How many times does it shoot?" the Governor affably asked,
as he approached one tough deputy toying with his gun.

"Six times, and if that doesn't get the job done, I got a little
one here for Number 7."

At 3:50 the phone rang in Kennedy's office; a sober Barnett
was on the wire: could they hold off sending Meredith until Satur-

day, the 29th?—the people were too excited. Kennedy said no, now was the best time—after all, the Governor was up for contempt on Friday, and it was important to square things away before then. Barnett changed tack—he was afraid people would say he was compromising.

"You're not compromising," the Attorney General cheerfully assured him. "You're standing right up there."

Johnson now came on the wire, stressing how touchy the situation was—he just couldn't get those deputy sheriffs out. Again, a plea for postponement; again, Kennedy was unimpressed.

Another call at 4:20. This time Barnett was more cheerful: all was set; and just to be sure, he and Kennedy went over the gun-drawing plan one more time.

"Get going," the Justice Department now flashed Memphis, and John Doar quietly dropped around to the house on Mississippi Street where Meredith was staying. They hurried out the back door, down an alley, into a waiting Border Patrol sedan, and were soon bowling down Interstate 55. This time there was quite a convoy—13 Border Patrol cars carrying around 25 marshals. All had empty guns and were well rehearsed on the role they would play. Overhead droned a Border Patrol plane, giving the federal party radio contact with the outside world.

At 5:35 Kennedy called Barnett to report that Meredith was on the way, and he took the opportunity to prod the Governor again about preserving law and order. Barnett's response seemed right out of Blackstone: he talked of using "reasonable diligence" . . . doing all that "a reasonable and prudent official" would do . . . doing everything he thought was "proper under the particular circumstances to protect the lives and health and persons of everyone." Kennedy was anything but reassured—he wondered if Barnett was trying to tell him something without actually saying it.

His hunch was right. At Oxford all efforts had failed to disperse the crowd. A phone jangled in the U.S. Attorney's office on Courthouse Square. Marshal Cecil Miller took the call. It was Colonel

Birdsong saying the mob was now out of hand, call off the attempt. Miller relayed the message on the hot line to Memphis, where it could be flashed to the Border Patrol plane escorting the convoy.

At the same moment Barnett was calling Kennedy. This time there was no legal doggerel—he said he was worried, nervous, couldn't handle the crowd. Kennedy—his misgivings had mounted all afternoon—quickly called off the show. A relieved Barnett assured the Attorney General that it was all for the best; otherwise a lot of people were going to be killed, and that would be (to quote the understatement of the day) "embarrassing."

The federal convoy had reached the little town of Como—less than 50 miles from Oxford—when the short-wave radio suddenly rasped orders to stop. Meredith's car pulled out of line, and John Doar phoned back for details. The directions were explicit—no leeway at all—there was nothing to do but return to Memphis.

McShane, keyed up to finishing the job, felt a natural letdown. Meredith was more philosophical. He had known setbacks before —expected to see many more again in the course of his long, long journey—this was just another stop along the way.

His NAACP lawyers were less patient. The Justice Department had told them nothing about the deal with Barnett, but they had an inkling something was up. Burke Marshall kept reassuring them that he had "special information" . . . they needn't worry, everything was going to be all right. None of it made any difference to Jack Greenberg, now head of the NAACP Legal Defense Fund. If there was a deal, as he suspected, he didn't believe Mississippi could or would keep it. Meanwhile it was ridiculous to add marshals "by twos and threes" at each new turn in the crisis. A real show of strength right at the start, he felt, would have turned the trick immediately, but this piecemeal commitment just encouraged the state to increase its resistance.

Certainly Mississippi was wilder than ever. So wild, in fact, that responsible men—even staunch segregationists—were showing signs of alarm. Paul Johnson, so recently the very symbol of defiance, now told the Senate that he was deeply worried. William Mounger, the dynamic insurance man whose firm controlled WLBT-WJDX, silenced his station's fiery editorials. Ole Miss alumni who had previously confined their efforts to keeping the University open began pondering some graceful way to sound a call for law and order—without, of course, making it look like treason. But like Ross Barnett before them, they all found that mass hysteria once set in motion wasn't so easily stopped.

"It is a privilege to resist the evil that seeks to destroy an honorable way of life," wrote Presley J. Snow from Philadelphia, Mississippi—a town that would later gain a certain fame of its own in the civil rights movement. "Let it be remembered that much of the hogwash known as the 'law of the land' in the nation today is a crime against the American people."

WRBC blared "Dixie" and "Go, Mississippi" more feverishly than ever, and to these favorites an exciting new song was added. On the 28th the Jackson *Daily News* carried it on its editorial page and urged everyone to learn it for the big football game with Kentucky Saturday night. Called the "Never, No Never" song, it urged "to hell with Bobby K," and happily boasted, "Ross's standin' like Gibraltar; he shall never falter."

Ironically, that same afternoon the Governor was back on the phone with Robert Kennedy urging the Attorney General to give him plenty of notice before Meredith came next time.

Nobody knew—the delirium rolled on. About this time the Jackson radio invented a new stunt. Listeners in automobiles were urged at a given signal to sound their horns together, to show their united support for Ross Barnett. Then the signal would be given, and a roar of claxons all over town showed the people how united they were.

In Oxford Mrs. Duncan Gray, the Episcopal minister's wife, looked at the Confederate flags on every car aerial and impulsively bought an American flag to fly herself. Better not do it, her husband warned, people were mad enough already. The thought in many

minds was finally spoken on the afternoon of September 28 when
State Senator Jack Pace stood up in the Capitol and offered "a petition to the United States Congress to sever relations with the State
of Mississippi."

Cooler heads called for lunch instead, but the fact remained that
for an amazing number of Mississippians the Civil War had really
come again. They were no longer fighting just to keep Meredith
out—or even for segregation in their schools. In a burst of fantasy
and nostalgia they were now picking up fallen standards . . . carrying on for those lost gray legions . . . keeping faith with Davis and
Forrest and all the rest.

Nor were they alone. "THOUSANDS SAID READY TO FIGHT FOR
MISSISSIPPI," cried the Jackson *Daily News*. "ALL SECTIONS VOICE
SUPPORT OF BARNETT," echoed the *Clarion-Ledger*. News stories
spoke vaguely of "tens of thousands" coming to help from all over
the land. It remained only to welcome the army of liberation.

8

"Bring Your Flags, Your Tents and Your Skillets"

IN AN OLD ABANDONED SCHOOLHOUSE NEAR THE LITTLE TOWN of Pavo, Georgia, eight men gathered on the night of September 28 and began laying their plans to rush to the relief of embattled Mississippi. At oil-rich Shreveport, Louisiana, a police officer who said he was acting as a private citizen prepared to sound a call for recruits. In the red-clay Florida hills north of St. Petersburg a local Citizens' Council man estimated he might raise as many as 500 armed men. At Mobile on the Gulf Coast 115 members of the Citizens for the Preservation of Democracy discussed their own plans to help—each volunteer would wear a red bandanna.

In sun-baked towns throughout the cotton belt dozens—even scores—of hot-eyed volunteers were preparing to march, not that there was any sign of the vast legions talked up in Jackson. Nor were they all coming on their own. Many needed, and were getting, considerable encouragement.

They were summoned by a private line installed in Alumni House on the Ole Miss campus. The phone was in Room 121, which along with Suite A next door formed the state's "command post" during these days of mounting crisis. Beginning September 27, several hundred dollars' worth of long-distance calls were made from this number to points all over the South. The gist was always the same: "Governor Barnett wants you and your friends to get on the campus for a showdown with the federal government."

Only those involved know for certain who made the calls. The place was like a bus station during these days. Aides, hangers-on, Citizens' Council stalwarts were constantly coming and going . . . making themselves at home . . . using the phone. The calls could have been placed by many people—or very, very few.

Only one thing is certain: Ross Barnett himself placed none of them and knew nothing of the project. He wasn't even there while the calls were being made. But as always, people were jockeying for position, capitalizing on his uncertainties—and using his name. The ultimate irony, according to Mississippi gossip, came when the Governor was even stuck with the phone bill.

Whoever made the calls, there's good reason to believe they no longer expected to stop the federals. Mississippi's ordinary citizens might still live in fantasy, but not so this particular segment of extremists. By now their real strategy lay in another direction. If it had to happen, they thought, make it as big a mess as possible . . . do whatever might call the greatest national attention to the raw deal they felt they were getting. Thus the same group that protested loudest about using troops against American citizens was secretly trying to bring this very thing about.

So the calls went out, and some were heeded—but why? What drove normally law-abiding citizens to answer the appeal of another state for volunteers to fight their own federal government? Some were people as lost in Confederate mythology as any Mississippian —they too heard those distant bugles. Others were simply anti-Negro. People in the Deep South like to say how fond they are of "our colored," but at crisis time other words simply pop out. "My friends," declared L. H. Perez, the fabled boss of Louisiana's Plaquemines Parish, in a pamphlet widely circulated at this time, "let's stop running from the negroes. If necessary, stand up and fight."

But a surprising number of those who headed for Mississippi were neither Confederate die-hards nor "nigger haters." They were simply fighting a growing federal colossus that seemed to have an insatiable appetite for interfering in their daily lives. Still far removed from an ever more urban America, they saw none of the forces shaping the government; they only saw the size, the waste, the controls, the regimentation, the end of "the way things used to be." And the pace was accelerating. The Supreme Court's apportionment decision the previous March threatened the time-honored setup in every state legislature. The White House crackdown on steel in April seemed to challenge a man's right to run his own business. The New York prayer case in June meant that "Our kid can't even say his prayers in school any more."

What was the world coming to? Grasping little of the complex forces at work, most were only too ready to accept the simple answer provided by local leaders: it was all a Communist conspiracy. The same Perez pamphlet that urged them to stop running away from Negroes also assured them that the 1960 Democratic platform was "a Communist indoctrination course" . . . New York State was "pro-Communist dominated" . . . the FEPC, the Full Employment bill and the protection of voting rights were all "evidences of surrendering to the Communist conspiracy." The Supreme Court was called "treasonable" four times in three pages.

Against all this evil was "the truth"—unquestioned and unsupported. The word was hammered home endlessly, starting with the very slogans of the bitter little weeklies that papered the area: "Look for the true meaning," proclaimed the Augusta *Courier;* "Truth, understanding, organization, loyalty, and love," boasted the *Crusader* of Baton Rouge; "Truth wears no mask," announced Albuquerque's *Citizen Courier.* A man who feels armed with the truth believes himself well armed indeed; these September days it helped many heed the siren call from Alumni House.

All this was, of course, a state of mind that had been flourishing since World War II, but this time there was something added that

immensely aggravated the bitterness: the President of the United
States. FDR had rescued them from the depression and that made
up for a lot . . . Truman was small-town and they felt they at least
understood him . . . Eisenhower was an authentic hero. They could
adjust to all these—but Kennedy! They never heard the eloquence
—only the flat Boston accent. They cared nothing about the style
that so appealed to the East—it only made him seem more remote
down here. And youth? It looked more like brashness to a people
who venerated age and tradition.

Here—complete with misspellings—is how the current issue of
the *States Rights Advocate,* bimonthly voice of the Montgomery
Citizens' Council, summed the man up:

> John Kennedy's Administration is unparalleled in the history
> of the United States for bunders and plain bad government.
> Kennedy was trainned in the school of Boston backstreet politics.
> The atmosphere was one of hoodlumism and corruption. It is no
> wonder that the present occupant of the White House, a descendent
> of a Boston salon keeper, has acted the way he has.

In their fear they joined extreme right-wing organizations—
sometimes big, well-known ones like the John Birch Society, but
more often small splinter groups that came and went. There was
Mobile's Citizens for the Preservation of Democracy . . . Florida's
National Christian Congressional Committee . . . and especially a
strange, shrill outfit called the National States' Rights Party,
founded by a Louisville chiropractor named Edward R. Fields and
now operating out of Birmingham.

But even these small organizations didn't play much of a part
themselves in the ragged mobilization now under way. They were
much too disarranged for that. Usually the central leadership had
little control over local units, and they in turn had still less over the
individual members. These various splinter groups are chiefly important in the clue they give to the fears and hates of many of those
who headed for Oxford. They were not latter-day fascists at all—

just small, deeply worried individuals who longed for an earlier America they saw slipping away. Now they were trying to do something about it in a desperate flash of frustration.

But one of them, though equally worried, was not small or unknown at all. Former Major General Edwin A. Walker was a national figure who had enjoyed a distinguished military career. A humorless young Texan who didn't do too well at West Point (220th out of 297 in the Class of '31), he made up for a lot with his drive and energy. In the doldrums of between-the-wars Army life, he threw himself into polo—23 years of it before he was through. In World War II he always sought the toughest assignments—rough, taxing commands in Kiska, Italy, the Rhone Valley. A man who would try anything, he ended up with 47 paratroop jumps to his credit.

Working on the Greek crisis after the war, he learned a lot about Communist tactics and was duly impressed. He learned more during the heart-breaking campaigns in Korea . . . and still more during a hitch in Taiwan. His passionate hatred of Communism led his political views ever farther toward the right, but still not so far as to collide with his military career.

Commanding the federal troops at Little Rock in 1957, he was a model of restraint. Whatever his private feelings, he showed none of the right-wing extremist's tone. "We are all subject to all the laws, whether we approve of them personally or not," he told the student body of Central High, "and as law-abiding citizens, have an obligation in conscience to obey them. There can be no exceptions; if it were otherwise, we would not be a strong nation but a mere unruly mob."

Yet it was all boiling up inside. In 1959 he joined the John Birch Society and tried to resign from the Army, feeling that, blocked by a "fifth column conspiracy," he wasn't doing any good. The Army refused his resignation and assigned him instead to Germany in command of the 24th Division. Here the depth of his feelings began to emerge in talks and information activities for his troops.

The situation came to a head in April 1961 with a slashing attack on Walker by the *Overseas Weekly,* a private newssheet catering to servicemen abroad. A subsequent Army investigation endorsed his anti-Communist training program, but it also found he had made derogatory remarks on the leftist influence or affiliation of Harry Truman, Dean Acheson and Eleanor Roosevelt; had called 60% of the press and radio Communist-influenced; had provided a service where his men could phone Flak M 813 and get their Congressmen's records—from data provided by the ultra-rightist Americans for Constitutional Action.

The investigation concluded that Walker had indeed broken regulations by trying to influence his men's voting, and that he had not complied completely with regulations by making speeches derogatory to past public officials. He was orally admonished.

That fall the General was ordered to the Pacific. The new job had important training responsibilities, but Walker felt the program was doomed to failure. So badly designed, in fact, that it couldn't be merely stupidity. Rather, it was part of a sinister, Communist-influenced, "no-win" policy which he was now convinced had the whole government in its grip.

He would have none of it. In November 1961 he resigned from the Army to devote himself entirely to public life. In the process he gave up $15,000 a year in retirement benefits; he wanted to feel completely free to speak his mind.

In April 1962 he appeared before a Senate subcommittee investigating the possible muzzling of U.S. military leaders. He charged that he was "a scapegoat of an unwritten policy of collaboration and collusion with the international Communist conspiracy," but failed to back it up. He objected to books by Walter Millis and John Gunther, but it turned out he hadn't read them. He declared that the Government was infiltrated by Communists, but he declined to name any. He also doubted Russia's space achievements and suggested the famous Soviet photo of the far side of the moon was "very likely a picture out of our own *Popular Mechan-*

ics." Leaving the hearing, he tossed a punch at a questioning reporter.

Now, less than six months later, the General was more than ready to tackle this new cause. To him it was not a question of race; it was a matter of saving the country. The states formed the last bastion of freedom, and the "no-win" Communist-infiltrated federal government was moving in on them. Something had to be done. On the night of September 26 he sounded his call for action in a telephoned interview over Shreveport's radio station KWKH:

> It is time to move. We have talked, listened and been pushed around far too much by the anti-Christ Supreme Court. Rise to a stand beside Governor Ross Barnett at Jackson, Mississippi. Now is the time to be heard. Ten thousand strong from every state in the Union. Rally to the cause of freedom. The battle cry of the Republic. Barnett, yes; Castro, no. Bring your flags, your tents and your skillets. It is time. Now or never. The time is when and if the President of the United States commits or uses any troops, Federal or State, in Mississippi. The last time in such a situation I was on the wrong side. That was in Little Rock, Arkansas, in 1957, and 1958. This time I am out of uniform and I am on the right side and I will be there.

What did he hope to accomplish? At the time, Walker said the crusade would be simply "a movement of the people to be heard" under their constitutional right of protest. Later, discussing it with a visitor, he added another and perhaps deeper aim. The federal move, he felt, was the first overt step in the take-over of power from the states, and he wanted to observe for himself how it was done. Then he could go forth and better alert the country on the danger it faced. If he could get others to join him, all the better—they too could go out and help wake up America.

In sounding his call, Walker always stressed his intentions were peaceful. "I certainly advocate no violence," he assured the reporters who soon came swarming to his gray stucco home in Dallas.

Yet at the same time he did little to discourage his followers from bringing their guns. When asked on September 27 if his volunteers should go armed, the Associated Press quoted him as merely saying, "The Administration has indicated it will do whatever is necessary to enforce this unconstitutional action. I have stated that whatever is necessary to oppose that enforcement and stand behind Governor Barnett should be done." Did this mean he advocated physical force? "The decision for force will be made in Washington . . . we will move with the punches."

And when a *New York Times* man also asked him on the 28th if people should bring guns, Walker again seemed to miss an easy chance to say no. According to the paper, he simply replied, "That's their own decision."

Asked about this later, Walker maintained that it wasn't his business what they brought. People had a constitutional right to bear arms, and he wasn't going to ask them not to exercise their right. That was their own business. "If I ask someone to have lunch with me in Dallas, I'm not going to tell him not to bring a gun."

So nothing was said on this point, or where the volunteers were to go, or what they were to do when they got there. Answering the phone in his comfortable suburban home, casually dressed in tan sport shirt and slacks, Ted Walker did not look like a "man on horseback," but he assured visitors that "thousands" were prepared to join him. He was ready to go at any time, "if and when they use federal troops."

Saturday afternoon, September 29, a small private plane headed east from Dallas. There were no federal troops yet in Mississippi, but General Walker was now flying to Jackson anyhow, piloted by his friend Joe Allred.

At Jackson's airport Walker was met by Ney Williams, the Citizens' Council anesthesiologist, and there soon followed a Mississippi ritual that must have seemed strange indeed to the deadly serious General. They drove around town for a while, switching football tickets back and forth for the all-important Ole Miss–Kentucky game at Memorial Stadium that night.

Around five o'clock he held a press conference at the Sun-n-Sand, a pleasantly cheerful motel where the setting seemed almost ludicrous with its background of children laughing and splashing in the pool. "I call for a national protest against the conspiracy from within," the General solemnly intoned as the TV camera whirred. Interviewed by the Memphis *Commercial Appeal,* he again told of the mighty host already heading for Mississippi—"thousands and possibly tens of thousands of people from Florida to California."

An optimistic estimate. On the other hand, there was no reason to take lightly the thin stream of dusty hard-tops and pick-up trucks now converging on the scene. What these people lacked in numbers they often made up in fear and hate—grim men carrying shotguns and rifles behind the seat or back with the spare tire.

And more were promised. At Birmingham, Eastview Klavern No. 13 ordered its members to assemble, prepared to march this same Saturday, the 29th. At Shreveport 3,000 people packed a mass rally in the courthouse square during the evening. Interesting plans emerged: 150 cars from Shreveport plus 60 cars from Monroe would meet at Tallulah 8:30 Sunday morning, then proceed in convoy to Jackson.

Wires were flooding Governor Barnett's office on the third floor of the Capitol. Dr. Edward Fields telegraphed from Birmingham that his National States' Rights Party would "place our lives and fortunes at the disposal of your supreme authority as governor of the sovereign state of Mississippi." The Anniston, Alabama, KKK wired that hundreds of its members "are on a stand-by alert waiting for your call to protect the state sovereignty of Mississippi."

Appalled by the prospects, Barnett desperately tried to fend them off. Aside from his natural distaste for violence, the Governor now had an added reason for acting. Friday, the 28th, the Fifth Circuit found him in contempt of court and ordered him to cleanse himself by October 2 or face a fine of $10,000 a day. So he was all for anything to discourage outsiders . . . without, of course, making Mississippi look any less determined to resist to the end. This proved a large order, yet Barnett's executive secretary, Hugh Boren, managed to sidetrack a group of 57 Montgomery volunteers, and the Governor himself cooled the ardor of Louisiana State Senator Willie Reinach who wanted to raise 10,000 "peace marchers."

But it was clear that this sort of fire once started isn't so easily put out. The cars continued coming, and among those reaching Oxford this Saturday night was a white Chevrolet compact carrying two men. They drove up to the Mansel Motel . . . checked in . . . and went to Room 17. One, the driver, was a young oil man named Louis Leman; the other, who was registered by Leman as "John Waters," was a tall, serious man in a white Texas hat. His real name was Edwin A. Walker.

Certain other people were converging on Oxford too. They were not sporting Texas hats or the open shirts of the country people; more likely they were wearing the ties and dark suits that by now automatically marked a federal man for most Mississippians. ("I can spot one a mile away," was a favorite boast.) Marshal Cecil Miller of Miami walked the campus, getting the feel of the place . . . green Border Patrol cars cruised slowly down Sorority Row to the cold stares of the coeds . . . other new faces in town were busy setting up a communications center in the basement of the Post Office. When they crossed the courthouse square to the U.S. Attorney's office (another scene of growing activity), the gaffers loafing on the benches studied the strangers' black city shoes with silent contempt.

Even more activity was going on in Memphis, 78 miles north by car. Although across the state line, this friendly, easygoing river port played a big role in the life of the cotton belt. It was where the Delta planters did their business, where their families shopped and played, where the Ole Miss students loved to go whenever they could afford it. Everyone gravitated to Memphis, and by the same token Memphis was the natural jumping-off place for anyone going to northern Mississippi.

Marshals and deputies began pouring in from all over the country as the Justice Department's mobilization plan moved into high gear. They concentrated at Millington, the big Naval Air Station north of town—140 by the evening of the 27th . . . 402 by the 28th. First to come were McShane's 123 regulars, but 316 hand-picked Border Patrolmen were soon pulling in too—3 from Savannah . . . 12 from Buffalo . . . a whopping 164 from Texas. The Mexican border was left virtually unguarded—but the wetbacks never knew of their golden chance. By the 29th the deputized prison guards were also arriving—97 hard, riot-trained men from Leavenworth, Atlanta, Terra Haute. That evening a grand total of 541 men were on hand. If—as many Mississippians claimed—they represented a new Yankee invasion, it was a strange one indeed: 54% of the regulars, 81% of the Border Patrolmen and 47% of the prison guards were born and raised in the South. Assistant Attorney General Louis Oberdorfer, the Justice official sent down to take charge, came from Birmingham, Alabama.

By now the supporting forces were gathering too—FAA planes, FCC monitoring cars . . . nine Navy busses . . . other busses from the Bureau of Prisons . . . five Border Patrol transports . . . a convoy of 49 trucks and jeeps bringing the 70th Army Engineers from Fort Campbell, Kentucky. The wide variety once again drove home an important point for anyone who cared to note: the limitless resources the federal government can bring to bear when anyone seriously questions its authority.

Yet both Kennedy and Katzenbach still hoped to do the job with civilians. Everyone carefully stressed that the 70th Engineers were not to enforce court orders but simply to feed and house the marshals. And the Navy insignia was even painted out on its nine busses.

Nevertheless, the military was always there, whether temporarily painted out or kept under wraps as a last resort. Mississippians liked to say it was illegal to use troops, and they pointed to a section of the U.S. Code that says no one can use the armed forces "to execute the laws." But the statute had a big exception they didn't talk about: "except in cases and under circumstances specifically authorized by the Constitution or Act of Congress." The Constitution, of course, charged the President to see that the law was enforced. Also, a U.S. statute authorized the President to use troops whenever he felt "unlawful obstructions" made it impractical to enforce the laws "by the ordinary course of judicial proceedings." And still another law authorized troops where "domestic violence, unlawful combination or conspiracy" impeded the course of justice under the nation's laws. These provisions went back to the days of George Washington, who had his own states' rights troubles, and used troops to suppress the Whiskey Rebellion in Pennsylvania.

Robert Kennedy always knew it might come to this. Already on September 28 he had begun hedging his bet on a civilian solution. That afternoon he met with General Maxwell Taylor, Chairman of the Joint Chiefs of Staff, and other top military leaders. They decided that, if necessary, two MP battalions and a battle group from Fort Benning should move in.

The wheels started turning. To Assistant Attorney General Norbert Schlei at the Justice Department, this meant drafting the proclamation the President must issue before calling in troops. To Secretary of the Army Cyrus R. Vance, it meant a War Room incongruously filled with huge maps of Mississippi. To Pfc Charles Vanderburgh of the 716th MP Battalion at Fort Dix, it meant mystery and uncertainty. Orders first came at 5:00 P.M. on the 28th to be ready to move in four hours. This was postponed, but another alert followed on the 29th, and all that day they stood by. No one knew where they were going, but scuttlebutt said either Cuba or Mississippi. "Same difference," grumbled a Negro GI.

All the while the Justice staff still worked on its plans for a civilian solution. In Memphis Lou Oberdorfer turned his precise mind from taxes to transport—how best to fit the several hundred marshals he now had on hand into his grab bag assortment of busses, patrol cars, planes and a helicopter.

Saturday morning, September 29, Robert Kennedy got a new call from Barnett's adviser, Tom Watkins—more talk, but nothing seemed really changed. "We'd better get going with the military," Kennedy remarked as he put down the phone. Even so, he and Nick Katzenbach—always the practical idealist—remained dimly hopeful they might yet find some other way out. At least the Governor kept on dickering; and above all they still had one last untried, immensely powerful weapon—the personal intervention of the President of the United States.

It was 2:30 P.M. when John F. Kennedy made his first call to the Governor. Through informal contacts with his brother, the President was well aware of the present impasse. It all looked hopeless, but even while the White House staff began planning for the troops, Kennedy made his own special pitch to Ross Barnett.

The President's manner was mild and friendly—he carefully explained he had to carry out the Court's orders, but he wanted to work with Barnett and wanted his help. The Governor said Robert Kennedy and Tom Watkins were working things out, that Watkins was flying up tomorrow with a detailed plan—it was most important for the Attorney General to see him. The conversation ended, with Barnett cramming in a last-second inspiration: "Appreciate your interest in our poultry program and all those things."

Not very promising, but at 3:15 the President was back trying once more. In the wake of the last call, Robert Kennedy had again been in touch with Watkins; now JFK put him on the line to report. The Attorney General was discouraging; Watkins really didn't have much to offer. His only new idea was a sort of hidden ball play: while Barnett staged a huge diversion at Oxford on Monday, Meredith would quietly register in Jackson.

The Governor jumped at it . . . growing more and more enthusiastic. He and Paul Johnson would follow through.

The President, less captivated, came back on the wire. The real question, he pointed out, was what the state would do to preserve law and order—then the federal government could decide the next step. Barnett said the Highway Patrol would do the best they could. But, Kennedy pressed, could they do the job? Again, they'd do their best. And Barnett himself? He'd do everything in his power. Hopefully, the Governor now asked for a cooling-off period . . . maybe two or three weeks. Kennedy asked if Barnett would give his word to register Meredith then. As the fencing began again, the President broke off. The conversation ended with Barnett agreeing to call back later.

A baffling afternoon. The New Frontiersmen, who considered themselves students as well as practitioners of government, never had a better case study in the mysteries of decision-making. All sorts of ingredients went into the pot: determination to enforce court orders . . . the hope to avoid troops . . . the memory that marshals had worked before . . . belated recognition of Mississippi's recalcitrance . . . belief that Barnett desperately wanted some way out . . . fear that the Governor could no longer control his people. All these factors tugged this way and that. And with none of them decisive, Washington simply plunged ahead on all fronts. Men worked not knowing what they would finally do, realizing that in the end something totally unforeseen—chance, hunch or the act of some unknown palace guard in Mississippi—might shape the ultimate outcome.

So all afternoon JFK, his brother and Burke Marshall pondered Barnett's latest proposal . . . staff assistants drafted the Executive Order federalizing Mississippi's National Guard . . . Norb Schlei continued working on the President's proclamation . . . Lou Oberdorfer shaped up his marshals at Millington . . . General Abrams ordered the 2nd Battle Group of the 2nd Division to Memphis from Fort Benning . . . Pierre Salinger called on the networks for TV time, 8:00 P.M. Sunday night . . . Ted Sorensen, temporarily laid up in the hospital, began drafting the President's speech to the nation. As he scribbled off his thoughts, a stream of messengers rushed them to the White House.

At 7:00 P.M., another phone talk between the President and Barnett. They again discussed the diversion plan proposed for Monday: Barnett and Johnson would go to Oxford; Meredith would slip into Jackson and register; and this time the Governor satisfied Kennedy that the Highway Patrol would indeed maintain law and order. It was a deal.

On went the brakes. Salinger phoned the networks canceling the TV time, and the President decided to hold up his proclamation and Executive Order federalizing the Guard. At the Justice Department Norb Schlei continued working on both "just in case." He finally finished around 10:00 and took the papers home . . . he better have them handy.

Shortly afterward Barnett was calling Justice again, asking for Robert Kennedy. The Attorney General had gone home too, but it didn't take long to track him down . . . or break the news. The Governor announced the deal was off.

A resigned Robert Kennedy phoned Burke Marshall. It was a sorrowful moment for the Assistant Attorney General for Civil Rights; he felt sure this marked the end of their chances for a civilian solution. They would have to go in with troops on Monday, and that could well turn into a "second Civil War." But it had to be faced, and Marshall began setting the wheels in motion.

About 11:15 Norb Schlei got the phone call he always sensed would come. It was Marshall, telling him the deal had been repudiated—get over to the White House with the papers. It was just after midnight when the President, sitting at the long table in the Indian Treaty Room, issued the Executive Order calling for troops, and signed Proclamation No. 3497 commanding those in defiance "to cease and desist therefrom and to disperse and retire peaceably forthwith."

The bedlam mounted steadily at the football game in Jackson's

Memorial Stadium that night. Now it was half-time and the roar was deafening—louder than before the kickoff when the Ole Miss students displayed the largest Confederate flag in the world . . . even louder than when the Rebel team moved ahead of Kentucky, 7 to o.

A big screen on the field flashed the words to "Go Mississippi" and the crowd sang it again and again. Then, above the general bedlam rose a growing chant: "We want Ross! We want Ross!" Louder and louder it grew as more thousands took it up, until at last that was all there was—a mighty, thundering command from 46,000 throats.

Barnett stepped forward from his box onto the floodlit field and moved before a microphone. A great rolling yell went up, then gradually died as the Governor dramatically raised a clenched fist. "I love Mississippi," he shouted and the stadium again rocked with cheers. "I love her people. I love our customs."

That was all, but it's doubtful whether many heard more than the start. The crowd laughed, cried, hugged one another, swept away by a delicious feeling of defiance . . . of standing together in a truly great cause.

"It was like a big Nazi rally," a student later exclaimed, and his eyes still danced in happy recollection. "Yes, it was just the way Nuremberg must have been!"

"That night," another recalled, "people would have been glad to die for Ross." And it was perhaps because the mood was all too clear that one Mississippi mother dropped a few lines of advice to her student son:

> Your *great-grandfather* set out to fight the federals from Ole Miss with the University Grays, called the Lamar Rifles, nearly a hundred years ago—He didn't accomplish a thing! See that you don't get involved!!!!

It was a voice of sanity in what had now become a madhouse.

9

"I Always Wondered What It Would Be Like to Go to War"

JACKSON LAY HUSHED AND STILL IN THE YELLOW DAWN OF Sunday, September 30. Exhausted by its emotional binge the night before, now at last the city was silent. On most streets the only sound was the comfortably familiar thump of the *Clarion-Ledger* landing on the doorstep. Still half-asleep, the early risers opened the paper to see what the new day brought. . . .

"The courageous stand of Governor Barnett has electrified the South and in fact the entire nation"—the editorial drums began pounding again. Word from the Rockies said 98 out of 100 backed Barnett . . . the day's cartoon showed the Tenth Amendment dumped in the Kennedy wastebasket . . . Charlie Hills' column ranted against bowing to "the unleashed furies of the Congo" . . . and the federalized National Guard inspired the headline, "CALL-UP MAY PIT BROTHER AGAINST BROTHER." Significantly, the next two pages eulogized Lee's glorious march North in 1862. Strong fare—enough to free many a man from his Sunday torpor and start his blood rising again.

In Washington too the day began quietly. The corridors of the Justice Department had that dead look that government buildings always get on Sunday. Then here too the tempo started beating again. An unsmiling Kennedy turned up around 9:00 . . . then

Norb Schlei . . . and by 10:00 the underground VIP parking space was nearly full. Nobody expected much to happen before Monday; still, this crisis had taken so many unexpected turns. In Kennedy's baronial office Schlei and Burke Marshall restlessly tossed a football back and forth.

In New Orleans John Doar and James Meredith drove toward the airport through the same kind of bright, peaceful morning. Doar had been down to argue Paul Johnson's contempt case, Meredith to visit some friends. Alerted to come back to Memphis "just in case," both were now on their way. Soon they were winging north in the Border Patrol's green Cessna—Meredith taciturn as ever, Doar explaining the plans as far as he knew them. From his last contact with Washington, Saturday afternoon, he understood that one more major civilian effort would be made . . . on Monday.

This was the understanding at Millington too. By now Lou Oberdorfer had two alternatives elaborately worked out: one calling for busses, the other for planes and then busses in two carefully meshed stages. But whatever was done, he too assumed a civilian effort . . . again, on Monday.

The details were complete; everything checked out. The marshals were divided into 9 groups, each with 4 squads, each squad with 12 men. The groups were assigned to the busses so that they would arrive as a unit together with their equipment. The regular marshals had some 1.5 tear gas guns; the Border Patrol only gas grenades and gas billies. All carried arms (Colt and S & W .38s), but they were to be kept out of sight in shoulder holsters under jackets. If marshals were used, as Millington expected, it was still hoped to keep any display of physical force at a minimum.

With this thought in mind, all the marshals were also ordered to wear business suits. Their only identification consisted of yellow arm bands and white helmet liners that said "U.S. Marshal." It apparently occurred to no one that while this indeed meant they didn't look like soldiers, it also meant they didn't look like men who carried much authority at all.

At 11:00 o'clock all seemed ready, and a "dry run" was planned for noon. About this time the Cessna arrived from New Orleans, and John Doar joined the other Justice men, while Meredith retired to a wardroom with Marshal Cecil Miller. Here they both settled down with Cokes and sandwiches to watch a pro football game on TV. Again, nothing would happen until Monday.

At Oxford everyone was also thinking in these terms. At 11:00 Chancellor Williams sent word to Walter Hurt, faculty adviser and publisher of the *Mississippian,* to recruit a staff for a special issue of the student paper next morning. It would run statements by the Chancellor and other leaders urging the students to remain calm. Outside, a white compact rolled by the journalism building and on down University Avenue. General Walker was passing through the campus, sight-seeing on his way to pay his respects to Sheriff Joe Ford.

The sheriff was courteous, but made some remark about not needing outsiders. No need to worry, Walker said, he had not come to Oxford for any violence. He was just very interested in what was going on and wanted to see for himself. The General added that he would be happy to assist the sheriff, but Ford did not take him up on this.

Certain other people, not at Oxford, were thinking in terms of Monday too. To the east, 150 men from central Alabama arranged to rendezvous near Selma at 3:00 A.M. Monday and head up U.S. 82 for the University. To the west, certain leaders of Coahoma County offered to have a posse of 8,000 men available for duty at the University Monday morning. To the south, the radio called on war veterans of Forest, Mississippi, to assemble at 2:00 P.M. at the American Legion retreat to discuss what action to take.

In Jackson the drums were beating harder. People started collecting on the sidewalk outside the Governor's Mansion. Cars began driving aimlessly around the block, blowing their horns as directed by the radio. From the Citizens' Council windows across the street, pretty girls waved Confederate flags and stirred up those below. In the Mansion, Mississippi State Senator George Yarbrough, a burly cattleman with a deceptively soft voice, met with Barnett on an important assignment. He was going to Oxford as the Governor's official representative, aided by Senator John McLaurin, Representative C. B. (Buddie) Newman and Judge Russel Moore, who had been on the campus much of the week. As Yarbrough later described his job, it was "strictly to prevent violence—to keep the peace —to represent the Governor until the next attempt to bring in Meredith on Monday." McLaurin interpreted the assignment a little differently: he later told the New Orleans Citizens' Council that he and Yarbrough were ordered up "for the purpose of preparing defenses for the next day." Newman's actions perhaps spoke louder than any explanation—he quickly made out his will.

In any event, passions were blazing again by 10:45 A.M., when Ross Barnett put through a new call to Robert Kennedy in Washington. He immediately urged Kennedy to "postpone this matter."

"We can't do that."

"Then you had better have enough troops to be dead sure that peace and order will be preserved at the University." With that, the Governor proposed a brand-new plan, built around a show of military might. Facing the U.S. troops, he would have the state's forces drawn up in three rows—first, a line of 175-180 unarmed Highway Patrolmen . . . next, a line of 75-100 unarmed sheriffs . . . and last, a line of 200-300 unarmed soldiers. Barnett himself would stand in front of this curious army when Meredith presented himself. The Governor would deny his entrance, then the U.S. Army would draw its arms, and finally the forces of Mississippi would stand aside.

This weird re-enactment of Appomattox seemed utterly fantastic to Kennedy, but for the moment he managed to confine his reaction to rejecting it as "a foolish and dangerous show." Then, with the Governor apparently in a mood to negotiate again, he suggested an alternative which still seemed to avoid using troops: why not bring the marshals in this very afternoon? Meredith could still come tomorrow, but meanwhile the campus would be occupied . . . letting the Governor off the hook with a *fait accompli*.

Barnett wavered.

At this point the fragile Kennedy patience—already stretched to a point some considered a miracle—finally snapped. He well knew that the President was already under heavy fire for apparently dawdling these past two days. With a civilian solution in sight, it seemed worth it, but this military charade was a different matter. Now he abruptly warned the Governor that the President was going on the air in a few hours, would describe the earlier agreement, and say that Barnett was reneging.

"That won't do at all!"

"You broke your word to him."

"You don't mean the President is going to say that tonight?"

"Of course he is." As Kennedy once again ticked off the details ("We have it all down"), the Governor protested he never meant to break his word, then offered a sudden inspiration: "Why don't you fly him in this afternoon?"

This was it . . . the key to the agreement that ended the impasse: the President would say nothing about the deal if Meredith was safe on the campus by the time he went on the air. Burke Marshall and Tom Watkins, now on the line, began working the idea out. To Marshall everything hinged on the Highway Patrol's cooperation: "The state police will have to help keep order."

"That will be done."

With this flat assurance, the details now fell into place: (1) Robert Kennedy would give Barnett thirty minutes' notice before Meredith and the marshals started down; (2) Barnett would tell the Highway Patrol not to resist, but to cooperate in maintaining law and order; (3) Barnett would issue a statement saying he had to yield to overwhelming force, that there must be no violence, that he would fight on in the courts.

And so one more deal was hammered out, but not without a touch of bitterness. At one point Watkins complained that he would never have engaged in these conversations if they had not been in perfect confidence. The Justice Department's answer was that this confidence hinged on the agreement's being kept. In Burke Marshall's words, "Last night you were talking to the President of the United States about a national problem of great dimensions. He was willing to suffer criticism, to do anything he could to permit the Governor to get out of the situation. That's why he did it. That's why it's absurd to think you can reach an agreement with the President and then call it off."

Whatever both sides' feelings, the conversation ended on a note of mutual understanding. It was decided that as soon as Colonel Birdsong got to Oxford, Watkins would let Kennedy know; then the Attorney General would give his half-hour's notice and launch the operation. "If I am surprised, you won't mind if I raise Cain about it?" the Governor asked just before hanging up. No, Kennedy didn't mind that.

Outside the Governor's Mansion all continued the same. The crowd ringing the building steadily grew, cheering and singing its defiance. At the Capitol State Attorney General Patterson worked on his defense in the Governor's contempt case, unaware that any change was pending. Senator Yarbrough prepared to fly to his farm at Red Banks, then down to Ole Miss where he'd meet the rest of his group at 6:30. Judge Moore contacted 70 of the state's 82 sheriffs for a strategy meeting at the Oxford courthouse that night. At the University Chancellor Williams began planning the statement he would tape that evening, calling on the students to behave when Meredith arrived Monday morning. In town General Walker arranged for a press conference at the Ole Miss Motel at 4:30 P.M., then retired for a little while.

In contrast, Washington was springing to life. At the White House the networks were notified there'd be another change in the time for the President's TV address . . . 10:00 instead of 7:30 P.M. (By then it was hoped all would be over and Kennedy could simply congratulate the nation for passing another test.) At the Justice

Department Robert Kennedy passed out the assignments. His assistant Joe Dolan, already on the scene, would be the advance man working with the Highway Patrol. Nick Katzenbach would fly down to take over-all charge on the spot. Ed Guthman, Norb Schlei, two other top aides, would go along to help. Burke Marshall and himself would hold the fort in Washington. All this was soon under way.

Meanwhile, there was still no word from Mississippi that Colonel Birdsong had received his orders to cooperate. Burke Marshall now felt that they shouldn't wait any longer—many of the Border Patrol deputies would be coming down by car and he wanted them on their way. At 1:45 he called Tom Watkins and explained. Watkins understood; he had only one suggestion: "Can you kind of spread them out, not in one big group?"

Millington got the word some fifteen minutes later—about 12:00 local time, which was two hours behind Washington. It was already getting on in the day, so Lou Oberdorfer quickly scrapped the carefully devised plans for using busses. Instead, the men would immediately fly to Oxford in the five Border Patrol transports. This meant two separate airlifts, but it also meant getting more marshals on the scene in a shorter time—an immensely important factor.

Yet the switch also had its cost. It meant breaking up the groups and squads (so carefully matched with the busses) in order to fill the planes with as many men as possible. It also meant leaving much equipment behind to be brought down later. Finally, it meant the inevitable confusion that accompanies any sudden change, heightened because some of the men thought they were off on the dry run planned for noon. In the scramble, the Border Patrolmen left their gas behind; 36 men forgot their gas masks. Loudspeakers were brought along but mislaid somewhere in the rush.

Only Meredith seemed completely unperturbed. The plans called for securing the campus before bringing him in, so he and Miller just continued munching their snacks and enjoying TV. Outside the engines warmed up on the loaded transports. It was just 2:00 P.M.

when they rumbled down the runway, took off and headed south.

"Planes full of marshals heading south"—the word was quickly flashed to Jackson. It fitted all too well a rumor already current that the marshals were coming today to kidnap Barnett. Now the story raced through the capital. WRBC broke into its regular program, told listeners the Citizens' Council wanted them at the Governor's Mansion. From the Council windows across the street, Membership Chairman John Wright grabbed an amplifier and shouted down, "Take your place around the sidewalks of the Governor's Mansion. Don't let anyone through." Some 2,000 fell in line—"a wall of flesh," they called it—and cheered themselves hoarse, shouting defiance. In the Mansion a calm and very collected Tom Watkins quietly called Washington with a suggestion: before starting Meredith for Oxford, call the University and tell them that Meredith was on the way. Burke Marshall agreed.

At the University it was just another sun-drenched Indian summer afternoon. The campus was still deserted at 3:00 P.M. when Chancellor Williams met with Dean Love and Hugh Clegg, the Chancellor's plump ex-FBI assistant who had been assigned to the Meredith case "because of his connections." Now the three sat in Williams' study, preparing his statements for tomorrow.

Around 3:30 the phone rang—it was Burke Marshall with the astonishing news that Meredith was coming this very afternoon. Moreover, he was to register on arrival. Williams was appalled. The University wasn't remotely geared to do anything like that on such short notice. The files were locked up, the Registrar was off somewhere, and the Chancellor himself certainly didn't know how to register a student. For added support he put Clegg on the line, who poured out reasons against the idea: the students returning from Jackson would be still excited; it would be getting dark; above all, it was Sunday. Mississippians, Clegg assured Marshall, would never stand for such a breach of the Sabbath.

In retrospect it seems an odd argument. As events were to prove, Mississippians certainly didn't mind breaking the Sabbath when it came to keeping a student *out*. Nor did Governor Barnett, a most devout Baptist, ever raise this objection during the negotiations. It seems more likely that the University's massive and unexpected opposition was simply a conditioned reflex. It had been keeping Meredith out so long it just couldn't bring itself to face the fact that he was now really on the way. Whatever the reason, the University remained adamant. But this didn't deter Marshall: Meredith would arrive this afternoon anyhow.

So down the drain went Chancellor Williams' careful plans for tomorrow. Down, in fact, went all the plans for all the tomorrows. At last the University came face to face with the mundane realities of the moment: where to put the man . . . who would be with him . . . how many mattresses they would need. Everyone scurried into action—their new student might turn up any minute.

At the Mansel Motel General Walker was spending a leisurely afternoon. He handled a few phone calls, polished his latest statement entitled "On to Mississippi," and took a little nap. Then, shortly after 4:30, he drove over to the Ole Miss Motel for the press conference he had scheduled. Walking into the center of the courtyard, he found surprisingly few signs of interest. There were no cameras or equipment, just four or five reporters lounging around.

"Your press conference," one of them explained, "has sort of been scooped." Then he broke the news: U.S. marshals had come and were swarming over the University campus.

It was true. The first lift of marshals had reached Oxford's airport around 2:35, but nothing had happened until the Jetstar from Washington landed at 4:00. Then Katzenbach phoned Kennedy, confirmed that the deal was still on, and loaded the 170 marshals now on hand into five Army trucks. With Katzenbach leading in a Border Patrol car, they started out for the University, but almost immediately met a state police car with Joe Dolan and Colonel Birdsong. Dolan had done his advance work well—the Colonel was clued in. With the Highway Patrol car taking over the lead, the convoy continued on to the campus. Once clear of the airport, they encountered few people this lazy afternoon, although one startled man cried, "You know you're going to be carried out, don't you?"

The pale lavender clock on the Lyceum said exactly 4:30 as the convoy rolled to a stop at the colonnaded entrance. This graceful ante bellum building was both the sentimental and administrative heart of Ole Miss—the place where Katzenbach automatically assumed Meredith was about to register. At the moment it was locked and empty—no sign of life at all, except a few inquisitive squirrels in the tree-shaded circle out front.

Then Hugh Clegg hurried up, accompanied by campus Police Chief Burnes Tatum, a great oak of a man. Tatum unlocked the building, and the party trooped into Clegg's office, a pleasant room that incongruously featured a New England seascape of gulls and lobster pots. Katzenbach asked expectantly, "Will Meredith be registered today?"

"No," smiled Clegg, "Mr. Marshall gave in on that."

Blocked on this point, Katzenbach decided to place his men around the Lyceum, while three of the trucks went back to the airport for the next contingent and Dolan looked around for billets. Ultimately he hoped to bed down the marshals some place nearby, leaving a small guard at the Lyceum until registration time Monday.

With this apparently settled, Katzenbach cleared the University's arrangements for housing Meredith in remote Baxter Hall, then called Robert Kennedy—now at the White House—to report all was set and he was bringing in Meredith at once. The phone connection was an ordinary pay booth in the hall; left open from now on, it would ultimately run up one of the largest reverse-charge bills in history.

Outside the marshals dismounted, formed a line across the front of the Lyceum. They might have been in civilian clothes, but with their white helmets, yellow riot vests, they were anything but inconspicuous.

A small crowd quickly gathered. At first most were faculty members, often with wives and children. Grouped more or less by academic departments, they gave the scene an odd family-outing flavor. Then around 5:00 the students began returning from the big Jackson weekend. The crowd grew bigger and more boisterous. Soon they were singing fight songs and giving the school's "Hoddy-Toddy" yell. A self-appointed cheerleader, with the shaved head of every good Ole Miss freshman, started a rising chant: "Go to hell, JFK."

Meanwhile Joe Dolan was having little luck finding billets for the marshals. The Highway Patrol had the gym—so that was out—and the dorms all seemed to be full. The men at the Lyceum waited uneasily. Five more truckloads arrived at 5:00 . . . then another group in patrol cars at 5:55. As they came they were added to the line already there, until finally the building was completely ringed.

The crowd was growing too—ever more boisterous and noisy. Two boys pranced up and down wearing the inevitable Confederate uniforms. A group rushed to the flagpole with a Confederate banner, and this time they got it up. A boy appeared with a bugle and began blowing cavalry charge calls. The organized cheering grew louder—"2-4-1-3, we hate Ken-ne-dy!" The yells grew meaner —"Go to Cuba, nigger lovers!"—and, more ominously, "Just wait'll dark."

All this time Joe Dolan was still searching for billets—but by now it didn't matter. Without anyone's realizing what was happening, a transformation had taken place. The crowd, originally just curious, was now closing in with taunts and threats. The marshals, originally brought to the Lyceum to register Meredith, suddenly found themselves defending the place. Nobody on either side really planned it that way—it just happened. And by the time the situation was fully appreciated, it was too late to do anything about it. The marshals could no longer get away; they had to stay there. For the introspective political students of the New Frontier, it illustrated an important point: you don't always make the decisions; sometimes they're made for you.

All this was painfully clear by the time Katzenbach and Guthman slipped over to the Oxford airport to meet the Meredith party. The plane landed shortly after 6:00, and into the gathering twilight stepped John Doar, Marshal Miller and Meredith himself, looking neat as ever and carrying a thin, tan briefcase. His uneventful day at Millington had ended in midafternoon, when Doar suddenly announced that the time had come.

So now he was in Oxford, heading for the campus in a strongly guarded convoy led by a state Highway Patrol car—Colonel Birdsong had been true to his word. Deep in the line was the sedan carrying Meredith; and he in turn looked almost lost, squeezed in the back seat between Doar and Katzenbach. They sat mostly silent, tensely listening to the Border Patrol radio. It crackled with instructions, always referring to Meredith as "the subject." Finally Meredith attempted a mild joke: wasn't this a funny situation where the "student" had become the "subject"? It fell flat.

They came in the back way, up Fraternity Row, left on Rebel Drive, stopping at Baxter Hall on the northwest edge of the campus. In the dusk few students saw them as they entered the dorm and climbed to the second-floor counselor's apartment—a compact suite of living room and kitchenette and two bedrooms. Meredith quickly picked the innermost room—a white-walled cubbyhole furnished with two cots and a big battered wardrobe. Within five minutes Ole Miss' new student closed the door and began to study.

Katzenbach put Miller in charge of a 12-man guard, later increased to 24. Then he and Doar headed back to the Lyceum, so Doar could meet the University officials who would handle the registration next morning.

It was 7:00 now, and the crowd had taken a mean turn. The students began flicking gravel and lighted cigarettes at the marshals. The federal line remained stolid and expressionless, which only seemed to goad the people. "Shoot me! Shoot me!" screamed a blond boy darting up to the very edge of the line. The coeds were soon using barracks-room language that astonished the marshals. They never knew that girls—especially these sheltered Mississippi girls—even knew such words existed.

The Army truck drivers were a special target. Five of the seven were Negroes, and it did no good to explain that the Army, anyhow, was integrated and this was the way the unit came. White Mississippi considered it a calculated insult. "Your time has come, nigger," a young man yelled at a wide-eyed driver. "We'll get the other son-of-a-bitches tomorrow!"

A boy suddenly dashed from the crowd, grabbed a fire extinguisher off a truck, and shot a stream right in the face of driver John Miller. "Those things are cold," the boy exulted, returning to his friends. "I'll bet it froze his God-damned face off."

As the crowd's fury grew, Highway Patrolmen moved here and there, trying to keep some trace of order. Chancellor Williams, Dean Love and Chief Tatum also circulated among the students, begging them to go to their dorms. Probably no one would have listened anyhow, but it didn't help to discover that the loudspeakers were lost.

Shortly after 7:00 the crowd surged dangerously close—rocks began flying, and Marshal Al Butler wanted to use gas. "Hold it off for a while," McShane said, but it was increasingly clear that new trouble was coming. "You God-damn, Jew-looking, Yankee son-of-a-bitch," one man raged at a marshal who happened to be from Texas, "come night and we're going to kill you."

Suddenly three older men shoved through the students and up the Lyceum steps. It was Colonel Birdsong with Senators Yarbrough and John McLaurin. Yarbrough and his aides had arrived as planned that morning, but were amazed to find the campus already occupied. As the Governor's representative, Yarbrough decided to withdraw the Highway Patrol. Once the place was "invaded," he felt, it should be the federal government's job to keep order. Taking McLaurin along to lend support, he was now going to tell Nick Katzenbach so.

Another tense conference followed in Hugh Clegg's office. Yarbrough explained his decision, and to back up his authority he produced one more of Ross Barnett's handsome sealed proclamations. It said that Yarbrough was authorized to do anything necessary to prevent violence.

Katzenbach tried to reason with him: withdrawing the Highway Patrol wouldn't prevent violence; it would invite violence. It would be the worst thing that could possibly happen. Yarbrough was adamant. Desperately Katzenbach asked if Yarbrough had consulted the "best technical advice" on the problem. Since this was a question of crowd control, maybe Colonel Birdsong's opinion would be useful. Then he hopefully turned to the Colonel, but Birdsong replied that he just followed orders.

If the head of the Highway Patrol sounded dejected, he had a right to be. An "honest cop" with a fine reputation as a manhunter, he had been caught between the politicians for a week. As early as the 25th there were stories of political leaders taking over, deploying the troopers without consulting their superiors. The result couldn't help but endanger discipline.

Giving up on this tack, Katzenbach now turned back to Yarbrough: maybe he didn't understand . . . this was definitely against the Governor's orders . . . wouldn't he at least call Barnett? Yarbrough remained firm—he had already talked to the Governor and this had Barnett's blessing. No, he wouldn't phone him now. The decision was made. It was only a question of when. He mentioned 8:00 o'clock . . . Katzenbach urged at least 8:30 . . . Doar appealed for 9:00.

As they bargained over the time, wheels were turning elsewhere. Early in the talk Katzenbach had whispered instructions to alert Robert Kennedy. Within minutes the Attorney General was on the phone to Jackson, telling Tom Watkins that the agreement was broken again. Watkins promised to straighten things out. Next Kennedy called back to the Lyceum: Tell Yarbrough that if he wouldn't agree to keep the Highway Patrol on duty, the President

—due on television in half an hour—would expose the broken agreement to the whole nation.

Yarbrough still couldn't be moved. At this point, however, the Governor's Mansion in Jackson called. The Senator listened soberly for a minute, then announced that orders had been changed—the Highway Patrol would remain after all.

In later post-mortems Yarbrough always denied that he had already given any orders to withdraw—he just planned to do it. Assuming this is so, perhaps what happened next stemmed from some unknown associate who knew the Senator's intentions but acted without his knowledge. In any case, there is no doubt that at 7:25 the FBI monitored a Highway Patrol radio signal that all its cars had been ordered out.

For Lou Oberdorfer, now in charge of the Communications Center in the basement of the Oxford Post Office, it was the first intimation of danger. He had been on duty here since 4:35, but the campus was a mile away. Isolated and lost in a maze of radios, scan lines and transmission cables, he had no chance to see what was really going on. Now he knew the worst and tried to alert the Lyceum. But the FBI radio got through ahead of him; at 7:34 it flashed the first warning that the Highway Patrol was pulling out.

"I'm glad I don't have to hold them back," a trooper remarked to Marshal Jimmie Morrell as the crowd's fury grew. "What do you mean? What's the deal?" asked the startled marshal. But the trooper wouldn't say anything more, just ambled off into the dark. Indeed, by 7:40 most of them seemed to have vanished—both from the gates and the campus itself—and the few that remained showed a curious concept of law enforcement.

Marshal John Cameron asked one trooper to help move the crowd back; the officer snarled, "To hell with you, you son-of-a-bitch, I didn't invite you down here." When a boy darted out and slashed at an Army truck tire, a nearby patrolman told him, "Don't fool around letting the air out that way, just cut the valve stems right off."

A flicker of photo flash bulbs suddenly drew the crowd's attention. The national press was a hated thing—a symbol of Yankee interference—all the more so since the television people had indeed staged some scenes that past week. TV cameraman Gordon Yoder of Dallas had nothing to do with that, but it didn't help him now. Spying him with his equipment, the mob beat and pummeled him as he struggled to his station wagon, where his wife sat waiting. It was little safer inside. Leaning halfway through the window, a boy howled at Mrs. Yoder, "You nigger-loving bitch, you Yankee bastard." Actually, Mrs. Yoder happened to be from Jackson, Mississippi.

A frightened coed rushed up to an officer and begged him to do something. "Go talk to your federal buddies about it," he replied. But some troopers finally did come and rescue the couple, leaving the crowd still kicking and beating the car to pieces.

Exhilarated by this taste of raw violence, the mob now turned on other "Yankee" newsmen—a Louisiana reporter, an Atlanta photographer. Seizing the Atlanta man's camera, a boy slung it down again and again on the pavement. Chemistry professor William Herndon—one of the few faculty men still around—snatched it from the boy, then was beaten to the ground himself from behind. Scrambling to his feet, Herndon shouted he was going to start taking names. The students had an answer for that—they clubbed him down again. This time Chief Tatum rushed up, rescued Herndon and hustled him off to the safety of the Lyceum.

Bricks, stones, bottles were now flying—the rest of the truck tires slashed. A rock clipped Marshal Ed Bartholomew on the thigh—"Next time we'll get you in the head," a voice shouted from the dark. A pop bottle, several stones and a piece of brick rained down on Marshal Dan Pursglove, and a dose of acid caught Marshal Stan Spofford—strong enough to burn holes in his clothes. A fiery Coke bottle landed by Marshal Robert Erwin, spewed burning gasoline around his feet . . . another bottle bowled over the man three down from him. Around 7:45 Marshal Cameron urged gas . . . McShane at first said no . . . then as more rocks cascaded down, he ordered the gas guns "at ready."

At this moment Senator Yarbrough suddenly appeared on the Lyceum steps. Overruled on his decision to withdraw the Highway Patrol, he had volunteered to come out and try to calm the crowd. Seeing the marshals put on their gas masks, he rushed up to McShane and begged him to cancel the order. This was done, and as the marshals took off their masks, Yarbrough plunged into the crowd. Again and again he shouted that he was the Governor's representative, that all would be well, that they should calm down.

At the same time, a number of Highway Patrolmen suddenly re-appeared—apparently not all, but enough to convince some Justice men that the Governor's orders had filtered through. The storm of missiles seemed to let up.

Then from the rear came a new cascade, and someone threw a burning newspaper on the canvas top of one of the trucks. Again the crowd surged forward; again the marshals put on their masks; again the crowd pulled back. The Highway Patrolmen seemed to be making some progress, particularly to the left, and the marshals once more took off their masks.

In the Lyceum Ed Guthman reported to Kennedy that it looked like they might use gas. The Attorney General said he hoped it wouldn't come to that and asked to talk to Colonel Birdsong. When Guthman brought the Colonel to the phone, Yarbrough came in too and got on the line first. He told Kennedy he wanted Barnett to fly up and talk to the students. Kennedy thought this was a dreadful idea.

Outside the storm had burst again. Professor Herndon was amazed to see a boy race by, literally frothing at the mouth. Bricks and bottles rained on the marshals; then a two-foot length of lead pipe crashed down on one man's helmet, sending him sprawling.

This last was enough for McShane. At 7:58 he gave the command to fire.

The center of the marshals' line erupted with a series of muffled blasts. Catching the sound, the rest of the line swung into action too. Firing spread up and down the line and around the building—including those spots where the Highway Patrolmen were trying to push the crowd back.

The troopers were caught squarely in the middle, with their backs to the marshals. The guns fired raw gas, not projectiles as later claimed by irate Mississippians, but the effect was bad enough. The wax wadding that packed in the gas could give a man a mean crack and, of course, the Border Patrolmen (lacking guns) began hurling grenades as hard as they could.

Highway Patrolman Welby Brunt—hit by either wadding or a grenade—fell stunned to the ground. As he struggled to his feet gasping for breath, he got a big dose of gas at point-black range and fell back again unconscious. A county sheriff raced to his rescue—and none too soon. Brunt's life was barely saved.

Other patrolmen staggered away cursing and crying, and Chief Tatum caught a bad dose too. "That's the dirtiest trick I've ever seen," exploded Officer Gwin Cole, as he groped his way into the Lyceum, tears streaming down his face.

The people in the building already knew what had happened—there was no mistaking those muffled pops. Colonel Birdsong had just taken the phone to discuss with Robert Kennedy what more might be done to forestall a riot; now it was all so clearly too late. Katzenbach raced in, grabbed the line: "Bob, I'm very sorry to report we've had to fire tear gas . . . we had no choice."

In the White House it was 9:59—just one minute before the President was due on the air with his calm reassurance that Meredith was safely in. JFK was already in his office, seated at his desk before a battery of microphones and cameras. Robert Kennedy and Burke Marshall were next door in the Cabinet Room, where most of the telephoning was done. When the flash came, Burke Marshall rushed to alert the President, but found his way blocked by a jungle of wires and cables. Stumbling over and around them, he reached the President's door just as Kennedy began, "Good evening, my fellow citizens."

In the Lyceum a furious Colonel Birdsong tore into Nick Katzenbach for gassing his men. Badly needing the Highway Patrol to stay on the job, Katzenbach did his best to patch things up. He poured out apologies: he was terribly sorry . . . it was most unfortunate that the troopers were hit . . . the marshals weren't meant to fire right where they were standing.

Mississippi later magnified the apology into a confession of guilt for the whole affair—something he certainly never intended. But the open-fire order would remain controversial. State leaders still argue that it wasn't necessary, nor was there adequate warning. The federal officials disagree—and they are backed up by many of the University people and nearly all of the newsmen present. One student leader has privately remarked, "Actually, they waited too long."

Certainly the marshals had taken merciless abuse for an hour and a bad beating for the last 30 minutes. At least eight were injured by flying missiles. While some Highway Patrolmen were back in action at the end, and while they were indeed having some luck holding back the crowd—especially on the northeast corner of the Lyceum—the situation as a whole was getting worse, not better.

Nor did the crowd need greater warning. The sight of the masks —nearly ten minutes before gas—was enough. The students knew what this meant, and most easily scampered to safety. The real victims, ironically, were those Highway Patrolmen who were doing something to help. With their backs to the marshals as they pushed against the crowd, they couldn't see the preparations and were caught unaware. Here loudspeakers would again have helped, and the failure to have any handy remains perhaps the most serious mistake made by the federal government.

But charges, countercharges and post-mortems would all come

later. At the time there was only wild confusion. Smoke billowed
out from the Lyceum as the marshals continued pumping tear gas
into the night. Shadowy figures in T-shirts raced about the circle
in front, pausing occasionally to hurl rocks and bottles at the
federal lines. This circle quickly became the main battlefield—the
first 80 yards served as no-man's land . . . the flagpole in the center
was the rioters' front line . . . and the Confederate monument on
the far side became an appropriate rallying point. The trees that
studded this area—and the comfortable brick buildings surround-
ing it—gave generous opportunity for cover and strategy. Finally,
the new Science Center under construction nearby offered an
arsenal of bricks and stone that exceeded the dreams of the most
bloodthirsty rioter.

Yells and howls filled the murky night. It was a setting made
for rumor, and the story soon spread that the federals had killed
Colonel Birdsong. The troopers, now completely out of action
and collecting by the gym, clamored for revenge. They were unarmed, but their guns were handy in the patrol cars. A quick-
thinking Senator Yarbrough hustled the Colonel, alive and
unharmed, to the spot.

Another story couldn't be stopped so easily: the rumor that a
coed had also been killed by the opening blast. Nothing could
better fit the popular notion of brave Southern womanhood and
federal bestiality; the students struck at the line of marshals with
new fury.

"Even among law-abiding men few laws are universally loved.
But they are uniformly respected and not resisted," the President's
calm voice came over a small radio in the YMCA building on the
circle. To the little group listening his patient tone seemed utterly
incongruous against the background of mounting explosions and
breaking glass. Jeers and howls split the night; somewhere, someone was pounding on metal. And still the quiet voice talked on,
now addressing the students themselves: "You have a new opportunity to show that you are men of patriotism and integrity. For

the most effective means of upholding the law is not the state policeman, or the marshals, or the National Guard. It is you. . . ."

"Oh, hell, the story's all over," remarked French newsman Paul Guihard to his photographer companion, Sammy Schulman, as their car entered Oxford, heading for the University. They were covering the crisis for Agence France-Presse, but now the President's speech suggested everything was settled. Still, they might as well wind it up; so they parked just inside the campus and Guihard plunged into the night. Nobody knows what happened next, but within minutes he apparently met someone who didn't like foreigners at a family affair. When they found his body half an hour later, it was lying near a dorm hundreds of yards from the rioting, shot from behind at a range of less than a foot.

"Nauseating, nauseating," muttered another man in Oxford, also listening to the President's speech. General Walker had interrupted his dinner at the Mansion House Restaurant, a mile from the campus, to hear it on somebody's portable. Now he returned to his table expressing his feelings about Kennedy's whole point of view.

As he paid his check, a man rushed up: "There is trouble going on, on the campus." Getting into his car, Walker told the news to his companion, Louis Leman, then suggested, "Let's drive on out there."

In the circle by the Lyceum, two young clergymen were still trying to restore peace to this fierce Sabbath night. Senator Yarbrough, Chancellor Williams, all the other peacemakers had failed and gone; but Duncan Gray, the young balding rector of St. Peter's Church, and the University's Episcopal chaplain Wofford Smith just wouldn't give up. They were both gentle individuals and were amazed at the power they often had in getting wild-eyed boys to drop their bricks and bottles. These the two ministers carefully collected and trundled off to the YMCA, where they placed them in a neat pile inside the doorway.

It was like bailing out the ocean. Soon the uproar grew still louder, as a line of automobiles entered the campus. It was a convoy of 17 Border Patrol sedans bringing 102 more marshals hurriedly summoned from the airport by Lou Oberdorfer. As the cars reached the driveway that ringed the circle, the students bombarded them with bricks and bottles. The marshals huddled low beneath a shower of breaking windshields. Somehow they all got through.

The riot raged on—a steady hail of missiles crashing into the embattled line of marshals, who kept mechanically pumping gas into the night. It did little good, for the wind was blowing the wrong way. Besides, the boys seemed to thrive on the danger and excitement; soon they were even picking up the sputtering grenades and tossing them back at the marshals. Carried away, they compared themselves to the patriots of '76, or (and this they especially liked) to a band of Hungarian Freedom Fighters.

"We've got a leader! We've got a leader now!" Suddenly the cry rose above the general tumult. Duncan Gray glanced across the circle, and there in the glow of some lights he saw a small cluster of people around a tall man in a dark suit, wearing a white Texan hat. General Walker had reached the campus shortly before 9:00 P.M., striding in by the University Avenue entrance, trailed by Louis Leman and a few other friends picked up along the street. Halting under a lamp post at the entrance to the circle, he was quickly spotted, and there followed a brief, bizarre reception as well-wishers moved up to shake hands, request his autograph, ask for his views on subjects like Cuba and the Constitution while the riot raged on in the murky darkness.

Then he moved slowly toward the front, as word spread ahead that General Walker was here . . . they had a leader at last. Seeing him, but scarcely daring to believe his eyes, a senior came up and asked, "Where are you from?"

"I come from Dallas, Texas," the tall man answered, and the boy needed no more. Indeed it was so—the General had come.

"General, will you lead us to the steps?" another boy asked, but Walker said no, there shouldn't be violence, it wouldn't do any good to close with the marshals. In fact, he seemed to discourage all efforts to involve him, most of the time fending off questions or turning them into queries of his own. Taking a stand short of the center flagpole, he said very little, just stood with a fixed gaze, staring into the night. Still, he *was* the General, and students continued rushing up, seeking a word, a nod, anything that might give them the moral support they so desperately needed. A boy hustled over, pulled up a grimy T-shirt and proudly showed Walker a scrape on his stomach.

A few minutes of this, and the General started back for the Confederate monument across the circle from the Lyceum. At this moment Duncan Gray suddenly pushed through and grasped his arm. "You can stop this," the minister begged. "You certainly can't let them do this . . . this is terrible!"

Walker said he couldn't do anything about it, but Gray kept on pleading, while the General twisted and turned, trying to avoid him. Finally, Walker asked who Gray was anyhow, and the minister replied that this was home—where he lived—and he was deeply upset by the damage to the community. He added that this was not Walker's home—he wasn't helping here at all. Then turning to the little group around the General—they too looked like outsiders—Gray pleaded with them all, "None of you are from this town. This is not your home. Why don't you get out?"

Then back to Walker, again appealing to him to help stop the violence. But the General had had enough. "You're an Episcopalian, aren't you?"

"Yes," answered Gray.

"Well, so am I, but I'm ashamed of it when I see people like you." And with that he finally broke away and strode off, still surrounded by his little group of admirers.

Now it was 9:10 and the dark night suddenly blazed with the glare of many headlights. A long line of cars appeared from behind the Lyceum, curved around the circle and on off the campus. As they passed, the crowd noticed they all carried state troopers.

The Highway Patrol was pulling out. First clue had come at 9:02, when the FBI monitored radio signals ordering all cars to leave and regroup at a road junction about a mile west of the campus. A voice designated as "A, Able" gave the order (he would give many more during the night), and it stirred some dissension. Some troopers felt they should be controlling the mob, but others wanted no part of it. As the cars left the gym parking area, one even tried to run down marshals Banter and Gartner. Another driver called out, "All right, you son-of-a-bitches, you asked for it, and now here it is!"

He knew what he was talking about. Removing the Highway Patrol cleared away the last trace of any official restraint the students respected. Now they could go about the serious business of the evening. Another storm of missiles rained down on the marshals.

Somehow General Walker saw it differently. According to his version, the students took the Highway Patrol's departure as a sign they had been deserted rather than released. Word was spreading that Barnett had sold them out, and they were getting "all riled up." The time had come, he felt, for some soothing words of reassurance. All evening long they had begged him to speak: now was the moment.

Mounting the base of the Confederate monument, he looked down on a sea of faces, lit by the pale glow of the lamp post across the street. "I want to compliment you students on your protest," he began, and launched into one of his favorite constitutional dissertations: "You can protest. You have a right to protest, but this is not the place for violence.

"Nobody came to Mississippi for violence," he declared. "If there is any blood shed at Oxford, it will be on the hands of the federal government." The truth and tragedy of the whole situation, he added, lay in a sign at the town's own airport which said, "Cuba, that way."

Carefully, he reassured them that Barnett had not sold them out. "I am not saying this, but I am telling you what I just heard at the courthouse this afternoon. The representative of your Governor was there, and he said that his orders and his desires had not been carried out with respect to what transpired on the campus." Then the General told the crowd that the man who really let them down was Colonel Birdsong. By escorting Meredith to the University, the head of the Highway Patrol had failed to do what Barnett wanted.

When Walker was later asked how on earth he was soothing the crowd by telling them that anybody sold them out, the General explained that dropping the business in Birdsong's lap was at least "one step lower."

At this point the Rev. Duncan Gray suddenly appeared again, struggling to climb on the monument too and make another appeal for peace. He never had a chance. Students hauled him down, and a sheriff hustled him off as Walker once again declared that Gray made him ashamed to be an Episcopalian.

That was all. The crowd now surged back toward the Lyceum, and the General resumed his stance, gazing into the night. He himself has always maintained he was a calming influence, and perhaps in individual cases he was. Certainly he led no charge, shouted no commands, performed no heroics. But he was a leader nonetheless, whose leadership lay in his very presence. He didn't have to do anything; just by being there Walker gave the mob a lift and lent a touch of stature to the vicious racists and irresponsible kids who carried on the riot.

The boys clearly sensed this, for as he stood there they would run up, show him their wounds, report their exploits, ask his advice. In addressing him, they tried to imitate the military niceties they remembered from a hundred Civil War movies. "General Walker, sir, why don't the marshals quit?" . . . "General Walker, sir, where are the thousands of supporters you said were coming?" . . . "General Walker, sir, what if we cut off their power?" The General gave them little encouragement—in fact, rarely spoke—although he did so occasionally and certainly discouraged one suggestion to shoot out the lights.

Just as well, for the marshals were now hard-pressed indeed. Most were Border Patrolmen who had had little riot training to begin with. Now their troubles were increased by the spur-of-the-moment nature of the whole operation. The carefully planned squads never did get back together after the sudden flight down. Nor did all the equipment ever catch up. Dressed in their business suits, they had no insignia of rank, and with everyone wearing gas masks, it was difficult to tell who their leaders were. Besides, the masks made it nearly impossible to speak, to give or receive commands.

Worst of all, they were running out of gas. To some extent this was their own fault. They were prodigiously wasteful with the stuff—sometimes tossing out grenades without even bothering to pull the pin. But whatever the cause, the shortage was there, and grew more desperate every minute. The ever-dependable Charles Chamblee had gone to the airport for more, but that was half an hour ago. Where was he now?

At 9:23 the crack of a rifle gave the question new urgency. Border Patrolman George Branch slumped to the pavement, wounded in the thigh. More firing followed—mostly shotgun blasts. A sophomore raced through the lines, crying that he hadn't bargained for this and wanted no part of it.

Stray birdshot caught another student in the hand . . . another in the stomach. In the upside-down world they lived they felt it must be the marshals, and they rushed into the YMCA to tell the Rev. Wofford Smith. The minister was horrified—and unquestioning. Waving a white handkerchief, he dashed across the lines begging the federal men to stop using guns against boys. He was quickly convinced that the marshals had not brought a single shotgun with them.

"Are you a priest?" a marshal asked, rushing up to Smith as he stood in the Lyceum main hall. It turned out the mob wanted a parley, and Smith soon found himself advancing toward the crowd. Beside him walked Marshal Floyd Park, who wildly waved a handkerchief with one hand and shined a flashlight with the other on the minister's round, fast-wilting collar.

The mob fell comparatively silent, forming a ragged, semimilitary line somewhat parallel to the federal defenses. In the background General Walker hovered, silent as ever but trying to listen. An emissary stepped forward, sporting the tell-tale shaved head of a freshman. But he had little to say, and finally suggested an upperclassman might do better.

A senior now came forward, and he had a much more specific objective: "We want to get Meredith." Smith gave his word that the Negro wasn't in the building and begged him to help stop the battle. Reassured, the senior shouted to the crowd that Meredith wasn't there, so break it up. Smith made a mental note that the boy wasn't remotely interested in preserving order, just in discouraging a useless attack on a building that didn't have his quarry.

Most of the students were different. They no longer really cared where Meredith was. By now they were mainly interested in fighting marshals—the hated federals—and this was probably the best explanation why the truce fell through. Even while the senior was still shouting to "break it up," bricks began flying again . . . the marshals braced themselves . . . and the war roared on. Where on earth was Chamblee and that gas?

He was coming. But it had been hard work collecting the gas at the airport. Then the planes bringing the deputized prison guards were arriving; it seemed a good idea to bring some of them too, and that caused still more delay. It was 9:17 when they were finally loaded, and 9:35 by the time Chamblee's rented red truck—led by himself in a government sedan—came rolling up University Avenue onto the campus. The students saw the headlights and swarmed over to meet the little convoy. As it curved around the circle to the Lyceum steps, they threw everything in sight. Ducking, the drivers made it; the marshals thirstily crowded around for the gas; and the prison guards scrambled out to take their place on the defense line.

They were none too soon. The gunfire was more than just that: it heralded a whole new element moving into the fight. The little country radio stations had done their work; the outsiders were arriving in force. From now on the crew cuts and T-shirts of Ole Miss would be less and less conspicuous—their place taken by duck-tail haircuts, long sideburns, the lean, hard figures of the men from the hills.

And still more were coming. A man in a white sheriff's car on Sorority Row was radioing some place in Tennessee: "Send reinforcements right away." Someone else was on a two-way radio in a black and white Mercury near Ricks Hall: "Better tell those people from Alabama to bring gas masks."

"They need help in there," a Highway Patrolman told a young Georgian named Mel Bruce who had hurried over from Decatur in his little green Nash Metropolitan. At that, the trooper was unusual, for he was still at the gates. Most were now collected at the road junction just west of the campus, bickering back and forth on their radios. When one car persisted in saying they should stop an approaching convoy of outsiders, a voice finally quashed him with "You're sick."

At the White House President Kennedy decided it was time to take a personal hand in the matter. At 11:45 Washington time (9:45 in Mississippi) he again called Barnett, personally urged him to get the Highway Patrol back on the job. The Governor, by now completely out of touch and bombarded with conflicting advice, assured Kennedy that this was being done. Then he begged the President to get Meredith away from the scene. Kennedy said they'd talk about that *after* peace was restored. Barnett suggested he go to the riot himself: "I'll get a mike and tell them that you have agreed to remove—"

"Now wait a minute!" broke in the President. He again stressed that nothing of the sort could even be considered with a riot going on. Restore order, and then they'd talk about Meredith.

Thanks perhaps to this intervention, a dozen Highway Patrolmen were back on duty shortly afterward, when a crowd of 250 outsiders came storming up University Avenue. A trooper stopped them, told them he couldn't possibly let through a group that large. Then he offered a helpful suggestion: "Count yourselves into groups of 15 to 20, then go on the campus through the wooded area back of the high school, another group behind Tyler Avenue, another down here."

Troopers were soon on duty again at the west entrance too. When an ambulance tried to get through, a patrolman told the driver he better not come back out that way with any federals, unless he wanted a speeding ticket.

At the Lyceum the situation was fast deteriorating—9:48, three marshals hit by shotgun blasts. Tear gas was low again too, and Chamblee set out once more for the airport for a new shipment coming down from Memphis. But even if he made it through the lines, gas was no match for this gunfire.

At 10:00 a heart-heavy Nick Katzenbach called the White House: he was afraid they'd have to have troops. Technically, of course, the actual decision was the President's, but it was really not that clear-cut. They had been working toward this step for an hour; now they simply agreed together that the time had come. For Katzenbach—believing almost to the end that he could do the job without troops—it was a moment of the bitterest disappointment.

Army Secretary Cyrus R. Vance, standing by at the Pentagon, got the word by scan line a few seconds later. He immediately notified General Abrams in Memphis, who alerted General Billingslea, who would be the field commander. Billingslea passed the orders on to his unit commanders, and in the darkened gym at the Millington Naval Air Station a sergeant's toe ultimately jabbed the side of a sleeping Pfc Charles Vanderburgh: get up, they were going in.

A far less plausible chain of command was at the same time operating in Oxford. Here the local National Guard unit was standing by at the town armory—about 65 men under Captain Murry

Falkner, nephew of William Faulkner and an engaging young insurance man in daily life. Officially designated as Troop E of the
108th Armored Cavalry Regiment, they were only ten minutes away,
and Katzenbach himself phoned the call to arms. The President, he
said, wanted Falkner and his men to come to the Lyceum right away.
Falkner was nonplused: he had never heard of getting military
orders this way. Briefly bewildered, he called his squadron commander, Lieutenant Colonel J. P. Williams. "Better do it," was
Williams' advice, "JFK is the Commander-in-Chief."

At 10:02 gunfire brought down a fourth marshal at the Lyceum.
Over the phone booth connection with the White House went another appeal for help on the Highway Patrol problem.

Ten minutes later Burke Marshall got through to Tom Watkins
in the Governor's Mansion . . . reported the troopers still weren't
cooperating. "We'll get them back," Watkins promised. The President tried Barnett again about the same time. The Governor replied
that he now had 200 men on the spot. He had done all he could.
Then he rambled off on a long complaint about the calls and wires
pouring in accusing him of giving up. Kennedy shut him off:
"Mississippi people don't want people killed—that's the important
thing."

It was after midnight now at the White House. The hurly-burly
of the early evening was over—the TV people and all their equipment gone. The group in the Cabinet Room and the President's
office narrowed down to six—JFK, his brother, Burke Marshall,
Ted Sorensen, a couple of other aides. The atmosphere was busy but
relaxed. As always when the crisis got big enough, the trappings of
bureaucracy mercifully vanished, and the scene was strikingly intimate. No special flaps—just six busy people fielding problems as
they came, making decisions which might affect the course of
federal-state relations for years to come. Sometimes the problems
were big: should the marshals be allowed to use firearms? No, said
the President; only if necessary to save Meredith's life. And sometimes they were of the small technical kind that hopelessly baffle

policymakers: how many gas grenades in a case? The Pentagon finally had to wake up the manufacturer on that one.

Through it all Robert Kennedy somehow maintained the easygoing camaraderie that so marked his relations with his staff. "How's it going down there?" he asked his beleaguered press aide, Ed Guthman, at one point.

"Pretty rough," Guthman replied, and by way of elaboration: "This place is like the Alamo."

"Well," said Kennedy cheerfully, "you know what happened to those guys, don't you?"

In the besieged Lyceum the marshals again asked permission to use their guns. No, said Katzenbach, hang on for five more minutes —the National Guard is coming.

They were indeed. Assured that his unconventional chain of command was valid, Captain Falkner piled his men into three trucks and four jeeps. Knowing nothing of the situation, he told the troops to bring rifles and bayonets, but no ammunition. Happily, he also had a hunch they might need gas masks. At 10:33 the little convoy rolled out of the armory, leaving only five cooks behind. As they headed up University Avenue, a scout car of rioters flashed by them, screaming curses, and sped on ahead to warn the mob.

No trouble till they hit the edge of the circle. Then a barrage of planks, rocks, bottles. There was gunfire too—one jeep picked up six bullet holes in the windshield. Falkner leading, the convoy plowed on, headed straight for a barricade of concrete benches now blocking the way. The Captain's jeep swung wildly around it; the trucks behind crashed through, scattering hunks of concrete in all directions. A sheet of flame now erupted from gasoline poured across the road . . . the men ducked and the convoy roared through, safe at last alongside the Lyceum.

The troops tumbled out and took their places on the south side of the building. Soon they were taking their beating with the rest, all the more frustrating because they had nothing—not even tear gas— to use in defending themselves. One brick-hurling student thought to himself, how typical of the cowardly Yankees to put unarmed Mississippi boys between themselves and the patriots.

But the rioters who supposed the National Guard would come over to their side—and some really thought so—were quite mistaken. The men, Falkner felt, had few emotional twinges about their role. They were there to protect lives and property, and that was that. Besides, it was increasingly clear that outsiders, not neighbors, now dominated the crowd. And finally, there were the casualties—fourteen of the Guard badly hurt coming through the mob. As Falkner wryly observed later, "It's hard to feel brotherly love toward someone who is trying to kill you."

The Captain was still getting his men into position when suddenly he heard a sound that sent a chill straight through him. It was the steady clank of approaching machinery, and he felt it could mean only one thing: the mob had broken into the armory, overcome the cooks and stolen his two tanks.

With sinking heart he studied the smoky darkness—and was rewarded by one of the few happy sensations he had all night. It wasn't a tank, but a small yellow bulldozer that the mob was now throwing into the battle. They found it near the new atomic accelerator, and Mississippi being a land of the soil, almost anybody knew how to start it up. At 10:50 it clattered toward the federal line, its scraper raised as a shield and a crowd of men deployed behind.

The federals fired a salvo of tear gas at point-blank range . . . the crowd wavered . . . and three marshals rushed forward. Marshal Ed Bartholomew tried to scramble up and seize the driver, who leaped out the other side, only to be tackled by another marshal. A wild free-for-all followed, ending when the marshals managed to carry their prisoner back to the Lyceum.

Meanwhile the mob recaptured the bulldozer, turned it again on the federals, this time driverless and with the throttle wide-open. At the last moment, Marshal Carl Ryan earned the evening's honors in gymnastics by jumping aboard and taking the controls. He quickly guided it into the federal line, where it became a bastion of defense.

The attackers' surprises were far from over. Twenty minutes later a fire engine suddenly loomed out of the darkness . . . raced by with a crowd of men hanging on the side, hurling bricks at the federals. Actually, the engine had been on hand for some time—originally brought to the circle to use its hose on the marshals. But they put that out of action, so now the plan was to use the truck instead for hit-and-run operations.

That's what it was doing when Marshal Ed Bartholomew— probing the no-man's land section of the circle—suddenly heard the roar of a motor ominously close. He stared hard into the darkness— the gas and smoke were exceptionally thick at the moment. Then suddenly, there it was—the engine bursting out of the night, bearing down on him fast. He tried to run for cover behind a tree, then saw he'd never make it. Turning, he spied a closer tree and ran for that. He was just in time. As he dived behind the trunk, the engine roared by, the boy at the wheel incongruously dressed in a sailor suit.

In a second the engine was gone again in the dark, but Bartholomew could hear the motor as it circled for another pass. He quickly loaded his gun, not with the ordinary "raw" gas, but with a special projectile-type shell the prison guards had brought. Five . . . ten seconds, then here it came again, heading right for him. He aimed and fired into the windshield, and the projectile exploded inside the truck, as the driver leaped out and tried to escape. Bartholomew had been through too much to let him get away now. There was another wild scuffle in the dark, and with the help of other marshals, he finally dragged one more prisoner into the Lyceum.

At 11:40 still another surprise hurtled out of the night. This time the rioters turned a cream-colored '53 Chevrolet into an improvised guided missile. Wedging the accelerator down with a brick, they aimed it at the marshals' line and let it go. Marshal Carl Ryan maneuvered the bulldozer into its path just in time to stop it.

The marshals were now experimenting too. Abandoning the "thin red line" type of defense, select teams began raiding the rioters, breaking up attacks before they got started. On one such foray they mistook two Associated Press reporters for rioters, captured them both, and beat them with billies for 200 yards back to the Lyceum. Other prisoners were also roughed up, later leading to angry charges of brutality issued by the state government. There undoubtedly were instances of harsh treatment, and it is also true that the marshals fired gas into at least one building. But such incidents happen in the heat of any pitched battle, and the wonder is not the marshals' atrocities but rather their discipline in the face of every kind of viciousness.

Later Mississippi also charged that the marshals used firearms on the crowd, but here the evidence is flimsy indeed. They did use their guns to shoot out the tires of the fire engine, and also to puncture its hose, but that's probably all. Certainly none of the evening's casualties could be traced to federal gunfire; extensive FBI tests on every marshal's pistol proved that.

Easier to make stick is the charge that by this time the whole operation was unsound. If the decision to act on Sunday lies at the Governor's door—and if the hollow square at the Lyceum was largely accidental—it was still the Justice Department's idea to use a large force of marshals wearing civilian clothes. It was one of those decisions based on the best of intentions which nevertheless don't come off. The men just didn't convey the necessary authority at this stage of the game. At best they looked, according to one observer, oddly comic in their rumpled business suits. At worst they looked positively frightening, prowling about in their helmets, stuffed vests and goggled masks. Far from suggesting the majesty of the law, to student George Monroe (peering down from his dorm) they looked like invaders from Mars. Watching them creep through the gas-filled haze around Falkner Hall, Monroe had one overwhelming impression: "I always wondered what it would be like to go to war—now I knew."

At the moment it was all too hectic for post-mortems. The marshals were again running out of tear gas. Reliable Charles

Chamblee had gone off again to the airport for another load at
10:27—over an hour ago. Where on earth was he?

He was having his troubles. First, his red panel truck was hopelessly smashed, and no one would volunteer to drive one of the
Army trucks through the mob. He finally found somebody, but then
they were stopped by the Highway Patrol trying to leave the campus.
A big trooper charged them with speeding and tried to drag the
driver out. Chamblee flayed at the officer with his billy while his
driver finally broke free. Then they took off—leaving most of the
driver's clothes behind.

At the airport Chamblee got the gas but lost the driver, who
apparently had had enough for the evening. Ultimately, a soldier
named Guy Spencer came up and offered to drive. This time they
stormed by the Highway Patrol, and coming against a wall of
people blocking the way, they simply set out cross-country. As they
bounced down a gully and up the other side, Chamblee thought to
himself what a great tank driver Spencer would have made.

Even so, it was 11:40 by the time they pulled up at the Lyceum.
Dumping some of the gas here, Chamblee took the rest to Baxter
Hall, where Meredith's guards were engaged in an intermittent duel
with the few rioters who knew the Negro was quartered here.
Meredith himself lay in bed, occasionally sleeping but more often
listening to the ragged gunfire in the night.

It was ever more deadly. Shortly after 11:00 a stray .38 bullet
instantly killed a local jukebox repairman named Ray Gunter, as he
stood on a cinder block watching the battle. Another shot hit
Marshal Graham Same in the throat, and now he lay gasping in the
Lyceum hall, anything but a reassuring sight for the other federals.

Happily a doctor had at last arrived. To the Justice men most of
Oxford's physicians seemed much too occupied with other matters
this violent night, but not Dr. L. G. Hopkins. He was an Ole Miss
grad and utterly opposed to desegregation, but he was also one of
those occasional people whose almost lonely sense of duty enables

them completely to put aside personal feelings in a crisis. He worked tirelessly all night long.

Outside the gunfire continued, and more was expected. The FCC monitors reported a bus of 50 armed men coming up from Jackson County . . . a convoy of 20 cars, each with four armed men, coming down Highway 6. Colonel Birdsong's troopers didn't seem to be stopping either group. McShane and Katzenbach began thinking in terms of the worst. They decided that if overrun, everybody would make a concerted dash for a last-ditch stand at Baxter. The only alternative was the Army. It was now nearly midnight—two hours had passed since the troops were called—Katzenbach anxiously asked where they were.

They were trying to get started, but there were all kinds of problems. Like everyone else, the Pentagon had been planning on Monday; now it took time to readjust. The Army's elaborate signal system just couldn't be set up on a moment's notice. Nor were men immediately available. The 2nd Battle Group, going to Memphis from Fort Benning, was diverted to Oxford—but they couldn't arrive before dawn. The 503rd and 716th MPs at Millington were handier, but they were bedded down far from the planes, and it took time to move troops in the dark. Also, their gas was gone—already sent to Oxford for the marshals—and now it took time to break open a new supply. Finally, at 11:50 the helicopters began taking off at three-minute intervals. About the same time other troops piled into trucks and headed down Interstate 55. Listening to them rumble by his home, one Ole Miss alumnus called it "the darkest moment of my life."

In these black hours before dawn there were dark moments for others too. For Nick Katzenbach there was the thought of wounded Graham Same lying in the Lyceum hall. For Dean Markham there was the dreadful moment when he heard that the Highway Patrol had gone over to the mob . . . a story that happily proved not true. For Burke Marshall there was the false report that a gang of really tough characters had broken into Baxter Hall and was about to get Meredith. For Robert Kennedy there was the feeling that the whole operation, all planned with such high hopes, had somehow gone astray. He considered it "the worst night I ever spent."

There were dark moments in Jackson too this frightening night. The usual swirl of advisers and aides swarmed through the Governor's Mansion, jockeying for a chance at Ross Barnett's ear. The Governor had issued a statement at 7:30, saying Mississippi was "physically overpowered" . . . she would fight on in the courts. William Simmons, his assistant Louis Hollis, the all-out Citizens' Council crowd took it for the surrender it was . . . rushed over from their offices across the street. With tears in his eyes, Hollis begged the Governor not to give up. Tom Watkins and the more realistic advisers desperately tried to counter the pressure, and one person especially close to the Governor was said to have lashed out at a top Citizens' Council leader, urging him to go away: he had already caused enough trouble. All the while the phones jangled with calls and wires protesting what seemed to be a "betrayal."

Finally, shortly before 12:00, Barnett went back on the air with a second statement, designed to stop the talk of a sellout. "I call on Mississippians to keep the faith and courage. We will never surrender." But he had already sent Lieutenant Governor Paul Johnson, a cool man who kept counsel with himself, to deal with the hotheads in Oxford.

In Washington the President added his weight. Two more calls urged Barnett to do something about the shooting. The harried Governor again protested he was doing all he could. Finally, Kennedy turned back to the Pentagon, trying to hurry the troops.

Secretary Vance didn't need to be told. He reported the 503rd MPs were airborne, the rest on the road. But he also knew they would still take time; so he called the Oxford Armory to make sure the whole Guard unit was in action. One of the cooks answered, and it turned out he wasn't about to be fooled by this man who called himself Secretary of the Army. "Who do you think you're kidding?"

he snorted, well coached by Captain Falkner on military security.

At 12:34 the guard at the Oxford airport heard the helicopters overhead. By 1:00 they began touching down, discharging the 503rd MPs. The copters continued landing at four-minute intervals, while the men already on the ground bustled about the field, sorting their equipment, reforming their units. Now it was 1:15, and still no sign of anybody moving toward the Lyceum. At 1:18 President Kennedy, with a touch of irritation, asked when they would be coming in.

There was no easy answer for the anxious President. Not knowing what to expect, General Billingslea had decided to wait for his whole force before moving—and this took time. True, the only enemy tonight was a disreputable mob half a mile away, but this in itself posed a puzzling problem of tactics, for America's Army was not designed to fight her own citizens. With nothing in the manual on that, it was getting ready to move in the only way it knew. The preparations went on. . . .

They were still loading at 1:32, when the Lyceum finally ran out of gas—this time for good. Nothing to do but wait . . . and hope the rioters didn't attack. It was perhaps a stroke of luck that at this point the mob had found a new diversion and was busy burning up automobiles parked around the circle. It was also about this time that General Walker finally left the campus. As he later explained it to a visitor, he had now seen what he came to see—the take-over—and there was no point in remaining any longer.

More bullets whined through the dark, slapped against the Lyceum. With no tear gas left, the marshals again asked permission to use their guns. The White House still said no, but the President sensed the greatest crisis yet might now be at hand. He made one more all-out effort to get the troops into action. Normally most poised when the going was rough, this time he spoke with emotion that startled his listeners. The night was, as he put it, "the worst thing I've seen in 45 years."

The troops at the Oxford airport got the point. They now

abandoned their reconnaissance plans, piled into four busses, and at 1:55 set out for the campus. At the Sorority Row gate they ran into a roadblock and a barrage of Molotov cocktails. Piling out of the busses, they marched through the flaming gasoline, bayonets fixed and in perfect order. The defenders broke and ran, howling warnings that the regulars had come.

Without breaking step, the soldiers continued on up the long hill toward the Lyceum—past the Tri-Delt house, where the coeds shrilled curses and threw books from the windows . . . past the pop bottles hurled from Delta Gamma . . . past the YMCA, where another batch of Molotov cocktails sent up billowing flames. Again the men marched right through, moving around the circle and up to the Lyceum portico at exactly 2:17 A.M.

It was like a western movie, where the cavalry arrives in the nick of time. Soon troops were pouring in from all directions—the 503rd's motorized convoy up University Avenue . . . the 716th's convoy in from Batesville. Here and there some units had anxious moments: a gang of rioters trapped four jeeps under an Illinois Central overpass at the edge of town, bombarded them with railroad ties. But most had little trouble. Approaching the west gate, the 716th was momentarily flagged down by the Highway Patrol. It was against orders, a patrolman coldly explained, to let anyone on the campus. A squad of MPs advanced with bayonets fixed. "You better not stick me with that thing, boy," the trooper shouted, but the soldiers kept coming and he jumped aside.

At the Lyceum General Billingslea conferred briefly with Nick Katzenbach. Then the troops deployed and methodically cleared the campus. Some of the marshals joined in, and Ed Bartholomew stopped a little green Nash pulling out of a side street near the main entrance. Mel Bruce of Decatur, Georgia, meekly emerged from the driver's seat. It turned out he had a pocketful of .30-caliber bullets, a 7.65 Mauser under the front seat and hands covered with brick dust. As with all others seized that night, an Oxford jury later found no evidence of wrongdoing.

It was dawn in Washington when the happy news came that the troops had really come. By now the little group at the White House had narrowed down to just President Kennedy, his brother and Burke Marshall; and at 4:30 the President—sure at last that all was well—headed off to bed. The Attorney General and Marshall cleaned up a few loose ends, and finally stumbled out into the early morning light. At 5:32 they both arrived back at the Justice Department, ready to start a new day's work.

Dawn was now breaking in Oxford too. The first light of the new day fell on a sea of rubble around the Lyceum. Here and there a burned-out car still smoldered; others sat battered and crumpled beyond repair. In Captain Falkner's jeep somebody counted nine bricks and an unexploded Molotov cocktail. There were casualties too: 160 marshals hurt—38% of those on hand. Some 28 had been shot.

Many of the wounded still lay in the Lyceum's main hallway. Blood-spattered and littered with cast-off equipment, it more than ever resembled Ed Guthman's Alamo. Guthman himself was taking stock, and around 5:00 he turned, bone-weary, to Nick Katzenbach: "What'll we do in the morning?"

"Why," said Katzenbach, looking mildly surprised that anyone should even raise such a question, "we're going to register Mr. Meredith at 8:00 o'clock."

At 7:55 John Doar escorted a trim James H. Meredith through the Lyceum hall and into the tidy blue office of Registrar Robert Ellis. Meredith wore a conservative suit, carried his slim briefcase, and showed no expression whatsoever. Inside, Ellis handed him a batch of forms, plus an extra one which he explained was for "late registration." As Doar, McShane and Guthman looked on, Meredith began filling them out. All was silent. No group of actors ever underplayed their parts more thoroughly, although in Ellis' case, at least, it was through no awed awareness that history was being made. He was simply so shocked he hardly knew what he was doing. It was all finished by 9:00, and Ole Miss's newest student went off for his first class, a course that probed the beginning of a subject to which he was now adding a chapter—Colonial American history.

Outside the Rev. Wofford Smith surveyed the battle-scarred circle. Then something up the flagpole, hanging limp in the early morning stillness, caught his eye. With firm step, he strode out to the pole, loosened the halyard and lowered the Confederate flag.

10

"You and I Are Part of This World, Whether We Like It or Not"

WAS IT REALLY THE END?

In some ways, yes. Meredith ultimately graduated on a sunny, peaceful morning in August 1963 that offered a striking contrast to the wild, bloody night when he arrived. More than that: from now on Mississippi abandoned official defiance as a weapon against federal authority.

In 1964 the state's new Governor, Paul Johnson, took a no-nonsense stand against public disorder. That fall two Negroes enrolled in the University with neither marshals nor fanfare. The same autumn saw three different school districts quietly desegregate under court orders—even rural Leake County allowed six-year-old Debora Lewis to go to class with the white children, although it did cost her father his job.

There was even some voluntary action. The Catholic school at Gulfport opened its doors to two Negro first-graders. Greenville desegregated its library. The Jackson Chamber of Commerce urged compliance with the new 1964 Civil Rights Act until it could be tested in court. The Hattiesburg police protected a civil rights picket line, and Ruleville hired a Negro policeman. Jackson's Mayor Thompson had already taken this step in 1963, and the 12 officers he picked were working out smoothly.

Yet there was another side of the balance sheet . . . going far beyond the 23,000 troops used to get Meredith in, the 500 needed to keep him there, and the $4,919,800 spent by the federal government to make its point. As for Meredith, he never won what he perhaps wanted most of all—to be accepted as an ordinary student. He ended up, as the Citizens' Council fondly pointed out, the most segregated man in America. He emerged brave as ever but critical of not only white Mississippi but the Army, the foundations that did so much for Negro education, and even the Negro leadership itself.

The University of Mississippi emerged torn and weakened. Discipline suffered, and at one point Ole Miss came close to losing its accreditation. Chancellor Williams, still struggling to do right by all, found himself attacked by both sides. "Contemptibly weak," scolded a racist pamphlet; "terribly weak," commented a liberal professor. The faculty dissidents spoke their mind (more freely perhaps than would be tolerated in many Northern colleges), but most went along with the old math professor who advised everyone, "Stick to your field." Disgusted, some forty quit, including most of the University's crack chemistry department. As classicist Richard Stewart explained, "You must finally decide whether you're going to be a missionary to Mississippi or teach your subject."

Most important of all, the people of Mississippi remained intransigent. They might make occasional concessions to reassure jittery tourists and investors—they might yield a few points because "you can't beat Washington"—but all this was a matter of tactics, not conviction. In their total opposition to any extension of civil rights, they still presented a nearly solid front. What Professor James W. Silver so aptly christened the "closed society" continued as closed as ever.

As usual, the leaders set the example. Governor Barnett hurled invective to the end, his language only slightly modified by the contempt-of-court case hanging over his head. He labeled the federal intervention as "military occupation"; he described the growing number of civil rights workers as "alien agitators, provocateurs and mercenaries"; he praised the local authorities for foiling these "racial scallawags." His successor, Paul Johnson, stood firmly against disorder—but no less firmly against voluntary compliance with the public accommodations section of the 1964 Civil Rights Act. He readily signed an avalanche of new state laws designed to curb the rights drive.

The legislature was never more ingenious. Sometimes it simply poured out its hate: Senate Concurrent Resolution No. 106 confined itself to that body's "complete, entire and utter contempt for the Kennedy Administration and its puppet courts" (another paragraph took care of "the grisly gang that work its wicked will"). Other times the lawmakers were practical indeed, churning out measures that offered a useful model for any totalitarian society. New laws controlled crowds, curbed picketing, struck at boycotts and punished "false" complaints to federal officials. Other acts beefed up the Highway Patrol and authorized communities to pool their police and equipment—welding all, if necessary, into one great defense force. Still not feeling safe, the Jackson police built a "tank."

The state's judges—who might have been a restraining influence—added fuel to the blaze. Judge M. M. McGowan snarled at the "spurious Fourteenth Amendment" and the "socialistic Sixteenth." Circuit Judge W. M. O'Barr attacked "the diabolical, political Supreme Court made up of political, greedy old men who are not qualified to serve as a judge of any court." Federal District Judge Harold Cox compared Negro voter applicants to "chimpanzees" and finally threatened to jail the U.S. Attorney General.

The Mississippi press made its own unique contribution. A few days after the riot the Jackson *Clarion-Ledger*'s columnist Tom Ethridge reported, "Campus talk is that Chief Federal Marshal McShane has volunteered to personally bathe Meredith and put him to bed every night at Ole Miss. Other marshals, reportedly envious, complain that McShane is pulling his rank on them by monopolizing the most pleasant duties." Two years later the *Clarion-Ledger* was still going strong. By now the Civil Rights Bill was the issue, and in a single editorial the paper called the measure "evil" . . . "fiendishly concocted" . . . "disgraceful" . . . "nefarious" . . ."diabolical." Desperately searching for something else as bad in the whole history of jurisprudence, the editor finally compared the proposed contempt proceedings to "sentences on the torture racks during the days of the Inquisition and Star Chamber proceedings."

As usual, the small rural papers added their bit. The Summit *Sun* suggested that the state strike Medals of Honor for riotous students. The Prentiss *Headlight* urged citizens to refuse to answer questions asked by FBI men, "and if you have difficulty getting them off your property, call the local law enforcement officers."

It was good advice. No group did more to bolster the spirit of resistance than Mississippi's collection of tough, fiercely independent sheriffs, deputies and town cops. Not that there weren't exceptions—Greenville's force, for instance, was a model of professional integrity. But for every Greenville there were dozens of rural communities where beet-faced deputies, bulging with holsters and cartridge belts, happily wallowed in defiance. Leaning back in the relaxed comfort of a barber chair, one Delta county officer told a neighboring customer how it was: "These outsiders are trying to make us do things, and we ain't a-gonna do it . . . we just ain't a-gonna do it."

The clergy were gentler but no less firm. Again there were exceptions—but not many. Seven Methodist leaders found this out on Easter morning 1964 when they tried to attend services with two Negroes at Jackson's Capitol Street Methodist Church. Turned back at the door, they tried again and soon learned that persistence meant jail. "Officer," an usher coldly told a hovering policeman, "take them away."

Church, police, press, political leaders—once again the juggernaut was too much for Mississippi's moderates. Right after the riot a few spoke up for law and order—notably 128 business leaders—but within months most of these voices either lapsed back into silence or were mercilessly suppressed. When 28 Methodist ministers declared themselves against discrimination in January 1963, their parishioners swiftly went to work. By June, 19 of the 28 had lost their churches through varying degrees of pressure.

So nothing was done, and the madness rolled on. June 12, 1963, NAACP field director Medgar Evers was murdered in ambush; June 21, 1964, three young civil rights workers were assassinated near Philadelphia—but these were just the headline cases, the ones that shocked the nation. All the while scores of little incidents were piling up that never made the papers but were no less real for that.

On lonely back roads, in sleepy courthouse squares, the toll steadily mounted during the "long, hot summer" of the 1964 civil rights drive. On a single, typical day—July 21—a civil rights worker was beaten in front of the Lexington courthouse . . . another volunteer's car was smashed at Greenwood . . . other workers were threatened at Tupelo, Aberdeen and Clarksdale . . . a Negro tavern was bombed at Laurel . . . a Negro Baptist church was burned to the ground at McComb. It all added up. Mississippi's "freedom summer" saw 3 workers killed, 80 beaten, 30 homes bombed, 35 churches burned, 35 shooting incidents and over 1,000 arrests.

In the midst of all this strife an unexpected casualty occurred: the Mississippi Citizens' Council. For ten years the Council had preached that defiance could be respectable—and the argument was convincing enough to win many of the state's leading citizens. But now it was increasingly clear that there was a flaw in the theory. While the Council was masterminding the defense, Mississippi had seen school desegregation, a new civil rights law and the "freedom summer." Apparently it was possible to be respectable or defiant, but not both at the same time. So the respectables went one way and the defiant the other, leaving the Council itself weaker than at any time in years.

Those who thought the Citizens' Council too tame slipped off to the KKK or the new Americans for Preservation of the White Race, which one shrewd Mississippian described as "like the Klan without sheets." Both organizations took strong root in the southwestern counties and the red clay hills. Both piously talked nonviolence, but the APWR urged prospective members to "stand up and fight," while the Klan finally showed its colors in a 1964 campaign leaflet:

> We are not going to sit back and permit our rights to be negotiated away by a group of Jewish priests, bluegum black savages and mongrelized money worshippers. . . . We will buy you a ticket to the Eternal if you insist.

The horrified respectables wanted no part of this, and decided that even the Council's brand of genteel defiance was only hurting the state's reputation. They too began quietly slipping off, looking for some other approach. But this didn't mean they were any less opposed to integration, or would work any less vigorously to prevent it. The situation was admittedly complicated, and trying to explain it to a visitor, they usually fell back on Mississippi's two favorite, all-purpose analogies: Reconstruction and football. It was, some explained, "just like last time" . . . and once again they told how their grandfathers played for time until the Yankees went away. Or it was, as one Ole Miss alumnus put it, like setting up a football defense: "We didn't get anywhere with a seven-man line, so now we're switching to a defense in depth."

Professed moderates remained as scorned as ever. "The failure of the moderates is one of the great lessons of history," observed pamphleteer Elmore D. Greaves early in 1963. "In all periods of historic crises the moderates have been incapable of governing."

"Don't you call me a moderate!" a Vicksburg lawyer begged a

visitor in 1964, and the visitor of course complied, although the term would have been considered an honor anywhere else in the nation.

The incident points up the heart of the problem. Mississippi and the rest of the country no longer operate on the same basic premises. In resolving any argument, the first step is usually to find some common grounds on which both sides can agree—then go on from there. But here there are no common grounds. The state and the nation have drifted so far apart that there's simply no bridge of ideas between them.

Hence it is useless to talk in terms of respecting court decisions, right or wrong. Supreme Court Justice Arthur Goldberg has remarked, "It is too late in our history to deny that the Constitution, as interpreted by the Supreme Court, is the supreme law of the land." But most Mississippians are more than ready to deny it. The wilder breed talk vaguely in terms of Patrick Henry and "Disobedience to tyranny is obedience to God." The more conservative element have come up with an elaborate mumbo-jumbo distinguishing the "law of the land" from the "law of the case." Under this theory a court decision affects only those directly involved—hence the *Brown* case might desegregate a school in Topeka, but has nothing to do with Mississippi. One wonders whether the state's legal scholars would argue the same about the earlier *Plessy* case, which concerned a Louisiana railroad but formed the legal basis for school segregation in Mississippi.

Nor can any discussion be based on "the good of the country as a whole"— there's still no common premise. Take the word of a perceptive planter's wife who watched the speeches at the 1964 Neshoba County Fair, a traditional jamboree drawing crowds from all over the state:

> I came home terribly depressed over the hopelessness of changing the attitudes of the majority of white Mississippians. The response to the speeches frightened me. On Thursday a leader of the John Birchers in Jackson spoke. It was what you would expect—

completely unreasonable—but the applause was deafening. Then the Governor spoke. To his credit he repudiated the sentiments just voiced, although he didn't call any names. However his meaning was clear, and he got little or no applause.

But what really shocked me was when he went on to say that the critics of Mississippi should remember that Mississippians had been among the first to volunteer in two world wars, and that if their country was in danger they would be second to none in coming to her defense. Then he paused (obvious time to applaud) and there was dead silence! Not a man clapped. These people have transferred their loyalty from the nation to the state. . . .

Perhaps this is unduly pessimistic, but certainly most people set Mississippi apart. There's the state, and there's the outside. "Why can't you leave us alone?" pleaded an Ole Miss senior. "We don't tell you what to do." It never occurred to him that the average American wouldn't mind if he did.

It follows that America's role in the world today is an even more meaningless starting point. Mississippi has no better friend than James Jackson Kilpatrick, the capable editor of the Richmond *News Leader*, yet even he conceded that the state cared "not a fig for the good opinion of mankind" at the height of the Meredith case. He could have carried it further. Any reference to the effect on underdeveloped nations brings charges of "bribing Africans at the expense of white children in the South." Perhaps the ultimate in the state's parochial approach came shortly after the 1962 Cuban missile crisis when pamphleteer Elmore Greaves charged that Kennedy really acted "solely to shift the public eye from his ruthless bludgeoning of Mississippi."

If lofty considerations of policy offer no common premise for attacking the problem, neither do such basic considerations as the need for law and order. Most Americans will always buy this— and so do the responsible people in Mississippi—but the fact remains that a great many people in the state rather like a little violence. After all, this was the place where five editors of the

Vicksburg *Journal* were shot in 13 years . . . where the London *Times* Civil War correspondent found even casual conversations had "a smack of manslaughter" about them. In milder form the people are still at it today. Talk to student rioters, and their eyes sparkle with the excitement of that rebellious night. In stamping out the KKK at Yazoo City, responsible local leaders found that the most likely members were men who enjoyed blowing up things for the sheer hell of it.

Finally, there isn't even any common premise in the most basic concept of all—the brotherhood of man. Whatever the current thinking elsewhere, most Mississippians continue to regard the Negro as inherently inferior. It does no good to bring up battalions of anthropologists, psychologists, ministers and educators. They have their own experts. And even if these were discredited, they still wouldn't change. As an old man put it in Tupelo, "There are some things I just know."

"Let's face it," declared a Bolivar County plantation manager. "They were monkeys a hundred years ago, and the whites have been around for 6,000 years."

"As different as silver and gold," intoned a mellow Ross Barnett, tactfully not saying which was which. But the county politician in his outer office laid it on the line: "Put this in your book—it's a criminal absurdity to attempt to educate an ape."

Then is there no hope?

On the contrary. Three new forces are at work which can lead directly to an infinitely better climate in Mississippi. More than that, these forces may do the job sooner than all the laws, court decisions, demonstrations and freedom summers put together.

First is the remarkable agricultural revolution that is sweeping the state. One mechanical cotton picker costs $18,000 but can do the work of 150 field hands—meaning an ever-growing trend to larger farms, higher production and fewer Negro workers. One Delta man with 2,000 acres needed 60 families in 1952; now he needs three. It all adds up: in 1950 some 42% of the state's employed were in agriculture; today the figure has fallen to 20%.

On the surface the change is in the scenery—the gleaming showrooms at so many Delta crossroads . . . the shiny red and yellow machinery . . . the lonely chimneys and empty cabins rotting in the fields. Beneath the surface the change is in statistics—in their way no less dramatic. Since 1940 some 680,000 Negroes have left Mississippi; 120,000 more should go by 1970. In 1940 the state was still 50% Negro . . . by 1970 the figure should be 39% . . . by 1980, only 33%.

Already a balance is appearing in many towns which is not out of line with the percentage of Negroes in many cities of the country. Take these examples:

Mississippi		*Elsewhere*	
Biloxi	13%	Atlantic City	36%
Greenville	49%	Baltimore	35%
Gulfport	21%	Chicago	24%
Hattiesburg	32%	Cleveland	29%
Jackson	36%	Detroit	29%
McComb	28%	Memphis	37%
Natchez	52%	New York	15%
Oxford	22%	Philadelphia	27%
Tupelo	24%	Pittsburgh	17%
Vicksburg	47%	Washington	55%

Of course a state-wide balance will not come overnight; long after cotton is completely mechanized, thousands of older Negroes will be living out their days in the Delta. Nor is a balanced population any guarantee against bigotry—Philadelphia, Mississippi, is only 32% Negro. "Balance" alone can never be a cure for deep problems of the human mind or spirit; but in certain situations it can help, and there's all too much evidence of the ugly role of fear in the presence of the opposite.

A second major force at work is Mississippi's current drive for new industry. The headlines have gone to NASA's new $400-

million rocket-testing center in Hancock and Pearl River counties, and to Standard Oil of Kentucky's $125-million refinery at Pascagoula, but these are just the show pieces. Less glittering but more important in the long run is the steady parade of small factories quietly moving in, slowly changing the face of the state: 1960, Borg-Warner's industrial saw plant at Greenville . . . 1961, General Cable's wire mill at Jackson . . . 1962, Air Capital's power mower factory at Tupelo . . . scores of others. Since 1960 Mississippi has been averaging over 80 new plants a year.

All this didn't just happen. Whatever might be said of Ross Barnett on racial matters, he was a bear on getting business, and his administration featured an all-out drive to bring new industry into the state. The climax came in 1961 when, in order to pave the way for Standard's giant refinery, he rammed through two changes in the state constitution and six new laws—all within 78 days.

In some ways the price of the drive has been high. The state income tax was slashed from 6% to 3%, meaning lower revenue. New plants get local tax exemptions for up to ten years, leaving a heavier burden for others. Municipalities are deeply involved in lease-back financing. Workers are saddled with the results of a promotion campaign that boasts how little they will accept— $1.66 an hour for a skilled machinist, $225 a month for a secretary.

But the returns are beginning to show too. New jobs are being created at a rate of 10,000 a year, and income is up. Delta payrolls doubled from 1956 to 1962, and the state's total income in 1962 jumped 9% in a year—fourth best record of any state.

All this doesn't mean that a Kemper County red-neck can soon discuss race relations with Martin Luther King. Despite the improvement, Mississippi is still the poorest state in the Union; and despite the inflow of industry, it remains overwhelmingly rural. Also, the present trend may be slowed or reversed by recent racial violence—Laurel lost one new plant and Greenville two during the "long, hot summer" of 1964. Finally, even under the best circumstances prosperity (like "balance") is no guarantee against bigotry—booming Jackson is proof of that. But it helps, and is one more ingredient that will at least set the stage for a new day.

In addition, there is a third great force at work in Mississippi. It is even more difficult to assess than the vast changes in agriculture and industry—and even more intriguing. This is the big question mark of Negro education. The state is still pouring money into Negro schools and curricula. The original purpose, of course, was to assure continued segregation, but ironically the result may be the opposite. It may turn out that the state has merely postponed a problem which will come back with even greater insistence. Already there are three times as many Negro high school students as in 1950.

And they are better equipped. Negro education in Mississippi still lags far behind white standards, but it is far ahead of Negro standards 15 years ago. Gone are the days when all a child got was a smattering of "figures"; 92% of today's Negro high school students take algebra, 36% geometry, 25% physics.

What to do with them? It is one thing, perhaps, to brush aside the 2,500 wretchedly trained high school kids turned out in 1950, but how about the 12,800 who will graduate from far better schools in 1970? What, in fact, to do with the 600 students trained in business law in 1964, when there are only six Negro lawyers in the state?

The State Sovereignty Commission (official watchdog of segregation) has no answer. In briefing spokesmen going out to explain Mississippi's position to the world, the Commission loads its missionaries with canned questions and answers. But the material doesn't help much when the discussion turns to the effects of the drive to improve Negro schools:

Q. What are you going to do when this great education program pays off and most of the Negroes have qualified themselves for equality?

A. I don't know. That probably will be a problem of the next generation.

That's not good enough. Thoughtful Mississippians must start facing the problem now. There are already four times as many Negro college students as 15 years ago. As they continue to graduate, one of two things will happen. They may leave the state— meaning that Mississippi, the poorest state in the Union, is in the expensive business of preparing educated Negroes for other areas. Or they may stay. But if they stay, they will no longer "know their place" like most of their parents. They have now tasted too much education for that. They will press far more diligently for the right to vote, serve on juries, enjoy the privileges of full citizenship. Taught to do something besides chop cotton, they are also likely to have greater purchasing power—and know how to use it. Jackson and Canton have already felt serious economic boycotts. In short, whatever the degree of outside influence in today's civil rights drive, tomorrow's will be home-grown.

So all these forces are at work—full of pitfalls and uncertainties, but no less real for that. Ultimately, they are what will give meaning to the thoughts expressed in Governor Johnson's strangely moving inaugural address in 1964. Johnson had ridden into office on a campaign of pure racism—and he would continue to man the barricades—but for a brief moment he seemed to catch a glimmering of the future as he reminded the crowd, "You and I are part of this world, whether we like it or not."

Few of the 1,700 honorary colonels present (all in Confederate gray hats) seemed very receptive, and indeed it was too early. It takes time to undo a century. Yet the forces continue working, and one day they will be felt.

Even so, the brightest future will not bring civil rights automatically to Mississippi—these forces will just set the stage. Nor will the people of the state automatically act—they will simply be far more receptive. Beyond that, they are trapped by the fears of the past. "Give us time," pleaded *DeBow's Review* in 1866 . . . William Alexander Percy in 1940 . . . William Faulkner in 1956. Even the best will continue to say so.

If there's to be any real change, the nation must do the prodding. This means civil rights organizations of every stripe—whether the NAACP's Legal Defense office with its highly specialized help or mass movements like Martin Luther King's SCLC. It means joint ventures too, like the 1964 "Mississippi Summer Project," provided they are responsibly conducted and real Communists are kept out. The Summer Project accomplished almost nothing on the spot—it reached few Negroes and made most of the whites more bitter—but it introduced hundreds of young volunteers to Mississippi. A few seemed to go out of their way to antagonize the whites—they only caused harm—but most worked quietly and with great dedication. These will presumably be the nucleus of the civil rights movement for years to come, and they will contribute a far greater understanding of the state's fears and problems than those who preceded them.

Prodding must also come from broader groups—church denominations, unions, bar associations, trade groups, industries doing business in the state. The whole country, in fact, has a role to play, if only the indirect one of setting a better example. Mississippi is thoroughly aware of Northern hypocrisy on schools, jobs and housing.

But the federal government has the biggest role. "Outsiders!" is still the most effective rallying cry of embattled Mississippians, but even the most ardent concede that Washington has some responsibility toward its Negro citizens, while the more sophisticated know that the state pays into the national treasury only a dollar for every $2.40 it takes out.

What, then, does this mean for the federal government? It means pushing voter suits and the whole new area of litigation opened up by the 1964 Civil Rights Act. It means banning segregation at federally financed facilities, as has been done at Jackson's new jet airport. It means a better job on U.S. hiring practices: the Veterans Administration has employed a top Negro secretary in Jackson—and a Negro deputy marshal was appointed in 1964—

but until recently few Negroes (except mailmen) held federal jobs in Mississippi above the level of janitor.

Above all, it means keeping at it—not just in spurts, but all the time; not just in Washington, but in Mississippi itself. "You've just got to keep going back," John Doar liked to say, and one April evening in 1963 he took a moment to elaborate a little on this philosophy. He had spent another hard day on back-country roads; now he sank into the chrome comfort of a Jackson motel and briefly reflected on what made him keep going: "Laws and court decisions and speeches up in Washington mean nothing. You've got to come *here* and chip away. You'll lose some games and win others—you've got to expect that. You'll think it's taking forever— you've got to expect that too. But the only alternative would be police state methods, and in this country we don't want that. So you do the only thing you can do. You come down, fight, be patient when you lose, and come back again. It's the only way."

The arch-segregationists know this well. That's why the heart of their strategy is to hang on. "We survived the war and Reconstruction," philosophized a Greenwood man. "I guess we can live through this new invasion. . . ." To these people it is all an endurance contest, and they are betting they can outlast John Doar.

John Doar would outlast *them*. And there are already signs that persistence is working. Some are big developments like the appeal for decency by 650 citizens of McComb, and the Mississippi Economic Council's call for "adjustment" to the Civil Rights Act. Others are small straws, but no less important, like hiring a Negro beer salesman in Jackson—that was always a white man's job. Yet these signs can be deceptive. With the state's monolithic state of mind, it's questionable how long any of the recent reforms would last if federal pressure were withdrawn.

But there is more to persistence than showing that the federal government means business. An equally important part is getting to know Mississippi better. Many Justice men concede that there has been far too little understanding in the past. This might help explain, for instance, why there was so little rapport during the negotiations with Barnett over Meredith. To the crisp New Frontiersmen, used to quick decisions, the Governor's initial courtliness sounded like accommodation. (To a good Mississippian, on the other hand, it might be difficult to conceive of wrapping up a deal with a single phone call.)

A more recent example was the Civil Rights Commission's suggestion that the President consider cutting Mississippi off from federal aid. Whatever else may be said of them, Mississippians don't scare easily, and the only effect was a storm of indignation. "Just like last time," they thundered again, and the air was filled with references to Northern bullies, Yankee tyranny and the "crime of Reconstruction!"

For the past lives on in Mississippi, and time has a way of standing still. This is easy to forget for the impatient reformer who advises from afar, but a constant reminder to the visitor who comes to learn. High on the wall in State Attorney General Joe Patterson's office is a handsome clock that seems permanently stopped at 4:30. It is very old, quite run-down, and appears as though it might need a little oil. Yet it looks essentially sound and is perhaps better made than many clocks today. Shaking it vigorously would probably do no good; but with enough patience and persistence, Joe Patterson's clock—like the state of Mississippi—should be able to run again.

Acknowledgments

"If you put all we got to say about the nigger into the book, no one man could tote the book," explained the old logger from the hills. But he tried, and so did the dozen other men gathered in the back room of the Belmont Café that rainy afternoon in Calhoun City.

Their anxious desire to talk was typical, and if this book contributes any insight into the ways of Mississippi, it is because over 150 people from all parts of the state generously gave their time and help. They were every kind—Delta and hill people, racists and moderates, whites and Negroes. And far from clamming up before the "outsider," they seemed to welcome the chance to pour out their innermost hopes, thoughts and fears.

Governor Ross Barnett and myself share few beliefs in common, yet he couldn't have been more courteous or generous with his time. It was the same with other officials: Secretary of State Heber Ladner; Attorney General Joe T. Patterson; State Tax Collector William Winter; Superintendent of Public Education J. M. Tubb; Secretary E. R. Jobe of the Board of Trustees, State Institutions of Higher Learning. Miss Charlotte Capers' Department of Archives and History wants only to help—she is rightly regarded as one of the best in her field.

Members of the State Legislature were no less courteous. I'm especially indebted to Senators Herman DeCell and George Yarbrough, and to Representative James Walker, but other legislators too went out of their way to talk with me on various points.

The Citizens' Council, never far from the political scene in

Mississippi, was equally accessible. William Simmons, the Council's administrative head, gave me most of a morning. As we sat talking in his office, the conversation drifted at one point from segregation to our mutual affection for Colonel Fremantle, the English officer whose diary gives such a vivid picture of the Confederacy at war. It was hard to believe that two people could be so congenial on one subject, yet so far apart on another. Perhaps he felt the same way.

No Mississippian, but very much there, was former Major General Edwin A. Walker, and I want to thank him for the two hours he gave me in Dallas, explaining his fears for the country, his reasons for going to Mississippi and his views on what happened during the crisis.

Throughout my research, everyone connected with the University of Mississippi seemed especially helpful. Charles Fair, Chairman of the Trustees at the start of the Meredith case, gave up an afternoon to see me. Chancellor Williams was wonderfully generous with his time. Registrar Robert Ellis not only contributed his recollections but lent me his own set of the Court records of the case. Hugh Clegg, Assistant to the Chancellor and Director of Development, filled me in on important points—and, as a bonus, described that other eventful night in his career when he crossed paths with John Dillinger. In addition, I'm especially indebted to certain other members of the faculty and staff: Miss Vassar Bishop, Samuel F. Clark, J. Hector Currie, Dean Robert J. Farley, C. Nolan Fortenberry, William C. Herndon, former Provost Charles F. Haywood, Edward H. Hobbs, Walter H. Hurt, Barton Milligan, Binford T. Nash, Lawrence E. Noble, Provost Charles E. Noyes, John E. Phay, the Reverend Wofford K. Smith, Burnes Tatum, Egbert F. Yerby.

Special mention must go to two members of the faculty who not only helped me but took time from their own books to do so. Dr. Russell Barrett gave me valuable impressions of James H. Meredith—and no one was in a better position to know. Dr.

James W. Silver took the time to dig out a fascinating tape his son had recorded in interviewing Meredith, and also gave me an introduction to the local Negro community that proved immensely valuable.

The students too played their part. All thanks go to Jan Humber, Brad Lawrence, Semmes Luckett, Jr., George Monroe, Ken Robertson, plus several others who prefer to remain anonymous.

In the Oxford community three names stand out: the Reverend Duncan Gray, Jr., the courageous Episcopal minister who sailed against the wind; Murry Falkner, the capable captain of Oxford's own National Guard unit; and H. M. Ray, the dedicated U.S. Attorney for that area.

Numerous other Mississippians have gone out of their way to help me. It is impossible to name them all, but here is a good cross section that reflects every area and opinion: William Barbour, Dr. A. D. Beittel, Roy Campbell, Oscar Carr, Jr., Hodding Carter III, former Governor J. P. Coleman, G. C. Cooner, Jr., Chester Curtis, H. J. Doler, Frank Everett, Hardy Lott, the late Sam Lumpkin, Bill Minor, William Mounger, William Pearson, LeRoy Percy, William Reid, Farley Salmon, Oscar Scott, B. F. Smith, and Tom Watkins. It should be added that while Mr. Watkins was immensely helpful in his analysis of events, he was the soul of discretion on his role as Governor Barnett's adviser. None of my information on the negotiations with Washington comes from him—the Governor never had a more loyal friend.

Mississippi's Negroes helped too. For obvious reasons, none will be named—except one. Through a happy combination of circumstances I met Medgar Evers in January 1963. He immediately grasped my goal of getting every point of view, and undertook to put me in touch with other members of the Negro community in Jackson. Thanks to this entrée, I believe a number of opinions were expressed with a frankness that would otherwise have been impossible. I believe too that Medgar Evers' assassination removed a wise, responsible man who would have done wonders for the good of both races.

I also owe thanks to three Negro leaders of Memphis—that attractive Tennessee city that plays so big a role in Mississippi life: Jesse Turner, head of the local NAACP; the Reverend J. A. McDaniel, director of the Memphis office of the Urban League; and A. J. Willis, Jr., who was Meredith's lawyer. I'm likewise grateful to my friend Albert C. Rickey who made these meetings possible.

The NAACP Legal Defense and Educational Fund, which played so large a part in this story, could not have been more helpful. Jack Greenberg, the organization's Director-Counsel, gave me the run of the office—and the files. Mrs. Constance Motley, the Associate Counsel and in charge of the Meredith case, was always willing to help. Derrick Bell, who also worked hard on the case, was full of wise comment. Jim Nabrit was the kind of person a rusty, renegade law graduate could turn to without embarrassment for a clear explanation of any legal technicality.

On the federal government's all-important role, the Justice Department provided every kind of assistance. Attorney General Robert F. Kennedy made himself available; Deputy Attorney General Nicholas deB. Katzenbach, in charge at Oxford, never failed me; Burke Marshall, Assistant Attorney General for Civil Rights, amply demonstrated the unique mixture of consideration and patience that marked his approach to every problem.

In fact, the whole Civil Rights Division was wonderfully cooperative—A. B. Caldwell, John Doar, Robert Owens, Gerald Sterns and Linda Storer, to name only a few. A special word should be said for Charles Charubos, whose splendid clipping files saved me so much time.

Other Justice Department officials who contributed their time and knowledge: Joe Dolan, Ed Guthman, Louis Oberdorfer, Andy Phelan, Harold Reis, Jack Rosenthal, Norbert Schlei. John Siegenthaler was no longer in the Department by the time of the Meredith case, but his intimate knowledge of the place made him an invaluable source. In the U.S. Marshal's office, special thanks should go to Chief Marshal James McShane, his assistant John Cameron, and Marshal Cecil Miller, who was in charge of Baxter Hall the night of the riot.

The federal government's role in this story, of course, ultimately went far beyond the Justice Department. Much help came from Secretary of the Army Cyrus R. Vance on the military's involvement; from Don Coppock and Charles Chamblee on the Border Patrol's work; from Henry Geller and Michael Finkelstein on the FCC's probe of local radio station broadcasts; and from Arthur M. Schlesinger, Jr., on the sequence of certain events at the White House.

Finally, there is James H. Meredith himself. He must have been very baffled that day he returned to his Jackson apartment and found me on the floor playing with his little boy "Dachi." But he didn't show it—not even a questioning glance at the warm-hearted Mrs. Meredith who had let me in. Instead, he set a superb example of hospitality as he gave me dinner and shared his thoughts far into the evening. I shall always be grateful.

All these people gave so much help. Needless to say, they get only credit; none of the blame for any mistakes I may have made in treating this most complicated subject.

Besides those who have helped with information, there are others whose support and encouragement lies perhaps closer to home. My law school classmate Lomax B. Lamb, Jr. of Marks, Mississippi, was the starting point for all my research in that state. He has been an invaluable guide and friend. Evan Thomas was as patient an editor as always. Barbara B. Thacher assisted on research and last-minute checking. Florence Gallagher completed her fifteenth year of turning my scribbled foolscap into handsomely-typed pages.

Written Source Material

The written material on this subject can crowd an author out of his home. It is mountainous and endless, as scholars, journalists, lawyers, officials, and pamphleteers tirelessly grind out their thoughts. And add to all this a blizzard of legal decisions, court records, official reports, transcripts, logs and correspondence files—to say nothing of valuable books, magazines, and newspaper articles. This book probably depends on interviews more than anything else, but here—chapter by chapter—is the written source material that seemed most useful.

1. "The Worst Thing I've Seen in 45 Years"

Interesting details on the scene in the White House that eventful Sunday night can be found in Hugh Sidey's affectionate book, *John F. Kennedy, President;* in the October 1, 1962, *New York Times* and *Herald Tribune;* and in the December 31, 1962, issue of *Look.* All times given in this chapter come from the base radio log kept in Oxford and from the Justice Department log kept in Washington. The quote used for the chapter title is as recorded in the base radio log.

2. "Lest We Forget, Lest We Forget . . ."

Contemporary newspapers and magazines abound with stories on the utter desolation of Mississippi, as fascinated correspondents trouped South after Appomattox. The visit to Charles Langworthy, for instance, is described in the August 25, 1865, Chicago *Tribune.*

On Reconstruction, the pendulum of assessment has swung far in recent years. Once considered a political chamber of horrors (Claude Bowers' *Tragic Era*), it is more likely regarded by today's historian as a period of positive reform and innovation (John Hope Franklin's *Reconstruction after the Civil War*). Somehow the totality of the swing seems unsatisfactory, and this book has tried to start all over again with another look at firsthand sources: accounts like Charles Nordhoff, *The Cotton States in 1875;* Susan Dabney Smedes, *Memorials of a Southern Planter;* Robert Somers, *The Southern States Since the War.* Also W. L. Fleming's *Documentary History of Reconstruction* and contemporary local newspapers like the Vicksburg *Herald* and the Jackson *Clarion.* For events, but not editorial outlook, James W. Garner's somewhat later *Reconstruction in Mississippi* has also been noted.

Without trying to revise the revisionists, the view that emerges falls somewhere between John Hope Franklin and the relatively recent Southern-oriented studies: Hodding Carter, *The Angry Scar;* and E. Merton Coulter, *The South during Reconstruction, 1865-1887.* Whatever the truth of the matter, one thing is clear: it's not what Reconstruction was, but what Mississippians *think* it was that's important in trying to understand them today. And of that, there is no doubt—it is still regarded as a terrifying experience.

On Mississippi's painful journey from 1875 to 1950, the following books have seemed most valuable: George Washington Cable, *The Negro Question;* W. J. Cash, *The Mind of the South;* John Dollard, *Caste and Class in a Southern Town;* Ralph McGill, *The South and the Southerner;* William Alexander Percy, *Lanterns on the Levee;* Arthur F. Raper, *The Tragedy of Lynching;* Vernon L. Wharton, *The Negro in Mississippi, 1865-1890;* C. Vann Woodward, *Origins of the New South, 1877-1913* and *The Strange Career of Jim Crow.* Also the Supreme Court decisions *Plessy* v. *Ferguson,* 163 US 537; *Williams* v. *Mississippi,* 170 US 213.

The Mississippi Negro's steady drift backward emerges clearly in recent government research: the Civil Rights Commission's Biennial Report for 1961; the Commission's 1963 study *Freedom to the Free;* and especially the Department of Justice's Answers to Interrogatories in *U.S.* v. *Mississippi,* filed in the District Court at Jackson, Civil Action No. 3312. On the lag in Negro education during this period, Mississippi itself offers ample data: M. V. O'Shea's 1927 study, *A State Educational System at Work,* and the detailed reports issued in 1945 and 1954 by the Board of Trustees of the State Institutions of Higher Learning.

On Mississippi's economic and population patterns, see the Mississippi Economic Council's thoughtful *Blueprint for Mississippi's Economic Progress.* The U.S. Census obviously has useful statistics on the state's population, but the most fascinating compilation can be found in the splendid county-by-county survey, 1800-1960, published by the Mississippi Power & Light Co.

Meredith's early years are covered in articles, interviews and testimony: for instance, September 19, 1962, Memphis *Commercial Appeal;* September 21, 1962, Washington *Star;* September 21, 1962, *New York Times;* November 10, 1962, *Saturday Evening Post* (his own account). Also see Meredith's deposition taken June 8, 1961, Defendant's Exhibits 7 and 28, in the record of *Meredith* v. *Fair,* Fifth Circuit Court of Appeals, Docket No. 19475.

3. *"We Shall Overcome"*

For background on the Negro and his struggle, nothing can beat Gunnar Myrdal's 1,483-page classic, *An American Dilemma.* Though originally published in 1944, it remains a treasury of information. During the past twenty years, a host of articulate Negro writers have offered more food for thought: Martin Luther King, Jr., *Stride Toward Freedom;* Louis Lomax, *The Negro Revolt;* Carl Rowan, *South of Freedom;* and almost anything by James Baldwin. White writers have added to the picture—liberal books like Charles Silberman's *Crisis in Black and White;* segregationist-slanted works like Nathaniel Weyl's *The Negro in American Civilization.* For a splendid treatment of the Negro in business, see John Emmitt Hughes, "The Negro's New Economic Life," in the September 1956 *Fortune.*

The history of the NAACP Legal Defense and Educational Fund is well summarized in its pamphlets, especially *Equal Justice under the Law;* Alfred Baker Lewis, *Progress—at Very Deliberate Speed;* and the Fund's various Annual Reports.

Two examples of the "new" sociological thinking that helped set the climate for the *Brown* decision: A. L. Kroeber, *Anthropology;* Clyde Kluckholn, *Mirror for Man.* Numerous authorities are listed in the appendix to the NAACP brief when the case was argued before the Supreme Court; this important appendix is reprinted in 37 Minnesota Law Review 427 (May 1953).

The trend of Supreme Court decisions leading up to the *Brown* case is spelled out in Anthony Lewis, *Portrait of a Decade;* Albert P. Blaustein and Clarence C. Ferguson, Jr., *Desegregation and the Law;* and the Civil Rights Commission's study *Freedom to the Free.* The cases themselves make fascinating reading, each one moving a little closer to scrapping "separate but equal": *Missouri ex rel Gaines* v. *Canada,* 305 US 337 (1938); *Sipuel* v. *Board of Education,* 332 US 631 (1948); *Sweatt* v. *Painter,* 339 US 629 (1950); *McLaurin* v. *Board of Regents,* 339 US 637 (1950); and finally, *Brown* v. *Board of Education,* 347 US 483 (1954). Along with the *Brown* decision should be noted its companion case for the District of Columbia, *Bolling* v. *Sharpe,* 347 US 497 (1954).

4. *"You Are Obligated to Defy It"*

The first, comparatively mild reaction to the *Brown* decision, even in Mississippi, is apparent from the roundup of interviews in the Jackson *Clarion-Ledger* for May 18, 1954. Also noted by many observers: Harry S. Ashmore, *An Epitaph for Dixie;* Ralph McGill, *The South and the Southerners;* C. Vann Woodward, *The Strange Career of Jim Crow;* and, generally, the *New York Times.*

The surge of racism that soon gripped Mississippi is all too well reflected in Judge Tom Brady's *Black Monday.* The rise of the Citizens' Council is described in Hodding Carter III's *The South Strikes Back.* This small volume received too little attention when it first appeared in 1959; more than one writer has gone back to it later. In my own case, the Citizens' Council's "primer" is just one nugget originally discovered in Mr. Carter's work.

More recently, two other books have eloquently probed the Mississippi climate: James W. Silver, *The Closed Society;* and Frank E. Smith, *Congressman from Mississippi.* But perhaps the Citizens' Council's own leaflets offer the best clue of all to the state's mood. Especially the reprints of three speeches: Judge Tom Brady, *Segregation and the South;* Senator James P. Eastland, *We've Reached the Age of Judicial Tyranny;* and Dr. W. M. Casky, *The South's Just Cause.* In the face of all this, the dilemma and helplessness of men of good will is revealed in the famous interview with William Faulkner, in the March 22, 1956, *Reporter.*

There is much material on sit-ins, freedom rides, and the continued advance of the Negro during these years: for instance, Martin Luther King's *Stride Toward Freedom* on the Montgomery bus boycott; J. W. Peltason's *58 Lonely Men* on Little Rock; Louis Lomax's *The Negro Revolt* on the sit-ins; CORE's pamphlet *Justice?* on the freedom rides.

For Mississippi's countermeasures, see the Memphis *Commercial Appeal,* November-December 1960, on secret payments of state money; the Jackson *Clarion-Ledger,* March-April 1961, on the Billy Barton case at Ole Miss; the November 8, 1962, *Reporter* on Negro Clyde Kennard's attempt to go to the University. For examples of violence and sheer brutality, note *Administration of Justice in Mississippi,* issued January 1963 by the Mississippi Advisory Committee to the Civil Rights Commission; and *Chronology of Violence and Intimidation in Mississippi since 1961,* issued March 31, 1963, by the Southern Regional Council.

The segregationist's search for respectability has produced a vast amount of material. The current favorites in Mississippi: Wesley Critz George, *The Biology of the Race Problem;* Carleton Putnam, *Race and Reason.* Mr. Putnam, in fact, has been churning out data steadily for several years under the banner of the National Putnam Letters Committee. Two examples: *These Are the Guilty* and *Race: 11 Questions and 11 Answers.* For a sample of theological scholarship in Mississippi, see the Reverend G. T. Gillespie, *A Christian View of Segregation,* put out by the Citizens' Council.

Mississippi's eleventh-hour cavalry charge to improve Negro education is described in much useful material put out by the state government: the 1954 report *Higher Education in Mississippi* already noted; the 1961 survey *Public Education in Mississippi* by the Mississippi Legislative Education Study Committee; *Statistical Data, 1961-62, Bulletin SD-62* and the pamphlet *Financing Mississippi Public Schools,* both issued by the State Department of Education. Most of this material frankly indicates the dark as well as the bright side of the situation. Further details are assembled in the Justice Department's Answers to Interrogatories in *U.S.* v. *Mississippi* previously noted.

Details on Meredith's application to Ole Miss can be found in the NAACP Legal Defense Fund files; also in the Fifth Circuit's record of the case, Docket No. 19475.

5. "In the Eerie Atmosphere of Never-Never Land"

Ole Miss's colorful past is lovingly recounted in James Allen Cabaniss, *A History of the University of Mississippi.* For more recent developments, see the University's *Ten Year Report* (1946-1956) and the *General Information Bulletin,* published every year. Useful information on curriculum, faculty and expenditures can be found in the 1946, 1954 and 1961 state reports already noted. The University's side of the Meredith case is meticulously presented, from beginning to end, in its Report of November 15, 1962, entitled *The University of Mississippi and the Meredith Case.*

The correspondence duel between Meredith and Ole Miss can be traced in the NAACP Legal Defense Fund's files and the Fifth Circuit's record of the case, already noted. Highlights are more readily accessible in the Court's opinion, 305 F 2d 343.

The fifteen-month legal battle emerges in the series of court actions that followed: *Meredith* v. *Fair,* 199 F. Supp. 754; 293 F 2d 696; 202 F. Supp. 224; 305 F 2d 341; 305 F 2d 343; 306 F 2d 374. Quoted testimony comes from the Fifth Circuit's 1,350-page record.

On the problem of federal courts in the South, see J. W. Peltason, *58 Lonely Men;* "Judicial Performance in the Fifth Circuit," November 1963 *Yale Law Journal;* and the analysis in the July 19, 1963, *New York Times.*

6. "You've Just Got to Keep Going Back"

Just about everybody has tried his hand at describing Robert F. Kennedy. A random sampling: Robert E. Thompson and Hortense Myers, *Robert F. Kennedy: the Brother Within;* Helen Fuller, *Year of Trial, Kennedy's Crucial Decisions;* Harry Golden, *Mr. Kennedy and the Negroes;* Theodore H. White, *The Making of the President, 1960;* March 18, 1963, *Newsweek;* May 21, 1963, *Look.* For somewhat sharper comment, see Gore Vidal's essay in the March 1963 *Esquire.*

For background on Burke Marshall and his approach to the Civil Rights Division's work, see August 9, 1963, *Life;* July 23, 1963, New York *Post;* November 30, 1964, *New York Times;* and the books by Helen Fuller and Harry Golden already noted. John Doar is briefly but skilfully profiled in the September 3, 1963, *New York Times.*

Statistics on Negro voting in Mississippi are given in the 1961 and 1963 Biennial Reports of the Civil Rights Commission; the 1961 50 *States Report* of the Advisory Committees to the Commission; the Justice Department's Answers to Interrogatories in *United States* v. *Mississippi,* already noted.

Written source material for the Forrest County story is as follows: (1) testimony given in *United States* v. *Lynd,* Fifth Circuit Record, Docket No. 19576; (2) Petitioner's Proposed Findings of Fact in the contempt action that followed the case, filed by the Justice Department on April 30, 1962, as accepted by the Court on July 15, 1963; (3) Answers to Interrogatories, Appendix B 2, filed by the Justice Department in *United States* v. *Mississippi,* already noted. The incident involving "Mrs. Edna Carter" comes from other sources and a pseudonym has been used for her protection.

The question of vacating Judge Cameron's stays—and Justice Black's power to act alone—has stirred an immense amount of legal discussion. For arguments pro: the Justice Department's *amicus* memo in *Meredith* v. *Fair,* filed in the Supreme Court, August 31, 1962; also Burke Marshall's address to the Washington chapter of the Yale Law School Association, November 20, 1962. For arguments con: pamphlet reprinting address by John C. Satterfield, *Due Process of Law or Government by Intimidation;* editorial by Charles L. Bloch, "We Who Love the Law," November 1962 *Georgia Bar Journal.* The issue was also hashed over by the Fifth Circuit judges in their four-to-four split in *United States* v. *Barnett,* April 9, 1963, No. 20240. Justice Black's decision of September 10, 1962, can be found in 83 S. Ct. 10.

7. "Ross's Standin' like Gibraltar; He Shall Never Falter"

The quotes from Governor Barnett's TV speech are based on text as released by his office. For background on the Governor, see September 20, 1962, *New York Times;* September 21, 1962, Washington *Star;* September 30, 1962, Washington *Post;* January 5, 1963, Memphis *Commercial Appeal.* The James Jackson Kilpatrick quote is from an editorial reprinted in the May 8, 1963, *Congressional Record.* Interesting articles on the circle around Governor Barnett can be found in October 7, 1962, New Orleans *Times-Picayune;* and the Memphis *Commercial Appeal* on December 7, 1962, December 16, 1962, January 13,

1963, and June 9, 1963.

The buildup of hate and defiance in Mississippi can be traced in a number of places, but nowhere better than in the local press. The following newspapers have produced items: the Long Beach *Gulf Coast Gazette,* the Lexington *Holmes County Herald,* the Indianola *Enterprise-Tocsin,* the Prentiss *Headlight,* the Starkville *Daily News,* and of course the Jackson *Clarion-Ledger* and *Daily News.* (It should also be noted that a few papers showed commendable restraint; notably, the Greenville *Delta Democrat-Times,* the McComb *Enterprise-Journal,* the Pascagoula *Chronicle,* and the Tupelo *Daily Journal.*)

For the legal duel between Mississippi and the federal government, this book relies on *Meredith* v. *Fair,* 313 F 2d 532, 313 F 2d 534, and the statement of facts accompanying the Fifth Circuit's findings of April 9, 1963, in *United States* v. *Barnett,* already noted. For the less publicized negotiations between the Governor and the Attorney General, the source is information provided by the Justice Department.

Caught between was the University. Much light is thrown on the hectic Board of Trustee meetings by testimony taken at the contempt hearing before the Fifth Circuit on September 24, 1962. See also Ole Miss's official version in *The University of Mississippi and the Meredith Case,* already noted. For a shrewd appraisal of the University administration's strength and weakness, see Professor Russell Barrett's address at the University of South Carolina, November 30, 1962.

Meredith's attempt to register on September 20, 1962: see testimony taken at the contempt hearing brought against the University officials before the District Court on September 21; testimony taken at the September 24 hearing before the Fifth Circuit, already noted; an undated statement by Meredith himself in the NAACP files; his own account in the November 10, 1962, *Saturday Evening Post.*

Meredith's attempts to register September 25 and 26: see testimony taken at the contempt hearings brought against Governor Barnett and Lieutenant Governor Johnson before the Fifth Circuit on September 28 and 29. Also Meredith's own reaction, movingly written, in his *Saturday Evening Post* article, noted above.

Meredith's attempt to register September 27: see the account in the December 31, 1962, *Look,* already noted; also a very knowledgeable piece in the December 16, 1962, Memphis *Commercial Appeal.* The spot news coverage, incidentally, was good on all four attempts.

8. *"Bring Your Flags, Your Tents and Your Skillets"*

Here are some of the Deep South papers carrying stories on particular outside groups heading for the scene during the last week of September: Clarksdale *Press-Register;* Jackson *Clarion-Ledger* and *Daily News;* Lexington *Advertiser;* Memphis *Commercial Appeal;* Montgomery *Advertiser;* New Orleans *Times-Picayune;* Selma *Times-Journal;* Tupelo *Daily Journal.*

On right-wing splinter-group activities, nothing is more revealing than the odd little journals of this movement: *The American Nationalist,* Inglewood, California; *Common Sense,* Union, New Jersey; *The Thunderbolt,* Birmingham, Alabama; *The Crusader,* Baton Rouge, Louisiana; *Citizen Courier,* Albuquerque, New Mexico; and for total bitterness, complete with blazing red headlines, the Augusta *Courier.*

Many sources have been tapped in an effort to understand the complex role of General Walker. On his early career: the General's testimony in *U.S.* v. *Walker,* Federal District Court at Oxford, November 20-21, 1962, Docket No. W-C-29-62; also his testimony in *Walker* v. *Associated Press,* District Court of Tarrant County, Texas, June 8-19, 1964, Docket No. 31, 741-C. On his activities as Commanding Officer of the 24th Division: *Report of Investigation into Allegations against Major General Edwin A. Walker by "The Overseas Weekly,"* dated 22 May 1961, conducted by Lieutenant General Frederic J. Brown. (This so-called "Brown report" has an especially interesting analysis of the General's personality on p. 65.) The General's testimony before the Senate committee investigating the "muzzling" of U.S. military officers can be found in "Military Cold War Education and Speech Review Policies," hearings before the Special Subcommittee of the Committee on Armed Service, U.S. Senate, 87th Congress, Second Session, Part 4, April 4, 5, 6, 1962.

For the text of various statements given by General Walker before coming to Mississippi on September 29, see his testimony in *Walker* v. *Associated Press,* already noted. Several informal exchanges are reported, as indicated, in the Memphis *Commercial Appeal* and the *New York Times.*

The development of Washington's plans, including President Kennedy's role, comes largely from information provided by the Justice Department.

9. *"I Always Wondered What It Would Be Like to Go to War"*

For events Sunday morning: the *New York Times* and the Jackson *Clarion-Ledger;* General Walker's testimony in the Associated Press case; the University of Mississippi's official account of November 15, 1962; and the excellent article in the December 31, 1962, *Look*—all noted above. Information on the final arrangement between Washington and the Governor again comes from the Justice Department.

The ensuing riot has produced an immense amount of material covering every point of view. For Mississippi's side, see *Report of General Legislative Investigating Committee,* dated April 24, 1963; the same Committee's fuller Report dated May 8, 1963; and the Mississippi State Junior Chamber of Commerce pamphlet *Oxford: A Warning for Americans.* For the federal government's side see almost any account written at the time by correspondents on the scene. Perhaps the best spot coverage is contained in October 15, 1962, *Newsweek;* later, there is the *Look* article already noted.

On the participation of the National Guard, the November 1962 *National Guardsman* contains an interesting piece. Much has been written of General Walker's role; the account in this book is based on interviews, on the statements of several eye-witnesses, and on the General's testimony in the Associated Press case.

The chronology of this night has been understandably difficult to pin down. Times given in this chapter are largely based on logs kept by the Federal Communications Commission, the Border Patrol, the Base Communications Center in Oxford, and the Justice Department in Washington.

10. *"You and I Are Part of This World, Whether We Like It or Not"*

James Meredith's views emerge in many comments he has made since Oxford: for instance, his speech at the NAACP Convention in Chicago, July 5, 1963; another at a panel discussion sponsored by the NAACP

264   THE PAST THAT WOULD NOT DIE

Legal Defense Fund in New York, May 28, 1964; and his letter in November 27, 1964, *Time*.

The University's troubles following the riot are clear from statements issued by various faculty members. The Southern Association of Colleges and Schools' concern is spelled out in Chairman Henry King Stanford's *Statement on the Mississippi Situation*, dated November 28, 1962. Good background material can be found in Professor Russell Barrett's speech of February 22, 1963, before the regional AAUP meeting in Memphis. For an eloquent defense of Ole Miss at the time, see Chancellor Williams's address at Greenville, October 31, 1962.

Mississippi's continued recalcitrance emerges in a wide variety of material. A few choice samples: the October 17, 1962, *Gulf Coast Gazette* of Long Beach, seriously urging secession; Elmore Douglass Greaves's hate-filled pamphlet *The Blackamoor of Oxford;* Governor Barnett's bitter affidavit prepared for the state's next desegregation case, *McDowell* v. *Fair*, but ruled out on the objections of the plaintiff; the January 1963 issue of *The Citizen*, condoning violence as a last resort; any issue of the *Rebel Underground*, a clandestine campus paper which actually urged the "execution" of President Kennedy. A devastating home-grown indictment of this mood can be found in State Representative Karl Wiesenburg's pamphlet *The Oxford Disaster—Price of Defiance*, reprinted from articles in the Pascagoula *Chronicle*.

In Mississippi today the young people often seem more intransigent than their parents; and this is perhaps why, of the many excellent articles written since 1962 on the state, I was especially struck by Margaret Long's "A Southern Teenager Speaks His Mind" in the November 10, 1963, *New York Times Magazine*.

The scope and significance of the agricultural revolution now sweeping Mississippi is spelled out in the "reference study" appearing in the March 1963 *Industrial Development;* in the Mississippi Economic Council's booklet *A Blueprint for Mississippi's Economic Progress;* and in "Mississippi's Economy in Transition," June 1962 *Mississippi Business*, published by the University of Mississippi's School of Business and Government.

Current population trends are projected in the 1961 Report of the Mississippi Legislative Education Study Committee, already noted. Also see the April 1961, June 1962, and June 1963 issues of *Mississippi*

Business. The comparison between selected Mississippi and U.S. communities comes from the *1960 U.S. Census, General Population Characteristics.*

Data on Mississippi's industrial drive can be found in the State Agricultural and Industrial Board's annual lists of new and expanded plants; the Delta Council's brochure *Five Years' Progress in Northwestern Mississippi* and the same organization's *Facts on Northwest Mississippi.* For interesting details on NASA's giant new installation in Hancock and Pearl River counties, see "The Space Program and Mississippi's Economy" in April 1963 *Mississippi Business.*

Long-range projections on Negro enrollment in Mississippi high schools and colleges are contained in the 1961 Report of the Legislative Education Study Committee; also in the annual *Statistical Data* released by the State Department of Education.

Index

267

ABOUT THE AUTHOR

Walter Lord first qualified to do this book by being born in Baltimore, Maryland, that borderline city between the North and the South, where exposure to all points of view about the issues between races was part of his birthright. He received his early schooling in Baltimore, and in 1939 he was graduated from Princeton University.

During World War II he was with the Office of Strategic Services, and he worked in London in 1944 and 1945. He took his law degree at Yale, then did editorial and advertising work in New York City, where he still lives.

He now devotes full time to writing, and his grateful readers have enthusiastically received and applauded such bestselling books as *A Night to Remember, Day of Infamy, The Good Years* and *A Time to Stand.* The latter won the 1962 Summerfield Award for the best book of the year about the history of the Republic of Texas.